Building Our
House on Rock

The Sermon on the Mount as Jesus'

Vision *for* Our Lives

As Told by Matthew and Luke

BUILDING OUR
HOUSE ON ROCK

THE SERMON ON THE MOUNT AS JESUS' VISION *for* OUR LIVES

AS TOLD BY MATTHEW AND LUKE

Dennis Hamm, SJ

the WORD
among us®
press

Published by The Word Among Us Press
7115 Guilford Drive
Frederick, Maryland 21704
www.wau.org

15 14 13 12 11   1 2 3 4 5

ISBN: 978-1-59325-181-9

Imprimi potest: G. Thomas Krettek, SJ
Provincial, Wisconsin Province of the Society of Jesus
May 26, 2009

Cover design by John Hamilton Design

Made and printed in the United States of America

Library of Congress Cataloging-in-Publication Data
Hamm, M. Dennis.
Building our house on rock : the Sermon on the mount as Jesus' vision for our lives as told by Matthew and Luke / Dennis Hamm.
   p. cm.
Includes bibliographical references (p.   ).
ISBN 978-1-59325-181-9
1. Sermon on the mount—Criticism, interpretation, etc. I. Title.
BT380.3.H36 2011
226.9'06—dc22
                          2010043317

Contents

Introduction

E ven after two thousand years of prayer, preaching, and commentary, we are still learning how to read the gospels. With more biblical scholars alive today than have ever existed, we are coming to appreciate, now more than ever, the role and skill of the gospel writers. After all, the human authors of the gospels are still our main interpreters of the words and deeds of Jesus of Nazareth.

Over those two thousand years, Jesus' Sermon on the Mount has intrigued scholars and laypeople alike and has been the subject of much study and debate. Many books have been written about Jesus' teaching and what he meant by it. In this book I want to pay special attention to the distinctive ways in which the evangelists Matthew and Luke present and interpret the teachings of Jesus in the Sermon on the Mount and in the Sermon on the Plain, Luke's version of these teachings.

At first this attention to similarities and differences may feel like scholarly fussiness. My hope is that you will soon begin to appreciate the authorial brilliance and pastoral wisdom of both Matthew and Luke as they mediate the sayings of Jesus for their respective audiences to help them live the faith. Such study eventually affects our own faith and life.

What we call the Sermon on the Mount is, of course, Jesus' speech in chapters 5 through 7 in the Gospel of Matthew. But there is another briefer version of that speech in Luke 6:20-49, which is sometimes referred to as the Sermon on the Plain (because Luke pictures Jesus speaking these words at the *foot* of a mountain, on a plain; see 6:12, 17). And Luke has conveyed much of Jesus' teaching that Matthew transmits in his longer version of the Sermon in other contexts in his gospel. Because Matthew's version of the Sermon is so much fuller, Luke's version has suffered comparative neglect over the centuries, much as the short Gospel of Mark had been overlooked because almost all of Mark's narrative shows up in Matthew and because Mark *lacks* much of the *teaching* of Jesus that appears in Matthew and Luke.[1] Now I hope you will take the time to savor with me what we learn when we seriously consider Luke's version of the sayings of Jesus that appear in Matthew's Sermon on the Mount.

THE GOSPELS: A FAITH UNDERSTANDING OF HISTORICAL REALITIES

Before going further, it's important to review a recent phase in the history of gospel study because it sheds light on the approach I have taken here. You may have heard of a research project called the quest for the historical Jesus. This is a rather recent scholarly endeavor, just a little over one hundred years old. Aware that the four canonical gospels are not simply collections of historical data such as archival records but rather documents meant to interpret the memory of Jesus' words and deeds for the living of Christian faith, many scholars have tried to access "the Jesus behind the documents." The means for this quest have been the use of such tools as the history of first-century Palestine, archeology, first-century Roman and Jewish texts, comparative cultural studies, and certain criteria used to assess the historical authenticity of words and deeds attributed to Jesus.

However, some of these criteria rely on assumptions that don't necessarily assure us of historical accuracy. For example, one criterion—whether the sayings of Jesus are discontinuous with the Judaism of his time—presumes that Jesus' controversies on particular interpretations of the Mosaic law entailed a full-scale rejection of it. Yet there is no reason to assume that Jesus' prophetic critique of some of the leaders of Israel meant that he was rebelling against the essential traditions of this people. Another criterion—whether Jesus' sayings were discontinuous with the early church—presumes that the gospel writers put words in Jesus' mouth to validate their traditions and that

Jesus' followers failed to follow and transmit their master's teachings. But there is no reason to think that the early bearers of the apostolic tradition readily departed from the teaching of their Lord and Master, for whom they were willing to die.

Still, as the historical Jesus project has continued, the labor of some painstaking and careful scholars has yielded important insights, three in particular.[2] First, we have learned much about the historical context of Jesus and the early Christian communities, especially about the diversity of first-century Judaism. Second, this study has led us to take seriously the Jewishness of Jesus. For all the startling newness of the good news that he embodied and preached, that preaching can only be fully understood as spoken by an exponent of what scholars call second-temple Judaism, the faith and practices of the people of Israel that developed after the Babylonian exile in a variety of expressions.

Third, the quest for the historical Jesus has further clarified the nature of the four gospels. Now we understand better than ever that the Gospels of Matthew, Mark, Luke, and John are indeed expressions of a *faith understanding* of the historical realities of the public life of Jesus of Nazareth. While the historical quest yields a picture of a "marginal Jew"—Jesus, the craftsman from Nazareth, who taught and healed and was crucified by the Romans—the gospels proclaim that Jesus was also the long-awaited Anointed One and, quite unexpectedly, also the Son of God, the Wisdom of God made flesh, and the risen Lord of the end-time people of God. The gospels claim, moreover, that Jesus' death and resurrection occasioned the promised end-time outpouring of the Holy Spirit that enables those who through baptism and faith become communities of disciples to live the way of life that Jesus taught his first followers.

Now more than ever, it is clear to us in the twenty-first century that the Jesus we Christians know and try to follow does not come to us straight out of history, without interpretation. Rather, Jesus has been *mediated* to us by the authors of the gospels who transmit the faith understanding of their communities, an understanding eventually affirmed by the universal church as inspired. The results of historical-Jesus research are guesswork—educated and instructive guesswork, to be sure, but guesswork nonetheless. The four gospels remain for Christians the definitive interpretation of the *meaning* of the person and teaching of Jesus of Nazareth. All else is commentary and application. The labors of historical-Jesus research have helped us appreciate that truth now more than ever.

THE GOSPEL AUTHORS AS LITERARY ARTISTS

In our own time, when there are more biblical scholars—men and women, lay and clerical—studying and analyzing these four relatively short documents, we have a greater appreciation than ever for the insight and craftsmanship of the authors of the gospels. We are discovering that Matthew, Mark, Luke, and John were *literary artists*. Some readers might find that a scary thought, suggesting that authorial creativity might somehow *come between* the person of Jesus and us would-be disciples. But this is really not the case. Let me explain.

I have spent the greater part of the past thirty-three years teaching Scripture, mainly to bright undergraduates. When we study the four gospels, we do a lot of comparing of the gospels, one with another, especially Matthew and Luke with one of their putative sources, Mark. In this we are replicating what New Testament scholars have been doing for the past sixty years or so. As you might expect, this comparative study reveals plenty of differences among the gospels.

Some people are troubled when they first confront these differences. It is natural to think of them as "discrepancies" and to compare the evangelists to witnesses in a trial whose testimonies fail to agree. The next natural thought is to "excuse" the evangelists for their differences with the idea that such differences are to be expected in any human testimony. After all, four witnesses—even four participants—in a traffic accident will come up with variant versions of what happened, even minutes after the event. So, the thinking goes, why should we expect otherwise from the evangelists?

But this kind of explanation is misguided. Comparing the four evangelists to four eyewitnesses who cannot agree is the wrong analogy. It turns out to be a false way of framing the data. Detailed comparative analysis of the four gospels reveals that the differences among those documents are not random variations due to faulty human witnesses; these differences are usually *deliberate* changes, omissions, abbreviations, expansions, additions, and rearrangements. These alterations have been made to highlight certain themes and emphases that the author intends to communicate to a particular audience, at a particular time in the growth of the early church.

The practice of comparing a piece of writing with its source to seek the "mind" of the author who rewrote it is called redaction criticism. Here "criticism" is used in the technical sense of thoughtful analysis—as in art or literary criticism; "redaction" simply means editing or rewriting. The fruit of several decades of this kind of analysis of the gospels has taught us that those fascinating differences, far from being random variations, are the result of patterned editing. In each gospel the pattern of this editing of the tradition turns out to be coherent within the particular gospel taken as a whole. In Luke's case the variations are part of patterns that are reflected in the whole of a *two-volume* project, the Third Gospel and the Acts of the Apostles.

This state of biblical scholarship yields some fascinating and pastorally valuable consequences for our understanding of the Sermon on the Mount in Matthew 5–7 and the Sermon on the Plain (Luke 6:20-49), along with Luke's other parallels to some thirty-eight verses in Matthew's Sermon on the Mount. It no longer seems reasonable to think of the Sermon on the Mount as a direct record (a "tape," if you will) of what Jesus said on a particular occasion in one place, and to think of Luke's Sermon on the Plain as a record of what Jesus said, much more briefly, on another occasion in another place. It makes more sense to understand both evangelists working from sayings of Jesus available to them in written form.

The consensus of scholarship understands the data of our documents in the following way.[3] Matthew and Luke both had access to a version of the Gospel of Mark and a collection of Jesus' sayings that scholars have dubbed "Q" (for *Quelle*, the German word for "source"). We do not have a manuscript representing the text of Q. What is called Q is a hypothetical source posited to explain the fact that both Matthew and Luke follow Mark's arrangement of the episodes of Jesus' public life, death, and resurrection. However, when it comes to the majority of Jesus' *sayings*, both authors have access to a common body of sayings that do not appear in Mark, but they arrange those sayings in different ways. For example, whereas Matthew transmits the Lord's Prayer in the middle of the Sermon (6:9-13), Luke chooses to have Jesus teach that prayer on the road to Jerusalem (11:1-4) and to link it with a parable of the friend at midnight (11:5-8) special to Luke.[4]

Matthew mainly arranges the sayings in five major speeches that punctuate his rendition of Mark's narrative, while Luke prefers to present those sayings in other ways, especially as taught by Jesus during his journey from Galilee to Jerusalem. Indeed, Luke expands that journey, which occupies a single chapter in Mark (10), into a nine-chapter section, apparently to accommodate material that came into his hands without a narrative framework. Of the sayings of Jesus that Matthew "packages" in his Sermon on the Mount, Luke incorporates about a fifth of them in his Sermon on the Plain, and around a third of the rest, he conveys in other parts of his narrative. While a few scholars think that Matthew worked with a copy of Luke, most understand Matthew and Luke to have worked independently of one another, using a version of Mark and the sayings source called Q. What does this mean when it comes to the Sermon on the Plain and the Sermon on the Mount? If neither Matthew nor Luke is reading the other's work, it means that both have access to a sermon, embodied in Q, which begins with beatitudes; addresses issues of love of enemies, nonviolence, and judgment; and ends with the similitude about the wise and foolish builders. Each evangelist, then, elaborates that speech in his own way, according to how it fits his respective narrative of Jesus' life and works.

COMPARING MATTHEW'S AND LUKE'S RENDITIONS

Given that we have a growing respect for the evangelists' differences, along with their artistry and the integrity of their works as unified wholes, and given that we also have a deeper appreciation of the evangelists' role as our primary interpreters of Jesus' meaning, I am moved to try to write a fresh book on Matthew's Sermon on the Mount with attention to Luke's rendition of much of the same teaching.[5] In each case, our main framework will be the canonical context. That is, we will attend especially to the Old Testament background that throws light on these teachings. Second, our main framework for attending closely to Matthew's understanding of Jesus' teaching will be the rest of Matthew's gospel. Similarly, our main tool for hearing Luke's understanding of Jesus' teaching will be Luke's rendition of those teachings in his Sermon on the Plain and in his way of contextualizing other sayings that parallel Matthew's Sermon throughout the whole of his work, in both the Third Gospel and the Acts of the Apostles.[6]

Finally, since Matthew and Luke were passing on the teachings of Jesus for the purpose of serving "the life and mission of the church" (the theme of the 2008 synod of the world's Catholic bishops on the Word of God), I will give my interpretations of how these teachings speak to us today, as we attempt to live as followers of Jesus. Since this book means to be informative in a basic way and also to be pastorally suggestive, the format will be the following:

Taking one unit of teaching at a time—sometimes a cluster of verses that seem to go together, sometimes a single verse, when it calls for that kind of attention—I will first give the passage in the 1986 New American Bible translation, the version currently used in Roman Catholic liturgies. (I have taken the liberty of using italics in these passages when necessary to make a point.) When I occasionally use a translation of the Bible other than NAB, such as the New Revised Standard Version (NRSV) or the New International Version (NIV), I will cite it after the Scripture verse quoted. I have also made occasional reference to other translations, including the King James Version (KJV), the Rheims, the Jerusalem and New Jerusalem Bibles (JB and NJB), the New American Standard Bible (NASB), the Good News translation, and the Christian Community Bible.

Second, using the scholarly and pastoral tools at my disposal (dictionaries, articles, commentaries, concordances, and some forty years' experience of teaching and preaching), I will grapple with the question of what the teaching meant *then*, that is, in the first century, both before and after that first Easter.[7] I will follow the structure of the teachings in Matthew's Sermon on the Mount. Then, where the Gospel of Luke has a parallel version of the saying or passage, I will do the same study of Luke's version in Luke's context, meaning the whole of Luke–Acts, where the complete documentary context seems pertinent.

Third, I will do my best to apply that understanding of the original meaning of Jesus' teaching in the context of the two gospels to the life and mission of the church *today*. This is the challenge for any Christian; it is especially the work of the homilist. At the end of the day, application is a deeply personal matter. But since we are participants in a faith community with a long history of interpretation, I will also try to recognize how some postbiblical exponents of the Christian tradition have understood a given passage and how their applications of the text might help us actualize the teaching of Jesus today. Since Jesus' teaching on the nonviolent response to hostility and on love of enemies has been a particular challenge over the centuries and offers a special challenge to us today, I shall devote some extra space to a review of the development of the Catholic magisterium on war and peace.

It's important for me to note that in addition to referring to the original Greek of the gospels when that seems helpful, I will sometimes refer to the Greek version of the Old Testament. This may seem pedantic. But the fact is that the authors of the New Testament wrote in Greek, and the version of the Bible they were most familiar with was the Greek translation. When they wrote in Greek, the words they used carried associations absorbed from their use in the Greek Scriptures. And when the evangelists quoted the Scriptures of Israel, it was usually the Greek version that they cited. The Greek Old Testament is known as the Septuagint—"the Seventy"—so called because of the legend that a group of seventy translators independently came up with identical translations. So the Roman numeral for seventy—LXX—has become the conventional sign for the Septuagint. When you see LXX next to a Scriptural citation, it is not a reference to some obscure manuscript; it simply identifies the quotation as coming from the standard version of the Old Testament used in the early church (before the Latin version became the dominant version used in the Western world). When I quote a Greek phrase (in the more familiar Latin alphabet, of course), it is not with the expectation that you know Greek, but that you will recognize similarities and follow connections between a given Septuagint passage and the New Testament verse under consideration. Don't be put off by an occasional citation of a Greek word; sound it out, and you will likely remember it when you see it again. You will be surprised at the fresh connections you will begin to make.

Finally, a word about the label "Old Testament": Understandably, there is some Jewish sensitivity about Christians referring to the Hebrew Scriptures as "the Old Testament." It sounds like a dismissal, as if the New Testament supersedes the Hebrew Scriptures in such a way that the latter renders the former irrelevant and invalid. So in recent years, people have tried "the Elder Testament," "the First Testament," "the Jewish Scriptures," and "the Hebrew Scriptures." However, following the advice of two Jewish colleagues—one a highly respected local rabbi and the other an eminent New Testament scholar (yes, a Jewish scholar of the New Testament!)—I shall use the conventional label, the Old Testament.

There are several reasons for using this label. First, the evangelists more often use the Greek version, and the name "Hebrew Bible" refers to the Hebrew version. Second, the version most used in the Christian churches during the first fifteen centuries (and still used by most Christians today) follows the Greek canon, which contains seven more books than the Hebrew Bible. Third, the ordering of the books is different in the Christian Bible. Whereas the Jewish Bible is arranged in three parts—the Torah, the Prophets, and the Writings (hence the name Tanakh, an acronym derived from the Hebrew names of the three divisions: *Torah, Naviim, Khetuvim*)—the Christian Old Testament is arranged so that the prophets come last, as a bridge to the New Testament pointing to Jesus Christ as the fulfillment. "We have the Tanakh; you have the Old Testament," my Jewish New Testament colleague observes.

Now let us begin by seeing how Matthew and Luke prepare us to hear their versions of the Sermon.

Chapter i

Beginnings

Matthew and Luke Introduce the Speaker of the Sermon and His Audience

In our effort to hear clearly Matthew's and Luke's understanding of the teaching of Jesus represented in the Sermon on the Mount and on the Plain, we need to take seriously the way the evangelists prepare their audiences to hear their respective presentations of Jesus' "inaugural address." This label applies in both cases, most obviously in Matthew, because the Sermon constitutes the first of a set of five major speeches in his gospel. But it is also a kind of inaugural address in Luke; even though Jesus' earlier speech in the Nazareth synagogue, with his self-application of Isaiah 61, is a kind of "mission and identity statement" (Luke 4:17b-21), the Sermon on the Plain (6:20-49) is more obviously a summary of his moral vision, and it is addressed to a more inclusive audience. Like Matthew 5–7, Luke's shorter version of the Sermon is a description of what it means practically for Jesus and his followers to live out that mission. We now take time to approach the respective *settings* of the Sermon in the Gospel of Matthew and the Gospel of Luke: Who is talking? Who is the audience? And what time is it?

Who Is Talking?

In the first sentence of his gospel, Matthew announces Jesus as "the Christ, the son of David, the son of Abraham." Even more obviously than Mark's identification of Jesus in his opening sentence ("Christ, son of God"), Matthew's statement underscores Jesus' Jewish roots.

Not only is he the expected Anointed One ("Messiah" in Hebrew, "Christ" in Greek), but he is also "son of David" (as fulfiller of the prophecy of 2 Samuel 7, one of the sources for understanding "the Anointed One"). He is also a true "son of Abraham," implying that he is heir and implementer of the promise to Abraham in Genesis 12:1-3, especially the promise that "all the communities of the earth / shall find blessing in you." This promise anticipated the mission to the gentiles, what Isaiah will call Servant Israel's mission of being a "light for the nations" in Isaiah 49:6. Matthew's inclusion of the genealogy (1:2-16)—Abraham, through David, past the Babylonian captivity, to Joseph, and culminating in Jesus born of Mary—highlights how Jesus historically culminates and spiritually embodies the mission of the people of Israel. Even the focus on the number fourteen ("Thus the total number of generations from Abraham to David is fourteen generations; from David to the Babylonian exile, fourteen generations; from the Babylonian exile to the Messiah, fourteen generations," 1:17) point in that direction. The numeric equivalents of the Hebrew letters for the name David—*dwd*—add up to fourteen: $4 + 6 + 4 = 14$.

Matthew's fulfillment citations of Israel's Scriptures (such as 1:22, "All this took place to fulfill what the Lord had said through the prophet. . . .") proceed to underscore aspects of Jesus' identity and mission. For example, the reference to Isaiah 7:14 at Matthew 1:23 applies to Jesus the name Emmanuel ("God with us"), a theme echoed at 18:20 ("For where two or three are gathered in my name, there I am in the midst of them") and in the gospel's final verse, 28:20b ("And behold, I am with you always, until the end of the age"). Matthew 2:6b echoes 2 Samuel 5:1 to identify Jesus as the one "who is to shepherd my people Israel." And when Matthew describes the migration of Joseph, Mary, and Jesus to sojourn in Egypt, he quotes Hosea 11:1, "Out of Egypt I called my son" (2:15), where the prophet is applying "son" (of God) to the whole people of Israel. Matthew thereby

implies that Jesus is not only son of God in the sense of being generated by God but also in the sense that he embodies the vocation of
his people Israel. This sonship will be confirmed by the voice from
the heavens after the immersion at the Jordan: "This is my beloved
Son, with whom I am well pleased" (3:17).

One of the things that makes Matthew's introduction of John the
Baptist different from Mark's is that he presents him as an announcer
of the coming of the kingdom, saying, "Repent, for the kingdom of
heaven is at hand!" (3:2). Since this is the first time Matthew mentions
the kingdom of heaven, it is important to hear this announcement
correctly. The next thirty times that this phrase occurs in his gospel,
it names the main topic of Jesus' preaching. It has to do with what
time it is in sacred history.

WHAT TIME IS IT?

Matthew's genealogy of Jesus is already a profound statement
about the *time* of Jesus; it is the culmination of the history of Israel,
the goal of biblical history. But equally important—and initially puz-
zling—is John the Baptist's announcement that *the kingdom of heaven
is at hand* (3:2). Unfortunately, we speakers of English have a problem
hearing accurately the phrase "kingdom of heaven" (the literal translation of the Greek would be "the kingdom of *the heavens*"). To our
ears, the phrase sounds like the name of a place, as in "the kingdom
of England." In other words, it sounds like "the kingdom which is
heaven," or simply another way of saying *heaven*, understood as the
transcendent realm of God. In fact, "kingdom of heaven" in Matthew
means what "kingdom of *God*" means in Mark, as a quick comparison of parallel passages in Matthew and Mark reveals (compare, for
example, Matthew 4:17 with Mark 1:15).

It helps to know that the word translated "kingdom" (*basileia* in
Greek) can also be translated "reign"; in other words, *the exercise*

of royal authority or power rather than the territory over which that authority is exercised. And what exactly does kingdom, or reign, of God mean in its first-century Jewish setting? It means the *end-time manifestation* of God's reign or kingship, the divine saving intervention that first-century Jews were anticipating. When John and then Jesus announce the imminence of the reign of God as "good news," it cannot simply refer to the *perennial* reign of the Creator's ongoing rule of the universe. An announcement of divine reign in *that* sense would simply be a statement of a commonly known and well-accepted fact; it would not be *news*. In that sense, God's reign is always "at hand."

What makes the announcement news is the implied apocalyptic framework of the phrase. Jewish apocalypses, of which the biblical Book of Daniel is our most familiar example, picture history as being divided between "the present age," in which some tyrant is ruling Israel's life, and "the age to come," in which Israel's true king, the Lord God, will intervene in a number of ways: by raising up his Anointed One, pouring out his Spirit, restoring the scattered twelve tribes of Israel, bringing peace and justice, and enabling Israel to become a "light for the nations" (Isaiah 49:6). To announce that the reign of God is "at hand" in *this* sense is to announce good news indeed. This is what the kingdom or reign of God means in the New Testament writings generally.

The reign of God was understood as future with respect to the Baptist, but Jesus announces the kingdom or reign of God as *inaugurated* in his ministry—most clearly in places like Matthew 12:28: "But if it is by the Spirit of God that I drive out demons, then the kingdom of God has come upon you" (and see the parallel saying in Luke 11:20). Jesus also speaks of the *future fulfillment* of that inaugurated kingdom, as when he teaches his disciples to pray "Your kingdom come" in the Lord's Prayer (Matthew 6:10 and Luke 11:2). So the formula that commentators often use to summarize Jesus' teaching about the kingdom as "already and not yet" present is a good way to put it. The kingdom of God is *already inaugurated* in Jesus' life, death, and resurrection, but it is *not yet fulfilled*. It remains to be fulfilled in the growth of the church and finally in the second coming of Christ. Understood in this way, it is perfectly correct to say that the end times *have already begun* with Jesus. It is the *end* of the end times that remains in the future—of whose precise time, Jesus taught, "no one knows, neither the angels in heaven, nor the Son, but the Father alone" (Matthew 24:36; see also Mark 13:32).

The Kingdom of Heaven

In modern English, Matthew's usual phrase for the same reality, the "kingdom of *heaven*," can throw us off and lead us to think that Jesus' sayings and parables that use that phrase refer to heaven as the realm of God to which good people go after death. It really means the reign of God already inaugurated by the life, death, and resurrection of Jesus—with implications, to be sure, regarding the future resurrection of the just.

Why, then, does Matthew use the phrase "kingdom of heaven"? Part of the answer may be that Matthew is exercising the customary Jewish restraint and reverence regarding the name of God. Traditional Jews have always avoided saying the sacred name represented by the four letters YHWH (the so-called tetragrammaton or "four-letter word") by substituting another name, *Adonai* ("my LORD"). In the same way, Matthew prefers "kingdom of the heavens" to "kingdom of God." The four exceptions in his gospel (12:28; 19:24; 21:31, 43) prove the rule. Matthew 12:28 is especially telling; it is what Jesus says in the Beelzebul controversy about the source of his power to heal and deliver from evil spirits: "But if it is by the Spirit of God that I drive out demons, then the *kingdom of God* has come upon you." In this way Jesus interprets his actions of healing and deliverance as signs of the inauguration of the long-awaited reign of God. Since kingdom talk occurs in eight places in the Sermon on the Mount (5:3, 10, 19 [twice], 20; 6:10, 33; 7:21), it is important to hear accurately how Matthew understands this language. The phrase refers to the reign of God already inaugurated in the life, death, and resurrection of Jesus. And like all of the gospels, the Gospel of Matthew views the life and teaching of Jesus through Easter glasses. What time is it? The time of the author of the Gospel of Matthew, and consequently the time of the readers, is the end times already inaugurated by Jesus. Like Mark, Luke, and John, Matthew is always thinking of Jesus as the risen Lord of the community, and he presents the story of Jesus always in this light of the Easter reality in which the writer and his audience now live.

Since Matthew does not shy away from using *ho theos*, the usual Greek word for God, in many places apart from the phrase "kingdom of God," there may also be another motive besides reverential restraint that explains his preference for "kingdom of heaven": The phrase connotes the transcendent nature of that reign. The source of that exercise of divine authority comes from beyond this world. This emphasis is evident in a statement like "I will give you the keys to the kingdom of heaven. Whatever you bind on earth shall be bound in heaven, and whatever you loose on earth shall be loosed in heaven" (16:19, addressed to Simon Peter; and see 18:18, the same mandate addressed in the plural to the community).[8] Another useful effect of the phrase "kingdom *of heaven*" is that the expression sharpens the contrast with the Roman Empire. Clearly, this was the *earthly* kingdom of the Mediterranean world, a kingdom whose lord was the emperor and whose "peace" (*pax Romana*) was achieved by violence and domination.[9]

When Matthew presents John the Baptist as saying that he is baptizing in water but the one coming after him will baptize "with the holy Spirit and fire" (3:11), the author expects his audience to hear in this imagery an allusion to such prophecies as Ezekiel 36:26-27 and Joel 3:1-5. First-century Judaism could understand these texts as prophecies of Messianic times, with water representing the end-time outpouring of the Holy Spirit and fire symbolizing purification for the righteous and punishment for the unrighteous.

Matthew has John interrupt the scene of Jesus' baptism at the Jordan with this objection: "I need to be baptized by you, and yet you are coming to me?" But Matthew, uniquely, has Jesus answer this way: "Allow it for now, for thus it is fitting for us to fulfill all righteousness" (3:14-15). We dare to attribute this dialogue to Matthew, rather than to a tradition unknown to the other evangelists, because of its focus on "righteousness," which is a theme special to Matthew. "Righteousness" is absent in Mark but introduced seven times in Matthew's gospel, five of them in the Sermon on the Mount. Matthew uses "righteousness" (*dikaiosynē*) in the biblical sense of doing the will of God, being faithful to the covenant. Thus Matthew answers a question inevitably raised by Mark's account of the baptism of Jesus: "Why should the sinless one go though a ritual of repentance, and one administered by a lesser person?" Answer: "Don't trouble yourselves with questions of superiority and inferiority. Each in his own way is called to do the will of God." This is a good lesson for a Christian at any time, and a helpful preparation for hearing the Sermon on the Mount, which is all about fulfilling the will of God.

Matthew's rendition of the Q tradition about Satan's tempting of Jesus (4:1-11; par. Luke 4:1-13) shows Jesus reliving the experience of Israel in the wilderness as told in Deuteronomy 6–8. But where Israel proved to be a rebellious "son of God," Jesus shows himself a true Son of God by obeying. Compared to Luke's version, Matthew highlights that one lives "by every word that comes forth from the mouth of God" (4:4, quoting Deuteronomy 8:3). And while Luke presents the third trial on the pinnacle of the Jerusalem temple (with Satan saying in effect, "Jump! God will send his angels to catch you"),

Matthew's sequence emphasizes as the top trial the devil's offer of all the kingdoms of the world spoken on "a very high mountain" (4:8). Again, the reader/audience is being prepared for the Sermon, which will spell out what it means to live by the word of God and which will be presented on "the mountain." These are the first two of seven geographically vague but symbolically powerful references to "the mountain" in this gospel.[10]

When Matthew comes to Mark's report of Jesus beginning his public ministry in Galilee (4:12-17), he elaborates this debut with another formula citation. He quotes Isaiah 8:23–9:1, Isaiah's prophecy about relief coming to people oppressed by an alien empire (*light to those dwelling in darkness*), applying that language to the long-range import of Jesus' public life. Although his immediate preaching addresses fellow Jews in the synagogues of Galilee, his message will eventually become light to the gentiles through his disciples. Like the narrative about the gentile magi worshiping Jesus as king, this passage forecasts the mission of the church to the entire world.

A Carefully Crafted Setting

After the account of Jesus' calling of his first disciples—two sets of brothers, Simon Peter and Andrew, and Zebedee's sons, James and John, who drop everything to follow him (4:18-22)—Matthew provides a carefully crafted setting for the Sermon.

Anyone following Matthew's rewrite of the Gospel of Mark will immediately notice that he omits the exorcism of the demoniac in the Capernaum synagogue (Mark 1:21-28). This omission is not arbitrary. One may reasonably conjecture that, as in the scene of the baptism at the Jordan, Matthew sees in this episode a question that he is eager to answer. The action of Mark's demoniac story is Jesus' mastery of an unclean spirit oppressing a man in the synagogue congregation. The episode is framed with references to Jesus' *teaching*. It begins with the statement that Jesus entered the synagogue and taught, and the report that "the people were astonished at his *teaching*, for he *taught* them as one having authority and not as the scribes" (verse 22). After the dramatic account of the deliverance, Mark reports, "All were amazed and asked one another, 'What is this? A *new teaching with authority*'" (verse 27). Strangely, while the account was about the deliverance from demonic oppression, the people at the beginning and at the end are said to be responding primarily to Jesus' *teaching with authority*. This raises the question: *What is this teaching* that Jesus gives with authority? The only hint about Jesus' teaching given thus far in Mark's narrative is the summary at Mark 1:15: "This is the time of fulfillment. The kingdom of God is at hand. Repent, and believe in the gospel."

Matthew sees in the statement about Jesus' teaching authority and in the implied question about the precise content of his teaching an opportunity to present some of that teaching in the form of an inaugural address, the collection of Jesus' sayings that we have come to call the Sermon on the Mount. Our best evidence that this is what our author is doing is first, Matthew's omission of the deliverance action in Mark 1:21-28, and second, the inclusion of Mark 1:22 ("A new teaching with authority!") as a *response* to this speech presenting the core of Jesus' moral teaching: "When Jesus finished these words, the crowds *were astonished at this teaching for he taught them as one having authority, and not as their scribes*" (Matthew 7:28-29).

Matthew appears to have modeled his description of the setting of the Sermon on Mark 3:7-13, where Mark provides a summary of Jesus' healing ministry and its effect throughout a wide geographical area—"A large number of people [followed] from Galilee and from Judea . . . [and] from Jerusalem, from Idumea, from beyond the Jordan, and from the neighborhood of Tyre and Sidon" (3:7-8). Mark describes this assembly as a single event—something like Pope John Paul II's 1979 visit to the Living History Farm in Iowa—a gathering that would have required complex logistical planning. It seems best to understand it as a summary of what happened over a longer period in Jesus' public life. Matthew draws on many of Mark's details, though with a more concentrated geographical range of the pilgrims' origins (Galilee, the Decapolis, Jerusalem and Judea, and beyond the Jordan, 4:25). Matthew makes it more clearly a summary by prefacing that description with a summary introduction:

> He went around all of Galilee, teaching in their synagogues, proclaiming the gospel of the kingdom, and curing every disease and illness among the people. His fame spread to all of Syria [the name of the Roman province that included all of Palestine], and they brought to him all who were sick with various diseases and racked with pain, those who were possessed, lunatics, and paralytics, and he cured them. (Matthew 4:23-24; see the parallel summary at 9:35).

The geographical references may be an effort to evoke the kingdom of David; "the mountain" of the next verse, Matthew 5:1, may be a symbolic venue meant to recall both of the most prominent mountains of the Jewish imagination—Sinai (the mount of the original covenant with Israel) and Zion (the temple mount as the venue of the end-time restoration of Israel and the gathering of the nations).[11] Whether or not Mark intends symbolic meaning for the mountain of Jesus' appointment and commissioning of the twelve (Mark 3:13), or in the mountain that is the venue of his personal prayer (6:46), or in the mountain of the transfiguration (9:2-9), Matthew's mountain, mentioned seven times (4:8; 5:1; 14:23; 15:29; 17:1; 24:3; 28:16), surely invites symbolic interpretation. Given Matthew's interest in Jesus as Son of David elsewhere in his gospel (see Matthew 1:6, 17, 20; 9:27; 12:23; 15:22; 20:30, 31), it makes sense to read his setting of the Sermon on the Mount as a presentation of Jesus as the end-time Davidic messiah presiding over the end-time gathering place (Zion).

Moreover, since Jesus explicitly compares his teaching in the Sermon with specific Mosaic laws, commentators also perceive allusions to Moses. Matthew can embrace both ways of understanding Jesus, but the geographical setting given here, including in four quadrants the extent of David's kingdom in its prime, is more evocative of the messianic restoration of Israel under the end-time king reigning from Zion than a memory of Moses' Sinai. Mosaic allusions, however, will soon follow.

To Whom Does Jesus Speak?

5:1When he saw the crowds, he went up the mountain, and after he had sat down, his disciples came to him. 2He began to teach them. . . .

"The crowds" would seem to be the vast assembly just described in the previous verse, who are said to have "followed" Jesus (4:25). When we read that Jesus goes up the mountain in response to seeing the crowds, it is not clear if he does so to withdraw from the crowds or to find a better perch from which to be heard—as will be the case when he gets into the boat to teach parables to the crowd in chapter 13. The fact that his disciples approach him, seemingly apart from the crowd, suggests *some* kind of separation from the crowd. Does the "them" that Jesus begins to teach include the crowds as well as the disciples? Matthew clarifies his picture of the audience at the close of the Sermon: "When Jesus finished these words, the crowds were astonished at his teaching, for he taught them as one having authority, and not as their scribes" (7:28-29). So it is Matthew's meaning that the crowds are being taught right along with the disciples.

And who exactly are those disciples? Up to this point, our author has mentioned only four who are singled out to follow Jesus in a special way—Peter, Andrew, and the brothers Zebedee (4:18-22), who drop everything to follow him. We will hear other references to "the disciples" in chapters 8 and 9, but only at the commissioning of "his twelve disciples" (10:1) will we meet the group of the twelve; Matthew skips Mark's account of the *choice* of the twelve. He seems to presume that his readers already know about the inner circle of twelve. Regarding the audience of the Sermon, now that we have read of their response, it is clear that Jesus teaches both the inner circle of disciples (whatever the number) and the crowds. Notice, though, that "the crowds" is not shorthand for all people. The crowds here have been described as those who are *following* Jesus because they have come to know him as preacher of the "gospel of the kingdom" and as the healer of "all who were sick with various diseases and racked with pain" (4:23, 24). One has to meet Jesus before one can decide to follow him or not.

Luke's Picture of the Who, What, When, and Where of the Sermon

Since our purpose is to listen to both Matthew and Luke as each mediates the teaching of Jesus, let us now turn to the way Luke sets up his readers to hear Jesus. The similarities and differences are fascinating and instructive.

In the Third Gospel, Jesus as speaker of the Sermon on the Plain (6:20-49) has been introduced even more elaborately than in Matthew—two and a half chapters more elaborately. Gabriel has announced Jesus as "Son of the Most High," heir of "the throne of David," and ruler "over the house of Jacob" (1:32, 33)—both of the latter expressions referring to the end-time restoration of the twelve tribes of Israel. Mary has sung a canticle celebrating her motherhood of Jesus as the fulfillment of God's promise to Abraham (1:46-55), and

Zechariah has sung his song about the coming visitation of divine day-break "to shine on those who sit in darkness and death's shadow, / to guide our feet into the path of peace" (1:78-79). The angel of the Lord has announced his birth as Messiah and Lord to shepherds (2:11). And at the presentation of Jesus in the temple, a Spirit-prompted elder, Simeon, identifies the child as the fulfillment of Isaiah's promise of a Servant of the Lord who will become a "light to the nations" (Isaiah 49:6, cited in Luke 2:32), while the prophetess Anna identifies the child as the one who will bring about the expected "redemption of Jerusalem" (2:38). John the Baptist has hinted at Jesus' universal mission by applying the words of Isaiah 40:5: "And all flesh shall see the salvation of God" (3:6). And if Matthew uses a genealogy to highlight Jesus as the culmination of Israel's life with God from Abraham forward, Luke provides a genealogy of his own that extends *backward*—past Abraham, through Noah, *all the way to Adam*—to underscore the universality of the mission of Jesus and his followers (3:23-37). He will continue the story of mission to the whole world in volume two, the Acts of the Apostles.

There is even more to Luke's preparation. Luke introduces Jesus' public ministry with the account of his debut in the synagogue at Nazareth. In Luke's version of this moment, Jesus reads Isaiah 61:1-2a and applies it to himself in a one-line homily ("Today this scripture passage is fulfilled in your hearing," 4:21). Since Luke's first mention of kingdom preaching occurs at 4:43 ("To the other towns also I must proclaim the good news of the kingdom of God, because for this purpose I have been sent"), Luke apparently understands Jesus' application of Isaiah 61 to himself as a proclamation of the kingdom of God. So that brief homily in the Nazareth synagogue is a kind of mission-and-identity statement, not yet the moral *teaching* to come in the Sermon on the Plain.

In subsequent episodes, Jesus recruits his first disciples—Peter, James, and John—with the miraculous catch of fish (5:1-11). Then comes the call of Levi (5:27-39). When, at 6:12-16, we come to Luke's description of the choice of the twelve, we read:

> [6:12]In those days, he departed to *the mountain* to pray, and he spent the night in prayer to God. [13]When day came, he called *his disciples* to himself, and *from them* he chose Twelve, whom he also named apostles. . . . [After listing their names, Luke says,] [17]And he came down with them and stood on a stretch of level ground. A *great crowd of his disciples* and a large number of *the people* from all Judea and Jerusalem and the coastal region of Tyre and Sidon [18]came to hear him and to be healed of their diseases; and even those who were tormented by unclean spirits were cured. [19]Everyone in the crowd sought to touch him because power came forth from him and healed them all.

When we bring to Luke's description of the setting for the Sermon on the Plain the same attention to detail that we gave to Matthew's setting of the Sermon on the Mount, a number of items stand out:

1. As with Matthew, we are reading another variation on Mark 3:7-13 (the mountain; a summary description of Jesus' healing ministry to a large assembly drawn from a broad geographical range).

2. There is a distinction between Jesus' disciples and a larger group. But unlike Matthew's description, it is not simply a matter of the disciples (in Matthew, apparently the twelve) and a great crowd. In Luke's scene, we see three circles: "a great crowd of his disciples"; then the group of the twelve drawn from that larger group of disciples; and "a large number of the people from all Judea and Jerusalem and the coastal region of Tyre and Sidon" (verse 17). Given that the phrase "the people" (*ho laos*) carries for Luke the connotation of the chosen people of Israel (a connotation that the word has in the Greek

Scriptures), this label includes a group still larger than the crowd of disciples, yet mainly Jews. Within this assembly of the people and the disciples, the twelve comprise a small core.

3. The spatial setting is a plains area below "the mountain"—a piedmont.

4. Jesus clearly addresses the entire assembly. Indeed, Luke writes at the end of the speech, "When he had finished all his words *to the people*, he entered Capernaum" (7:1).

What is the import of Luke's setting of the Sermon on the Plain? Jesus has been identified as destined for the "throne of David his father"; he is Son of the Most High (1:32). Identifying himself with the prophetic figure of Isaiah 61 (linked with the Servant figure of the rest of the Book of Isaiah?), anointed "to bring glad tidings to the poor" and "to proclaim liberty to captives" (4:18), he comes in the role of a prophet of Israel. And because he *comes down from the mountain to speak to the people*, Luke's audience is prompted to think of Jesus as the long expected "prophet like Moses"—an idea that Luke will emphasize elsewhere (see Acts 3:22; 7:37). While Luke has not used fulfillment formulas like Matthew, he has emphasized in other ways that the coming of Jesus is indeed a fulfillment of Jewish end-time expectations. The "age to come" has begun in his own life and presence: "If it is by the finger of God that I drive out demons, then the kingdom of God has come upon you" (11:20), "finger of God" being another allusion to Moses' ministry (see Exodus 8:19). In his own way, Luke is describing the same Jesus as Matthew and announcing the same eschatological time.

What Luke is saying about the audience to whom the Sermon is directed is equally as important. Both Matthew and Luke make it clear that the Sermon is not abstract teaching about leading a successful life. The teaching is not simply advice about doing the right thing. It is all about *following Jesus*. In both gospels, the people to whom the Sermon is addressed—on the mount, below the mount—are those who have been following Jesus, those who have come to know him as preacher of the kingdom and as healer. The audience, *then*—in the time of Jesus and in the time of Matthew and Luke—and *now*, consists of those who have come to know something of the person of Jesus the Messiah and who desire to follow him.

Already, our study of the settings of the Sermon in both Matthew and Luke suggests a profound practical application for us who would be disciples of Jesus today: The Sermon on the Mount is not instruction for an elite group. It teaches basic Christianity. It is meant for anyone who would be a disciple of Christ. But notice: It is not directed to isolated individuals. It is directed to a community of people who have already known Jesus the healer. Now let us begin to hear afresh the Sermon itself.

Chapter 2

Four on the Plain
The Beatitudes (and Woes) according to Luke
(6:20-26)

The beatitudes (Matthew 5:3-12 and Luke 6:20-26, including Luke's "woes") invite our careful attention for several reasons. First, they set the tone for the whole Sermon; how we hear them affects how we understand the rest of the speech. Second, they show how Jesus—*and* Matthew and Luke as Jesus' interpreters—use this literary form in ways that resonate profoundly with the Old Testament. And finally, the similarities and differences in the two sets of beatitudes illustrate at once what is distinctive about each evangelist and what they have in common, as well as their fidelity to the preaching of Jesus.

Even though this book will follow the order of Matthew's Sermon on the Mount, treating the parallels in the Gospel of Luke as they are prompted by the Matthean text, we are going to make an exception to that procedure even as we begin our study. After reviewing Old Testament background on beatitudes and woes, we will make some preliminary observations about Matthew's and Luke's renditions of the beatitudes, and then we will proceed directly to an indepth study of Luke's four beatitudes (along with their opposites, the four "woes"). The reason for taking Luke's four before Matthew's nine will become obvious as we proceed: Luke's beatitudes appear to reflect an earlier stage in the transmission of Jesus' teaching.

For now, because those classic beatitudes standing at the head of the Sermon on the Mount and the Sermon on the Plain are part of a long Israelite tradition, it will help to revisit some examples of the beatitude format in the Old Testament.

WHAT IS A MACARISM?

When Jesus' original synagogue audiences heard him make statements that began, "Blessed those who . . ." and then went on to name a consequence, they recognized this as a familiar communication pattern, one that they had heard frequently in readings from their Scriptures. It occurred often in the Wisdom scrolls, such as Sirach and Proverbs, and appeared frequently in the Psalms. The typical Old Testament beatitude has two or sometimes three components:

1. An adjective—'*ashre* in Hebrew, or *makarios/makarioi* (singular/plural) in Greek—meaning in both languages "blessed" or "fortunate";

2. A subject (normally indicated in the third person, "the one who . . .") whose behavior or whose happy state is described in a clause, and sometimes a third element closely associated with the first two;

3. A description that elaborates either the blessed state or the piety that led to this happy consequence.

In the Bible a beatitude, or macarism,[12] is always a religious statement, never simply a description of a psychological state or feeling, because the key word, the adjective ('*ashre* or *makarios*), always describes a situation deriving from a person's relationship with God. That is why it is best translated "blessed" rather than "happy" or "fortunate." Even before it was used in the Greek translation of the Hebrew Scriptures, *makarios* was used in nonbiblical Greek with godly associations. Homer called the Greek gods *makarioi*; by extension, human beings were called *makarioi* when they were thought of as participating in the happiness of the gods. That background made it a good word to translate from the Hebrew *'ashre*, which had the same divine connotations. Psalm 1 provides a good biblical example of the beatitude form:

> Happy those who do not follow
> the counsel of the wicked
> Nor go the way of sinners,
> nor sit in the company with scoffers,
> Rather, the law of the LORD is their joy;
> God's law they study day and night.
> They are like a tree planted near streams of water,
> that yields its fruit in season,
> Its leaves never wither;
> whatever they do prospers. (Psalm 1:1-3)

We can see the formula at work here. The first element, "happy," translates the conventional adjective—*'ashre* in Hebrew, *makarios* in Greek—implying a blessed relationship with the Lord God. The description of the behavior of those who follow the Lord, the rest of verse 1 as well as verse 2a, constitutes the second element. And verse 3 ("They are like a tree planted near streams of water . . .") gives us the third element, the consequence.

That example demonstrates the *format* of beatitudes. As for the *content*, scholars observe that the Bible gives us two kinds of macarisms—wisdom beatitudes and apocalyptic beatitudes. *Wisdom* beatitudes focus on attitudes and behaviors that benefit a person in life here and now; *apocalyptic* beatitudes focus on attitudes and behaviors in the light of their consequence in God's future intervention in history. The beatitude we observed in Psalm 1 is a wisdom beatitude, as are most of the beatitudes in the Old Testament. An example of an OT apocalyptic beatitude is Daniel 12:12-13: "Blessed is the man who has patience and perseveres until the one thousand three hundred and thirty-five days. Go, take your rest, you shall rise for your reward at the end of days." Notice the switch from third-person mode, "he" ["the man"], to second-person, "you"—something that also occurs in the NT beatitudes. Most of the forty-four New Testament beatitudes are apocalyptic beatitudes. Witness, for example, James 1:12: "Blessed is the man who perseveres in temptation, for when he has been proved he will receive the crown of life that he promised to those who love him." As we will see, the beatitudes of Jesus are very much like his statements about the kingdom of God—apocalyptic in their emphasis on God's future action but something like wisdom beatitudes in their assertion that the future fulfillment has already been initiated in Jesus' present activity.

And what is the point of a beatitude? Is there a way of summarizing what a speaker is doing when he or she makes a statement in that format? I would put it this way: A beatitude is a kind of congratulation, spoken to affirm, encourage, and hold up as examples those qualities that either show that a person is blessed by God or assure future blessedness with God. Jesus' beatitudes are at once congratulations and challenges. But precisely what the macarisms of the Sermon are saying requires more careful study. Let us begin. We will first view Matthew's and Luke's beatitudes together. This will enable us later to hear them separately.

SEEING MATTHEW AND LUKE TOGETHER

We can learn a lot about the beatitudes by comparing Matthew's and Luke's versions, along with Luke's corresponding "woes." What follows is based on the version called the New American Bible (NAB) in the revised edition of 1986. To get as close to the original Greek as possible, where the NAB uses words for which there is no literal counterpart in the original (e. g., the verb "are" after "blessed"), I have dropped them. And where the word order of the Greek can be more directly represented, I have done so.

MATTHEW 5:3-12	LUKE 6:20B-26
[3]Blessed: the poor in spirit, for theirs is the kingdom of heaven.	[20b]Blessed: the poor for yours[13] is the kingdom of God.
[4]Blessed: they who mourn, for they will be comforted.	
[5]Blessed: the meek, for they will inherit the land.	
[6]Blessed: they who hunger and thirst for righteousness, for they will be satisfied.	[21a]Blessed: they who hunger now for you will be satisfied. [21b]Blessed: they who weep now for you will laugh.
[7]Blessed: the merciful, for they will be shown mercy. [8]Blessed: the clean of heart, for they will see God. [9]Blessed: the peacemakers, for they will be called sons of God. [10]Blessed: they who are persecuted for the sake of righteousness, for theirs is the kingdom of heaven.	
[11]Blessed are you when they insult you and persecute you and utter every kind of evil against you [falsely] because of me.	[22]Blessed are you when people hate you, and when they exclude and and denounce your name as evil on account of the Son of Man.
[12]Rejoice and be glad, for your reward will be great in heaven. Thus they persecuted the prophets who were before you.	[23]Rejoice and leap for joy that day. Behold, your reward will be great in heaven. For so their fathers did to the prophets.

[24]But woe to you who are rich,
for you have received your
consolation.
[25a]Woe to you who are filled now,
for you will be hungry.
[25b]Woe to you who laugh now,
for you will grieve and weep.
[26]Woe to you when all speak well
of you, for so their fathers did to
the false prophets.

A comparison of the two sets of beatitudes yields three important insights.

1. *Matthew and Luke have four beatitudes in common:*

- One for the poor (who already possess the kingdom)—the first beatitude in both gospels.
- Another for the hungry (who will be satisfied)—Matthew's fourth, Luke's second.
- A third for the grieving (whose lot will be reversed)—Matthew's second and Luke's third.
- And a fourth beatitude—Matthew's ninth and Luke's fourth—on being rejected for Jesus' sake (for your reward will be great in heaven).

2. *Matthew and Luke each incorporate those common beatitudes in their own phrasing and within a carefully crafted and distinct design.*

We will look at the difference in phrasing in a moment, but the design features can be noticed right away. Matthew has balanced and unified his first eight beatitudes carefully. The eighth echoes the first with "for theirs is the kingdom of heaven." The fourth and the eighth focus on righteousness, as something to be hungered for in the first case and as something to be suffered for in the eighth. Matthew's original audience would have heard the alliteration (repeated "p" sounds in this case)—and even a kind of rhyme between the second and fourth subjects—connecting the qualities that are congratulated in the first four: *ptōchoi*, *penthountes*, *praeis*, and *peinōntes* (poor, mourning, meek, and hungering).

Luke incorporates the common beatitudes in a quite different design of his own. He first presents the four beatitudes he shares with Matthew (about the poor, hungry, weeping, and excluded), and then he presents their opposites in the form of four "woes" (addressed to the rich, full, laughing, and well-thought-of).

3. In each case the design elements and word choices cohere with the larger themes and the structure of their respective gospels.

Matthew tends to favor balanced phrasing and repetition. He has a special interest in "righteousness" (see 3:15; 5:6, 10, 20; 6:1, 33; and 21:32), and he prefers the phrase "kingdom of heaven" over "kingdom of God." On the other hand, Luke's insertion of four woes addressed to the rich, full, laughing, and well-thought-of, contrasting with the beatitudes addressed to the poor, hungry, mourning, and rejected, reflects a strong theme in the Third Gospel: Encountering Jesus reveals one's inner disposition toward God and provokes a personal decision either to accept or to reject Jesus as mediator of the divine.

Beginning with the contrasts of the Magnificat ("He has thrown down the rulers from their thrones / but lifted up the lowly. / The hungry he has filled with good things; / the rich he has sent away empty,"

Luke 1:52-53) and Simeon's prophecy that "this child is destined for the fall and rise of many in Israel" (2:34), and climaxing with the contrasting responses of the two crucified with Jesus (one reviling Jesus, the other repenting—23:39-43), Luke underscores how encounters with Jesus reveal "the thoughts of many hearts" (2:35) in opposite ways. Indeed, the parable of the rich man and Lazarus (Luke 16:19-30) puts in story form the contrasts of Luke's beatitudes and woes. As the parable begins, the rich man—traditionally called "Dives" (Latin for "rich man")—is full and satisfied, and Lazarus is poor and hungry. After death the rich man is thirsty, and Lazarus is enjoying the eschatological banquet with Abraham.

Noting the difference between Luke's "poor" and Matthew's "poor *in spirit*" and between Luke's "those who hunger" and Matthew's "those who hunger *and thirst for righteousness,*" some commentators rush to the judgment that Matthew has "spiritualized" and somehow diluted what they take to be Luke's (and Jesus') references to the literally poor and hungry. Such commentators think that Matthew has softened and watered down the tough, edgy beatitudes of Jesus reflected in Luke's version. Careful attention to the Old Testament background and the gospel contexts of these beatitudes shows that this interpretation of the differences is not warranted. Let us see what a more careful reading of each version reveals.

Since Luke confines himself to the four Q beatitudes and provides the shorter, and possibly earlier, versions (poor, mourning, hungry, and rejected), we begin with his rendition.

LUKE'S FIRST THREE: POOR, WEEPING, AND HUNGRY VERSUS RICH, LAUGHING, AND FULL

When Luke reports Jesus' speaking the first beatitude to that vast healed assembly of disciples and other seekers—*"Blessed: the poor [hoi ptōchoi], for yours is the kingdom of God"*—how does Luke understand these words? We have three good tools to use in our search: dictionaries of ancient Greek; the Greek version of the Hebrew Bible (called the Septuagint, the version of the Bible that early Christian writers generally used); and, most pertinent, the rest of Luke's two-volume work—the Third Gospel and the Acts of the Apostles.

Lexicographers note that first-century Greek used two words that can be rendered "poor" in English—*penēs,* which denoted a person who had employment but was of slender means, and *ptōchos,* "begging, dependent on others for support."[14] The evangelists do not use the word *penēs* at all. They use *ptōchos,* which carried connotations from the Septuagint, especially in the Psalms and in Isaiah, where the word often refers to those who are so oppressed that they are in special need of God's help.

The Poor in Luke

In Luke only two *individuals* are termed *ptōchos*: the widow who contributed all that she had in the form of two copper coins (21:3), and the beggar in the parable of the rich man and Lazarus (16:20, 22). The seven other references in Luke are general references to the poor as a group.[15] They include those to whom the rich man is invited to give the worth of all his property (18:22), those to whom Zacchaeus resolves to give half his goods (19:8), and those among Jesus' list of preferred banquet guests (14:13, 21). Our best clue to Luke's specific meaning for "poor" as he uses it in his first beatitude is that his beatitude about *hoi ptōchoi* (6:20) stands in his gospel between two key Old Testament references to *hoi ptōchoi*: the quotation of Isaiah 61:1 at 4:18, and the allusion to that same seminal Isaian passage at 7:22. Our author has provided in those two references to Isaiah 61 the scriptural context in which he would have his audience understand *hoi ptōchoi* in the first beatitude. He means "the poor" as Isaiah means it.

What is Isaiah's meaning for the poor? In Isaiah 61, the passage quoted at Luke 4:18, *hoi ptōchoi* translates *anawim* ("the lowly" in the NAB) and stands in parallel with "the brokenhearted"; "the captives" ("the blind" in the LXX version from which Luke quotes at 4:18); "the oppressed" (added to Isaiah 61 from Isaiah 58:6); and "the mourning." In this setting, *hoi ptōchoi* are not some group or class to be distinguished from the brokenhearted, the captives, and the mourning; rather, *hoi ptōchoi* are the faithful in postexilic Israel who, even after the return, still yearn for the definitive saving intervention of God. Isaiah 61:1-3 is an application of the Servant-of-Yahweh imagery from Second Isaiah to the prophetic community of Third Isaiah.[16] This prophetic figure is portrayed as addressing the larger community of Judah (representing the full twelve-tribe Israel of old) and announcing to them that hoped-for salvation. In the Greek version of Second and Third Isaiah (i. e., chapters 40–66), *hoi ptōchoi* are the people as a whole in need of salvation by their God (chapter 41, especially verse 17, and 61:1).[17] The imagery of hungering and weeping also employs conventional Old Testament language for describing the people as a whole in need of help from their God (see the beatitudes in Psalms 34:6-10; 146:5-7; and Isaiah 26:6; 40:28-30; 41:17-20; 49:10; 55:1-3).

Even the needy who are not explicitly called *hoi ptōchoi* are touched in some way by the end-time manifestation of God's power shown through Jesus and his agents: the needy to whom John the Baptist exhorts the crowds to give their extra tunic or their surplus food (3:10); those reduced to borrowing and stealing (6:29-30); and the sick, maimed, blind, and lame, who if they were not supported by an extended family were reduced to begging, like the blind beggar of Jericho (18:35-43) and the man born lame in Acts 3:1-10. The two ideal descriptions of the life of the Jerusalem Christian community in Acts 2:42-47 ("all things in common . . . dividing them among all according to each one's need") and 4:32-37 ("There was no needy person [endeēs] among them"—verse 34, echoing the Jubilee text of Deuteronomy 15:4) show that the blessedness of the economically needy is already inaugurated in the life of a Christian community.

The teaching of Jesus after blessing infants at Luke 18:16-17 may be our best commentary on the essence of the poverty in the first beatitude: "Let the children come to me and do not prevent them; for the kingdom of God belongs to such as these. Amen, I say to you, whoever does not accept the kingdom of God like a child will not enter it." What makes children receptive is not their lack of financial resources, or their cuteness, but their spontaneous awareness of utter dependence on others. For adults, to receive the kingdom of God like a child means to know their utter dependence on God.

The next few episodes of the Gospel of Luke demonstrate that financial status is not the determining factor in the poverty that is congratulated in the first beatitude. First comes the rich official, who because of his attachment to possessions is unable to respond to Jesus' invitation to follow him. Jesus tells him, "How hard it is for those who have wealth to enter the kingdom of God!" (18:24). Then follows the encounter with the blind beggar of Jericho (18:35-43), who knows very well his dependency and his need. When he asks Jesus for sight, Jesus heals him ("Your faith has saved you"—verse 42), and he begins to follow Jesus. This thread of events comes to a climax with Jesus' encounter with Zacchaeus (19:1-10). Although this man is said to be rich and to have achieved this status dishonestly, Luke portrays him in a way that emphasizes childlike characteristics: He is short of stature and scampers up a tree in straightforward curiosity ("seeking to see who Jesus was"—19:3). In the sharing of hospitality that follows, Zacchaeus undergoes a conversion that results in a promise to recompense the victims of his greed fourfold and to give half his possessions to the poor. "Today salvation has come to this house," says Jesus (verse 9). Despite his financial wealth, this tax collector can be included among the "poor" of the first beatitude.

But Zacchaeus is a rarity. Shortly before this episode, in the aftermath of the encounter with the rich official (18:18-27), Jesus insists that wealth really is a danger to one's spiritual health. With wealth comes power, and with power comes the possibility of the delusion that one is autonomous, dependent on no one, least of all on (the invisible) God. "How hard it is for those who have wealth to enter the kingdom of God!" (verse 24). Jesus' listeners, thinking that wealth is a spiritual advantage—one can do great good as a benefactor—ask, "Then who can be saved?" Jesus says, "What is impossible for human beings is possible for God" (verses 26-27). Zacchaeus is apparently "poor" enough to recognize this by listening to Jesus.

The Rich in Luke

If we are to come to a full grasp of what it means to be poor in the sense of the first beatitude in Luke, we need to pursue its opposite. Who are the *rich* (*hoi plousioi*) to whom the "woes" are addressed? We have already met that exceptional rich man, Zacchaeus. But who are the woeful rich? If Luke's language about the poor, mourning, and hungry is rooted in the Hebrew Scriptures (in the Greek version he knew), especially in the psalms and Isaiah, does his language about the rich and satisfied also have its roots in Scripture?

A concordance search on the word for "rich" in the Septuagint—*plousios*—takes us to passages that seem to leap off the page in the direction of Luke's gospel. Notice, for example, Psalm 34 (33 in the LXX), especially in its LXX version (the version Luke knew and used):

This poor one [*ptōchos* in LXX] called out, and the
    Lord heard him, . . .
Taste and see how good the Lord is;
    happy [*makarios*] the man who hopes in him . . .
The rich [LXX: *plousioi*] grow poor and hungry,

But those who seek the Lord shall not lack any good thing . . .
The eyes of the Lord are upon the righteous,
  and his ears toward their prayer.
But the face of the Lord is against those who do evil things.
(LXX Psalm 33 [34]:7, 9, 11, 16-17, translation mine)

Here in a single psalm we have (1) a macarism; (2) a contrast between the poor and the rich in their relationship with God; (3) an apparent equation of the poor with righteousness and the rich with evildoing; and (4) a paradoxical linking of wealth with hunger and poverty with satisfaction. The Lukan beatitudes and woes are in this tradition. And it is clear that the psalmist is not simply equating "rich" and "poor" with economic status but with an underlying disposition regarding God.

If we search for examples of the woe formula in Luke's favorite prophet, we find that it is indeed Isaiah who uses this format most frequently, especially in Isaiah 5:8-23. There the prophet unfolds the meaning of the parable of the vineyard song (Isaiah 5:1-7), and he issues no less than six woes against the arrogant landowners whose land grabbing renders the countryside desolate and who are reprimanded for their indulgent feasting. They are, in short, addressed as being rich, full, laughing, and having their consolation now, with only doom to look forward to in the future.

The subjects of the four Lukan woes (the rich, full, laughing, and well-spoken-of) are so obviously the opposites of the subjects of the four Lukan beatitudes (the poor, hungry, weeping, and reviled) that one is justified in saying simply that the rich/full/laughing are those who fail to qualify as members of the end-time Israel because they reject Israel's Anointed One. But how does Luke's gospel specify the identity and character of the subjects of his woes?

Simply following Luke's use of the word "rich" does not clarify what he means by the *plousioi* who are the subject of the woes. In the Third Gospel, the rich are many things—sometimes bad examples (as in the case of the parable of the rich fool, Luke 12:16; and Dives, 16:19, 21, 22), sometimes morally neutral (the master of the wily steward, 16:1; and the temple benefactors, 21:1), and sometimes a good example (as in the case of Zacchaeus, 19:2). It turns out that our best clue to Luke's meaning of the "woeful rich" is his portrayal of the Pharisees.

Gospel scholarship today recognizes that the evangelists do not attempt to give us a historical snapshot of first-century Pharisees, who seem to have been generally decent folk, lay teachers of the Torah whose worldview was much closer to that of Jesus than the Sadducees. The gospel picture of Pharisees seems to derive from the evangelists' desire to use them as foils to Jesus; that is, the gospel writers invest Pharisees with qualities that are the opposite of the qualities they wish to highlight in Jesus.

For example, Luke calls the Pharisees "money lovers" (*philargy-roi*, 16:14). And passages in the Third Gospel do indeed portray the Pharisees as embodying the essence of "the rich" of the woes as contrasted with "the poor" of the beatitudes. Indeed, the money-lovers passage parallels the expression of the "woes" against the rich:

LUKE 6:24-26	LUKE 16:14-15
(description)	
you who are rich	who loved money
you who laugh now	sneered at him
all speak well of you	you justify yourselves in the sight of others
(consequent reversal)	
You will be hungry. . . , grieve and weep.	What is of human esteem is an abomination in the sight of God.

There is another parallel between this critique of the Pharisees in Luke 16 and the woes of the Sermon. The Pharisees exemplify a statement in the immediate context that resonates with the first Lukan beatitude. In the poem on mammon that precedes the money-lovers passage (16:8b-13), we read, "If you are not trustworthy with what belongs to another, who will give you *what is yours* [*hymeteron*]?" (16:12). That is, if you have not been faithful in your stewardship of earthly goods—managing what in fact belongs to Another (God!)—who will give you a recompense that you can call *your own?* Compare: "Blessed are you who are poor, for the kingdom of God *is yours* [*hymetera*]" (6:20). It may not be a coincidence that the rare, emphatic second-person plural possessive adjective, *hymeteros*, occurs only in these two places in the synoptic gospels. This repetition may be Luke's way of linking the two passages. Ironically, the Pharisees' efforts to *possess* what they should *steward for the Lord* disqualifies them from receiving the kingdom of God as a "possession" given by God.

The focus on money loving occurs also in Luke's version of Jesus' critique of the Pharisees, introducing another set of "woes" at 11:39-41:

> "Oh you Pharisees! Although you cleanse the outside of the cup and the dish, inside you are filled with plunder [*harpagēs* = "greediness"] and evil. You fools! Did not the maker of the outside also make the inside? But as to what is within, give alms, and behold, everything will be clean for you."

Like the wealthy landowners addressed in Isaiah 5, the problem with Luke's Pharisees is not so much their possessions as their possessiveness. Isaiah says of the rapacious landowners, "What the LORD does, they regard not, / the work of his hands they see not" (5:12b). That is the very point Jesus makes with the money-loving

Pharisees: "You fools! Did not the maker of the outside also make the inside?" (Luke 11:40). Their possessive approach to creatures has rendered them blind to the Creator. It is significant that the word for "fools" in this passage—*aphrones*—is a rare word used only twice in the gospels; the other instance occurs in Luke's next chapter, in the parable of the rich fool. Just when that landowner is making plans to pile up the produce of his land exclusively for his own enjoyment, he hears the voice of God: "You fool [*aphrōn*], this night your life will be demanded of you; and the things you have prepared, to whom will they belong?" (12:20). So the picture of the Pharisees in Luke illustrates the opposite of what the Lukan beatitudes affirm. These men are the very model of what the Lukan woes doom. Their greed has rendered them closed to right relationships with their neighbors and deaf to the word of God addressed to them in the person of Jesus. Thus, as Luke portrays them, the Pharisees turn out to be the opposite of those identified as the poor of the first beatitude.

In the language world of the prophet Isaiah, from which Luke (and before him, of course, Jesus) draws his inspiration, *the poor* and *the rich* are not primarily economic cohorts but descriptors of internal postures toward God and, consequently, toward other human beings. The poor, the mourning, and the hungry are not three distinct subgroups but parallel ways of referring to the same people—in Isaiah and in Luke. The same holds for the rich, the laughing, and the full.

Are the rich and the poor, then, simply metaphorical labels for an interior attitude? Do these statements say something to the literally rich and the literally poor? They do indeed. The episode of the encounter between the rich man and Jesus in all three synoptic gospels (Matthew 19:16-22; Mark 10:17-22; Luke 18:18-23) shows that Jesus insisted wealth was a danger to one's spiritual health. When the man, whom Luke pointedly calls "an official" (18:18), asks Jesus what he must do to inherit eternal life, Jesus tells him that in his case, keeping the commandments is not enough; he must sell all he has, distribute it to the poor, and follow Jesus. Interestingly, in Luke's version of this encounter, the man does not *go away* sad, as Mark tells it. Luke says, "But when he heard this he became quite sad, *for he was very rich*" (18:23). The rich ruler does *not* leave (as he does in Mark and Matthew) but remains for the speech that Jesus addresses directly to him:

> "How hard it is for those who have wealth to enter the kingdom of God! For it is easier for a camel to pass through the eye of a needle than for a rich person to enter the kingdom of God." Those who heard this asked, "Then who can be saved?" And he said, "What is impossible for human beings is possible for God." (Luke 18:24-27)

Jesus taught that wealth can indeed be a spiritual danger. The economically rich can suffer the delusion that they are fully in control and that they have no need for God. Conversely, the economically poor are more likely to be aware of their physical and spiritual vulnerability, and thus be open to the reality of their creaturehood and their need for the presence and support of their Creator. So while Jesus does not affirm economic poverty as a positive good, it can in this sense be advantageous. Yet Luke is careful to avoid the idea that literal wealth predestines a person to spiritual doom. His version of the encounter of the rich ruler with Jesus, with the rich man remaining for the little sermon from Jesus, leaves the ultimate response of the man open; we are not told how he responds. This nuance of storytelling anticipates the hopeful note of Jesus' further statement, "What is impossible for human beings is possible for God" (18:27).

Luke's Fourth and Last Beatitude (and the Final Woe): Hated and Rejected versus Well Spoken Of

Taken alone, there is nothing specifically Christian about the first three Lukan beatitudes and woes. They could well be understood as the words of a Jewish prophet speaking in the spirit of Isaiah. It is the last beatitude (and its corresponding woe), along with the full context of the gospel narrative, that renders the beatitudes and woes Christian. For here the listeners finally meet a reference to Jesus (as Son of Man) and to what it means to be his follower:

6:22 "Blessed are you when people hate you, / and when they exclude and insult you, / and denounce your name as evil, / on account of the Son of Man.
23Rejoice and leap for joy on that day! Behold, your reward will be great in heaven. For their ancestors treated the prophets in the same way. . . ."
26"Woe to you when all speak well of you, / for their ancestors treated the false prophets in this way."

We know from the rest of the gospel that "the Son of Man" is Jesus' way of referring to himself. As for the reference to prophets, Jesus had identified himself with the prophetic figure of Isaiah 61 in the synagogue of Nazareth (Luke 4:18-19), had applied to himself the maxim about prophets getting no respect in their hometown (4:24), and had compared himself to the Israelite prophets Elijah and Elisha (4:25-27). There are other places where the role of prophet is applied to Jesus and his disciples; see 7:16 (after the raising of the widow's son at Nain); 9:8 (Herod's opinion); 9:19; 11:49 ("I will send to them prophets and apostles"); 13:33 ("It is impossible that a prophet should die outside of Jerusalem"); and 24:19 ("Jesus the Nazarene, who was a prophet mighty in deed and word").

The Last Beatitude Illustrated in Acts

The early Christian community that assembled the sayings of Jesus in the Q document kept the last beatitude with the other three and, by that means, made them explicitly Christian—linked with the following of Christ. The evangelist Luke found the last beatitude characteristic of Christian life as he knew it in his own day, for he made it thematic in his portrait of church life as sketched in his narrative in the Acts of the Apostles. For Luke, disciples are prophets, spokespersons for God, who face the likely prospect of persecution. Besides the places in Acts where certain disciples are called prophets because they have the special role of prophet within the community (such as Acts 13:1; 15:32; 21:10), there are other places where the followers of Jesus are associated with the prophetic tradition in a broader sense.

For example, the very imagery that had earlier been assigned to the infant Jesus at the presentation, "a light for the nations" (Luke 2:32), from Isaiah 49:6 describing Israel as the prophetic Servant of Yahweh, is later applied to Paul and Barnabas in Acts 13:46-47. This prophetic image from Isaiah is tellingly employed once again in Acts 26:22-23, where Paul, in his defense before Agrippa, speaks of the events of Jesus' life fulfilling OT prophecies "that the Messiah must suffer and that, as the first to rise from the dead, he would proclaim light both to our people and to the Gentiles" (verse 23). This is a clear identification of the ministry of the disciples as an extension of Jesus' own prophetic ministry. Indeed, their ministry is the means by which Jesus as risen Prophet-like-Moses now continues his ministry and fulfills what was spoken of him by Simeon in Luke 2:32.

One passage of Acts in particular demonstrates the last beatitude. After telling of the arrest, flogging, and warning of Peter and John, the narrator continues:

So they left the presence of the Sanhedrin, *rejoicing* that they had been found worthy to suffer dishonor for the sake of the name. And all day long, both at the temple and in their homes, they did not stop teaching and proclaiming [*euangelizomenoi*] the Messiah, Jesus. (Acts 5:41-42)

Besides the convergence with the last beatitude in the elements of rejoicing in being rejected because of the name of Jesus, the use of the word for proclaiming, *euangelizomai*, is an enhancement of the theme of the apostles extending the prophetic ministry of Jesus, for Luke took this word from Greek Isaiah 61:1. The verb is used for both Jesus' ministry (Luke 4:18 and 7:22 [both citing Isaiah 61:1]; 4:43; 8:1; 16:16; 20:1) and also the work of the disciples (9:6). It is also used extensively in Acts to describe the mission of the church: It describes the preaching of the apostles (5:42); Philip (8:4, 12, 35); Peter and John (8:25); the disciples in general (11:20); Paul alone (13:32; 16:10; 17:18); and Paul and Barnabas (14:7, 15, 21; 15:35).

So for Luke (as for the Q community before him and as we shall see, for Matthew), the last beatitude climaxes the others and makes the following of Christ a matter of following Jesus the rejected prophet.

Let's summarize what we have learned from our study of Luke's beatitudes and woes and also see how they might apply to Christian disciples today:

- The key references to "the poor" [*hoi ptōchoi*] in the immediate context, in the quotation of Isaiah 61:1 at 4:18 and the allusion to the same at 7:22, suggest that Luke understands the poor of the beatitude as Isaiah does; they are the people as a whole who, still in a kind of spiritual exile, recognize their deep need for God.

- As in Isaiah, "the poor" is not a label pertaining to economic condition but an image—like the hungry, the thirsting, and the mourning—describing those who know their need for God.

- It follows, then, that the weeping and the hungry of the second and third beatitudes are not distinct groups, but different ways of speaking of the same people.

- Luke's featuring of people called "rich" in the rest of his gospel shows that he has a special concern for the place of possessions in the life of a disciple.

- His stereotypical description of the Pharisees as money lovers (16:14) and "full of plunder" (11:39) illustrates that he is using the *term* "rich" [*plousioi*] to evoke the mentality of the rich, full, and self-indulgent described in Isaiah 5:8-12.

- The reversals of the fates of the subjects of the beatitudes and woes are reflected in the reversals described in the Magnificat, in the prophecy of Simeon, in the parable of the rich landowner, and in the parable of Dives and Lazarus.

- The last beatitude is about rejoicing when you are excluded and being reviled on account of the Son of Man because your reward is great in heaven. This rejection shows that you are following in the footsteps of the prophet Jesus. This last beatitude (and its corresponding woe) identifies the lot of the poor, weeping, hungry, and reviled with the rejected prophet Jesus. In doing so, this beatitude announces the good news that one can share, even now, in the joy of the risen Lord. The image in Acts of the rejected disciples rejoicing (5:41) illustrates this in a narrative form.

None of this explaining takes away the paradoxical nature of the language of Luke's beatitudes and woes. Indeed, it was Jesus' practice to speak paradoxically when he taught about the cost of discipleship. He could say, "Whoever wishes to save his life will lose it, but whoever loses his life for my sake will save it" (Luke 9:24; and see 17:33). This way of speaking is something like a Zen koan in being a kind of "mind tease." But there is a big difference between a Zen koan and a paradox from Jesus. The purpose of a koan seems to be to empty the mind. The purpose of a paradoxical expression from Jesus is to move the listener from a conventional way of thinking about success, health, security, and happiness to a new understanding of one's relationship to God, self, and others. Taking his cue from Isaiah's language about rich and poor, Jesus calls us beyond conventional thoughts about wealth and poverty to what it truly means to be well-off. The crucial thing is not one's possessions or lack of them; rather, what is important is one's relationship to the source of all life—our Lord and God—and our relationships with the rest of creation, especially other persons.

With the last beatitude comes the insight that true wisdom about these relationships is revealed in the person and teaching of Jesus. It takes the full story of Jesus' life, death, and resurrection to unpack the meaning of the beatitudes and woes; indeed, when we read the Lukan beatitudes, we need the full story of Jesus *and the church*—the Third Gospel and the Acts of the Apostles—to hear them clearly.

Having labored hard to hear the beatitudes in their gospel and Scriptural contexts as mediated by Luke, we are now prepared to do the same for the more familiar nine beatitudes according to Matthew.

CHAPTER 3

NINE ON THE MOUNT

THE BEATITUDES ACCORDING TO MATTHEW

(5:3-12)

When we made some preliminary observations about the similar settings that Luke and Matthew provide for the Sermon, we noted some of Matthew's distinctive elements. The speaker is the long-awaited son of David. He is the *Son of God* in several ways: as Messiah (see Psalm 2); as embodying the vocation of Israel (which is called "son of God" by Hosea 11:1, quoted in Matthew 2:15); and even as generated by the Holy Spirit (Matthew 1:18, 20). He comes to fulfill all righteousness, and as Isaiah prophesied, to bring light to those who sit in darkness. The *mountain* he ascends is as evocative of a Davidic Zion as it is of a Mosaic Sinai. The audience, drawn from the four quarters of the territory that David once ruled when his dominion was at its height, are those who have been following Jesus and have experienced his healing. In the post-Easter perspective of our author, the Messiah is addressing end-time Israel restored.

The summary verse 4:23 provides a hint of the author's larger design: "He went around all of Galilee, teaching in their synagogues, proclaiming the gospel of the kingdom, and curing every disease and illness among the people." Five chapters later, another summary verse, 9:35, echoes 4:23 almost verbatim. Commentators have noted that this repetition brackets a schematic presentation of Jesus, first as Messiah of the *word* (chapters 5–7, the Sermon), and then as Messiah of *deed* (chapters 8–9). This is followed immediately by the mission charge to the twelve (chapter 10). Here Matthew omits Mark's separate account of a *call* of the twelve (Mark 3:13-19) and moves right to the *sending* (paralleling Mark 6:6-13). Then, in chapter 11,

Matthew says that John the Baptist hears in prison about "the works of the Christ" ["*ta erga tou Christou*"] (11:2), a strikingly formal and inclusive phrase that seems to refer to all that has been presented schematically in the preceding six chapters: the words and deeds of Jesus and also of the twelve. Seen within the story line of Matthew, then, the words that introduce the setting of the Sermon introduce more than the recital of a certain speech; they set the reader up for Matthew's interpretation of all the words and deeds of the Messiah and his followers.

Given that the summaries of 4:23 and 9:35 mention *teaching* and *preaching the gospel of the kingdom*, we can consider the beatitudes and the accompanying salt and light sayings of 5:13-14 as illustrations of "preaching the kingdom" and the rest of the Sermon as "teaching." The description of the crowds' response at the end underscores that understanding: "When Jesus finished these words, the crowds were astonished at his *teaching*, for he *taught* them as one having authority, and not as their scribes" (7:28-29). The beatitudes and the salt and light sayings are, after all, proclamation, and what follows is teaching and exhortation. Further, the beatitudes are a transitional expansion of the summary of Jesus' preaching given at 4:17 ("Repent, for the kingdom of heaven is at hand"). The first part of each beatitude expresses an aspect of the disposition that demonstrates conversion (repenting), and the second part of each beatitude is an expression of the experience of the kingdom either as inaugurated reality ("Theirs is the kingdom," 5:3, 10) or future reward (5:4-9, 11-12).

When we studied Luke's four beatitudes—the basic Q tradition of the beatitudes—we recognized that the language was rooted in the prophecy of Isaiah, not only for Luke and the Q community, but probably also for Jesus himself.[18] The same goes for Matthew. In fact, Matthew seems to have remodeled and expanded the four Q beatitudes in the light of Isaiah 61.[19] This becomes evident when we read the fuller context of that Isaiah passage from which Jesus' mission-

and-identity speech came (Luke 4:16-21) and which is the source of another key self-description, "The poor have the good news proclaimed to them" (Matthew 11:5; Luke 7:22):

The days of your *mourning* [*penthous sou*] shall be completed.
Your people shall all be *righteous* [*dikaios*].
    They shall *inherit the land* for ever . . .
(LXX Isaiah 60:20-21, translation mine)

The spirit of the Lord is upon me
    because he has anointed me.
He has sent me *to preach good news to the poor* [*euangelisasthai
    ptōkois*]
    to heal the broken hearted,
to announce release to captives,
    recovery of sight to the blind,
to proclaim the acceptable year of the Lord,
    and a day of recompense,
to *comfort all that mourn* [*paraklesai pantas tous penthountas*],
    that there should be given to *them that mourn* [*tois
        penthousi*] Zion,
glory instead of ashes, the anointing of joy to *the mourners* [*tois
    penthousi*],
    a garment of glory for the spirit of sadness.
And they shall be called generations of *righteousness* [*geneai
    dikaiosynēs*] . . .
(LXX Isaiah 61:1-3, translation mine)

Thus they **shall inherit the land** [*klēronomēsousin tēn gēn*] a
    second time . . .
(LXX Isaiah 61:7, translation mine)

Let my soul **rejoice** [*agalliasthō*] in the Lord.
(LXX Isaiah 61:10, translation mine)

The bolded phrases highlight the resonances between Matthew's beatitudes and this passage of Isaiah. Given the frequent references to *mourners* (four times here), it seems likely that Matthew altered Q's *weepers* to Greek Isaiah's *mourners* to conform the phrasing of the beatitude to this passage. The references to *inheriting the land* no doubt recalled the fivefold refrain in Psalm 37:11 (LXX Psalm 36:11) about the *meek* inheriting the land and provided a basis for that new beatitude. And the mention of *the righteous* and *righteousness* likely encouraged Matthew to insert that theme in the beatitudes about the hungry and the persecuted, his fourth and eighth, to underscore a key theme of his version of the Sermon (see also 5:20; 6:1, 33), which he has also inserted into the baptism account ("Thus it is fitting for us to fulfill all righteousness," 3:15) and in Jesus' challenge to the chief priests and elders about their failure to believe in John the Baptist, who came to them "in the way of righteousness" (21:32). Finally, Matthew's expression "be glad" [*agalliasthe*] in the elaboration of the last beatitude may well have been prompted by Isaiah 61:10.

However, discerning Matthew's sources only becomes important when it throws light on the meaning of his words in the context of his gospel. Let us put that background to use by reading carefully his version of the beatitudes.

THE POOR IN SPIRIT

5:3 "Blessed are the poor in spirit, / for theirs is the kingdom of heaven."

Over the phrase "poor in spirit," much ink has been spilled. Some read Matthew as "spiritualizing" or "diluting" what a (likely more original) Q beatitude may have said about the economically poor. For others, it is an escape; they hear Matthew saying that wealth is really no problem as long as you remain detached. Still others are thrown off by an accident of the English language; by analogy with idioms like "He is poor in math" or "This soil is poor in nitrogen," they hear "poor in spirit" as referring to someone who is dispirited or lacking in spirit, perhaps depressed.

In fact, the phrase is neither a watering down of Lukan "realism" nor a congratulation of the spiritless. First, to deal with the latter distraction, when the Greek language wants to indicate the good of which poor are deprived, it does so by means of the genitive case, not, as here, by the dative.[20] So it is the same kind of phrase as "clean of heart" in the sixth beatitude and "meek and humble of heart" in Matthew 11:29. It is a metaphorical application of what is ordinarily a physical quality to the human interior (which in the Bible is sometimes called *spirit*, sometimes *heart*). Most commentators are satisfied to cite the solution of J. Dupont, who finds a Hebrew parallel to Matthew 5:3 in a document from Qumran (1QM 14:7), where *anawei ruach* appears to mean "humble." By another route, however, Guelich may have come closer to Matthew's intent. He takes his cue from Matthew's alignment of the beatitudes with Isaiah 61 and suggests that it was necessary for the evangelist to add *tō pneumati* ("with respect to the spirit") if the word for "poor" was to be understood in a way that was faithful to its meaning in Isaiah 61:1. The word *ptōchoi* at Isaiah 61:1 is a rare use of that word to translate *anawim*, which, while retaining the socioeconomic element, puts greater stress on the relationship of the poor to God. "Ultimately, the poor *in spirit* of 5:3, viewed as an explication of Isaiah 61:1, is no different from Luke's *poor*, since each refers to those who stand without pretense before God as their only hope."[21]

If this interpretation of Matthew's phrase is correct, it must also be acknowledged that the socioeconomic dimension of "the poor" does not carry nearly the thematic weight in Matthew that it does in Luke. No individual is called *ptōchos* in Matthew; all five instances are "the poor" in the generic sense (here, and 11:5; 19:21; 26:9, 11). Indeed, Matthew describes only one individual as *plousios* ("rich")—Joseph of Arimathea (also called a "disciple," 27:57). The young man who goes away sorrowful (Matthew 19:22) is wealthy by implication ("He had many possessions"), but only Luke calls him *plousios* (18:23).

In chapter 2 we considered Matthew's preference for "kingdom of heaven" (literally, "kingdom of the heavens") over Mark's (and Luke's) "kingdom of God," and we found it to be virtually equivalent, the slight difference being the way that Matthew's phrase seems to emphasize the transcendent sovereignty of God's reign. We also saw that the synoptic evangelists understand this apocalyptic reign to have been inaugurated in Jesus' public life, and especially in his death and resurrection and in the outpouring of the Holy Spirit, and that Christians are to look for, and work for, its further coming in the growth of the church and, finally, in the second coming of Christ. But how about the meaning of the present tense in the promise of Matthew's first and eighth beatitudes: "For theirs *is* the kingdom of heaven"?

In Luke's case, we concluded that the reign of God was understood to have been inaugurated in the person and ministry of Jesus and accessible in the community of the church. Can we say the same of Matthew's first and eighth beatitudes? When is the kingdom of heaven possessed according to the rest of the Gospel of Matthew? John the Baptist and Jesus announce—and the twelve are instructed to announce—"The kingdom of heaven *is at hand* [*engiken*, perfect tense]" (3:2; 4:17; 10:7). This speaks of proximity and presence but not yet of possession. *Entering* the kingdom usually refers to a future activity (5:20; 7:21 [both here in the Sermon]; 18:3; 19:23-24; 20:21), although tax collectors and harlots are said to be entering the kingdom of God now (21:31). *Inheriting* the kingdom comes at the final sorting out by the Son of Man (25:34). Matthew, more than Luke, stresses the second coming of Christ and the final judgment that accompanies it. Accordingly, we *can* read the promise of the first and eighth beatitudes as referring to the kingdom's *ultimate* fulfillment at the *end* of the end time.

However, another series of statements and images from this gospel suggests that the "possession" is at least inaugurated in current Christian life. "The violent are taking it by force" (11:12). Jesus' casting out of demons by the Spirit of God is a sign that the kingdom of God "has come upon you" (12:28). The tax collectors and prostitutes enter it now (21:31). Those who are like little children own it (19:14). Perhaps most pertinent, two key parables of the kingdom of heaven present an image of at least *finding* the kingdom now before gaining total possession later: the hidden treasure and the pearl of great price (13:44-45). In both cases, the finder really does acquire the item that symbolizes the kingdom. Indeed, the parable of the hidden treasure might be considered a cameo of the first beatitude. The man plowing in the field actually *finds* a hidden treasure and *out of joy* sells all he has to buy that field; similarly, those who are poor in spirit in the presence of the kingdom of heaven made manifest in the Son of God can be called truly *makarioi*, "happy," for the kingdom of God is theirs for the taking—that is, for the giving, *"He sells all that he has"* (13:46). Both Matthew and Luke preserve the mysterious ambiguity about the time element in their expression of the consequence of the final beatitude. In both gospels the "is" verb is absent. The literal translation of the Greek is "Your reward, great in heaven." Like a future inheritance, although you come into possession of it later upon the death of the testator, it is as good as yours already.

THOSE WHO MOURN

[5:4]"Blessed are those who mourn, / for they will be comforted."

Two things help us capture Matthew's understanding of this beatitude—the Old Testament passage that seems to have inspired it (Isaiah 60–61), and Matthew's account of the debate about fasting (9:14-17; Mark 2:18-22).

When we explored the likely source of this beatitude in the passage from Isaiah, we saw that consoling those who mourn was a way of describing the divine rescue of Israel for which the people were still yearning even *after* their return from the Babylonian exile. Also, "to comfort all who mourn" is a description of the mission of the prophet described in 61:1-3. Indeed, consoling all who mourn becomes the dominant image of the oracle as verse 3 goes on to elaborate the kind of mourning that is meant: "To place on those who mourn in Zion / a diadem instead of ashes, / To give them oil of gladness in place of mourning, / a glorious mantle instead of a listless spirit." If indeed Isaiah 61 is the primary background for understanding it, Matthew's second beatitude is a variation on the first. Like "the poor," "those who mourn" is another description of Israel in need of God's rescue.

The passive voice of "for they *will be comforted*" is the divine passive, a Semitic circumlocution to refer to an act of God. Unlike the first beatitude, this one states the promise in the future tense. When is that future divine consolation supposed to occur? During the time of the church? Or at the final coming of the Son of Man? Matthew provides a clue in the other passage where he employs the word for mourning (*pentheō*), his rendition of the controversy about fasting (9:14-17; par. Mark 2:18-22). Matthew makes a point of associating fasting with mourning. Asked why his disciples do not fast like those of John the Baptist, Jesus answers, according to Mark's version, "Can the wedding guests fast while the bridegroom is with them? As long as they have the bridegroom with them they cannot fast. But the days will come when the bridegroom is taken away from them, and then they will fast on that day" (2:19-20). Matthew has Jesus answer this way: "Can the wedding guests *mourn* as long as the bridegroom is with them? The days will come when the bridegroom is taken away from them, and then they will fast [*on that day* omitted]" (9:15).

Several things should be observed regarding the way Matthew's redaction integrates with the rest of his gospel:

- In Matthew's retelling, this episode has been situated in the banquet scene at the home of Matthew the tax collector (9:9-13).

- The whole double episode (spanning 9:9 through 9:17) is dominated by the joy of the age of salvation; the banquet, the images of the bridegroom, the new garment, and the fresh wineskins for new wine all underscore the new era introduced by the presence of the messianic Son of God.

- The thrust of Jesus' answer in the setting of his ministry (Stage I) is that his *non-fasting*, and that of his disciples, is a kind of prophetic symbolic action signaling the inauguration of the messianic age (the kingdom).

- The reference to the days to come, when the bridegroom is taken away and they will fast, is best understood as a reference to the post-Easter (Stage II) practice of fasting in the early church for which Matthew writes.

- By introducing "mourn" for Mark's "fast" and by dropping the phrase "in that day," Matthew has highlighted the time reference as a period in which the community's practice of fasting is understood as expressing the pain of separation during the interim between Easter and the Parousia. (See the parables of the great banquet [22:1-14] and the wise and foolish virgins [25:1-2] for Matthean images of the return of the Son of Man as a bridegroom.)

- At the same time, fasting for the Christian is not a matter of retrieving "old wineskins" (9:17), for the sayings on fasting in the Sermon on the Mount (6:16-18) make it clear that Christian fasting is a new creation. In contrast to traditional Atonement fasting, Christians are to anoint their faces; that is, they are to fast in the manner of people preparing for a feast. Christian "mourning" is a new kind of mourning indeed. It is the mourning that prays "Thy kingdom come," feeling the gap between what has been inaugurated by Jesus and the completion that is yet to come.

Against the background of Isaiah 61 and in the full context of Matthew's gospel, the second beatitude takes on new life. Those who respond appropriately to the gospel of the kingdom of heaven, those who know their need for God's saving intervention in Jesus, are "happy mourners." They anticipate God's final comforting when the kingdom of heaven is fully established, and even now they share in the life of the messianic community, like the finder of the buried treasure selling all he has "out of joy" by performing the "mourning" practice of fasting with joy.

Another valid way of applying this beatitude is to hear it as a blessing on those who mourn in the sense of responding compassionately to the suffering of others. This is surely part of loving one's neighbor. It is also an inevitable side effect of living out what the church has recently come to call a "preferential option for the poor." In this sense, the "option" is the choice to pay attention to the suffering of those who are hurting because of oppression and injustice at home and abroad. This kind of solidarity is blessed in that it shares in the solidarity that Jesus chose to have with us. Such mourning also prompts action to remedy the suffering of others.

The Meek

5:5 "Blessed are the meek, / for they will inherit the land."

Because of the familiar phrasing of the King James Version, many may still hear the promise of the third Matthean beatitude as "the meek shall inherit the *earth*." Indeed, that translation has become so traditional that the New American Standard Bible and the New International Version still render the final phrase as "inherit the earth." The word in question is *gē*, the same word that appears in such English words as "**geology**" and "**geography**." Like its Hebrew counterpart, *eretz*, it can mean "the earth" as the counterpart to "heaven," as in "heaven and earth" when that phrase is used to include the universe in the two-storey worldview of the ancients. Or again like the Hebrew *eretz*, it can refer to a particular territory, as in "the land of Israel" or "the land of Goshen." One thing *ge* and *eretz* do *not* mean in the Bible is planet Earth as we think of it in our contemporary worldview. When the word appears with the verb for "inherit" in the Old Testament, it always refers to a particular territory, and is best translated "the land." Most English translations of the third beatitude acknowledge that background and translate the phrase "inherit the land" (such as Rheims, NRSV, and NAB 1986).

In our quest to hear the beatitudes correctly, the most pertinent background is Isaiah 60–61 and Psalm 37. The passage from Isaiah is the one Jesus reads at his debut in the synagogue at Nazareth and the source of the first and second beatitudes (the poor in spirit and the mourning). The Greek translators of Isaiah heighten the references they find before and after the verses on the poor and mourning at Isaiah 60:21 ("They shall always possess the land") and 61:7b ("They shall have a double inheritance"). In Greek, Isaiah 60:21 becomes "Forever, *they shall inherit the land*" and 61:7b becomes "Thus *they shall inherit the land a second time.*" In the context of Isaiah, this language is referring to Judeans, who are back from exile but living under an alien empire (that of the Persians) and who still yearn for full freedom in the promised land. This imagery of a second exodus parallels the other images of salvation in this passage—poor receiving good news, captives freed, blind seeing, mourners comforted, Jubilee happening.

The fact that it is the *meek* who will inherit the land takes us to a specific verse in another passage, Psalm 37:11 (LXX Psalm 36:11): "The meek [*praeis* in Greek, *anawim* in Hebrew] shall inherit [the] land." This verse, repeated four other times in this psalm, becomes a refrain that teaches that those who trust the Lord God in their troubles will ultimately find salvation. The adjective in question—*praüs*—is defined as "not being overly impressed by a sense of one's self-importance, *gentle, humble, considerate, meek* in the older favorable sense."[22] It is rare in the Septuagint and occurs only four times in the New Testament: Matthew 5:5; 11:29; 21:5; and 1 Peter 3:4 (of wives). Both of the other passages in Matthew (11:29 and 21:5) illuminate the beatitude in Matthew 5:5, for both apply to Jesus. In 11:29-30, which comes right after Jesus identifies himself as Wisdom incarnate, Jesus says: "Come to me, all you who labor and are burdened, and I will give you rest. Take my yoke upon you and learn from me, for I am meek and humble of heart [*praüs eimi kai tapeinos tē kardia*]; and you will find rest for yourselves. For my yoke is easy, and my burden light."

Notice that this passage, which comprises a set of wisdom sayings, has the feel of the beatitudes. Those who suffer are promised relief in paradoxical terms. Surprisingly, a yoke spells relief. The yoke is easy and the burden light. Although the "rest" is promised for the future, like the kingdom of heaven it is already somehow experienced in the

shouldering of the yoke. Like the beatitudes, this wisdom hymn captures the mystery of discipleship in which the joy is known in the
paying of the price.

The other instance of *praüs* in Matthew is equally significant. It
occurs in the fulfillment citation of Zechariah 9:9 at Matthew 21:5:
"Say to daughter Zion, / 'Behold, your king comes to you, / meek
[*praüs*] and riding on an ass, / and on a colt, the foal of a beast of
burden.'" Zechariah's picture is that of an unexpectedly peaceful
king, one not cast in the warrior-king mold of David. What is largely
overlooked is that the next verse of Zechariah's vision includes the
paradox of a *dis-arming dominion* over the whole earth:

He shall banish the *chariot* out of Ephraim,
  and the *horse* from Jerusalem;
The *warrior's bow* shall be banished,
  and he shall proclaim peace to the nations.
His dominion shall be from sea to sea
  and from the River to the ends of the earth. (Zechariah 9:10)

Matthew's citation of Zechariah 9:9 occurs in the middle of his
narrative of Jesus' entry into Jerusalem. In his redaction of these
events, Jesus is thrice hailed "Son of David," but his takeover of Zion
is exactly the *reverse* of the original David's takeover a millennium
before. The description of that event in 2 Samuel 5:6-12 tells how the
Jebusites mocked the would-be conqueror by saying, "You cannot
enter here: the blind and the lame will drive you away!" After David
does indeed take over, a saying arises, "The blind and the lame shall
not enter the palace" (5:8). Exactly reversing this taunt, when Jesus
enters Zion's temple as Son of David, Matthew makes a point of saying, "The blind and the lame approached him in the temple area, and
he cured them" (21:14). This Son of David begins to come into his
inheritance in a new, nonviolent kind of takeover.[23]

How Jesus is the meek one *par excellence*, who inherits the land/ earth in the fullest sense, is spelled out by another set of key episodes in Matthew's narrative: the first and final mountain scenes. The first scene occurs in the third temptation in the wilderness, when the devil takes him up to a very high mountain, shows him "all the kingdoms of the world," and promises to *give them to him*, if Jesus would only fall down and worship him (Matthew 4:8-10). Jesus refuses. The Son of God will come into his inheritance only through obedience to the Father (fulfilling "all righteousness"—3:15, 17). In the final mountain scene, after he demonstrates his sonship, trusting the Father even in the experience of abandonment on the cross, Jesus as risen Lord can say, "All power in heaven and on earth has been given to me" (28:18). The king has come into his inheritance, not by grasping, but by letting go to the Father. The meek one inherits the earth.

Now it becomes clear how "the meek will inherit the land/earth." Those who follow Jesus will, through their allegiance to him as risen Lord, share in his reign. They will do so first by extending his mission, "making disciples of all nations" (28:19), and ultimately when they "inherit the kingdom" upon Jesus' return at the end of the age (25:34).

THOSE WHO HUNGER AND THIRST FOR RIGHTEOUSNESS

5:6 "Blessed are they who hunger and thirst for righteousness, / for they will be satisfied."

The word translated here as "righteousness"—*dikaiosynē*—has been rendered in a variety of ways in English: "justice" (Rheims, echoing the Latin Vulgate's *iustitia*); "uprightness" (Goodspeed); "goodness" (Phillips); "holiness" (NAB 1970), "what is right" (JB); and "righteousness" (KJB, NIV, NRSV, and NAB 1986).

There is a reason for the variety. In biblical language, the Greek word *dikaiosynē* and its Hebrew counterpart *tsedakah* express such a rich concept that no single English word does it justice (no pun intended). "Righteousness" captures the root sense of *dikaiosynē/ tsedakah*, especially rightness of relationships. This language occurs mainly in "God talk" in the OT. It is mainly God who is said to be *dikaios* or to have *dikaiosynē* in the sense that God is faithful to covenant relationships with the people of God. A human being is said to be *dikaios* or to have *dikaiosynē* if that person is "right with God," that is, if that person lives out the covenant relationships with God and with neighbors. We receive the *dikaiosynē* of God as a *gift*; we pursue our own *dikaiosynē* as a *task*—enabled, to be sure, by the saving *dikaiosynē* of God. Significantly, the "home base" of the beatitudes, Isaiah 61, uses "righteousness" in both senses. Those who receive the end-time blessings of the Lord are called "oaks of righteousness, the planting of the LORD" (LXX Isaiah 61:3c), God's saving gift being the point here. A few verses later, the oracle of the Lord reads, "For I am the LORD who loves righteousness [*dikaiosynē*, as in verse 3] and hates robberies" (LXX Isaiah 61:8); "righteousness" here surely referring to right *human behavior* before the Lord. Although in contemporary American English we do not usually use "righteousness" in ordinary parlance, except sometimes to refer to moral arrogance, it is still the best word to capture the full range of the biblical term.[24]

Given the rich biblical possibilities of *dikaiosynē*, what is Matthew's meaning for that word in this beatitude? Is righteousness here the divine gift or the human task?

On the face of it, the clause "those who hunger and thirst for righteousness" seems open to either interpretation. One can hunger and thirst for God's ordering of relationships, especially if one is poor in the sense of being a victim of injustice. On the other hand, we have already heard Jesus' statement to John the Baptist: "It is fitting for us to fulfill all righteousness" (3:15), where the term refers to the human doing of God's will. And one *can* speak of *hungering* for righteousness in this sense, as when Jesus says in John 4:34, "My food is to do the will of the one who sent me and to finish his work." Our best hint as to Matthew's meaning may be Matthew 6:33, read in the context of the two verses preceding it, where Jesus says:

"So do not worry and say, 'What are we to eat' or 'What are we to drink?' or 'What are we to wear?' All these things the pagans seek. Your heavenly Father knows that you need them all. But seek first the kingdom [of God] and *his righteousness*, and all these things will be given you besides." (Matthew 6:31-33)

Here, seeking the righteousness of God is contrasted with seeking literal food and drink, the very image behind the metaphor of the fourth beatitude. In Matthew 6:33, then, what is sought (hungered and thirsted for) is not an action to do but a gift to be given by God—God fulfilling his part of the covenant, setting things right. Given the context, such would seem to be the meaning of the fourth beatitude. If we miss here the call to action possible in the other sense of *dikaiosynē*, the eighth beatitude will speak to that directly.

THE MERCIFUL

5:7"**Blessed are the merciful, / for they will be shown mercy.**"

Those drawn to simplistic generalization sometimes say, "The Old Testament shows a God of justice, but the New Testament speaks of a God of mercy." A simple concordance scan shows that idea to be utter nonsense. The ordinary Greek word for mercy, *eleos,* is used in the Greek Old Testament as a quality of God some 236 times and of human beings 60 times; in the NT, *eleos* is a quality of God twenty times and a human quality seven. Matthew uses *eleos* three times, and two of those are citations of Hosea 6:6. In the Greek Old Testament, the verb meaning to show mercy, *eleeō,* describes an action of God one hundred times and a human action thirty times.

Matthew's triple use of *eleos* ("mercy") is clearly his redaction of the received tradition. As noted, the word occurs twice in reference to Hosea 6:6 ("I desire mercy, not sacrifice"). In the first instance, Matthew adds it to the Markan account of Jesus' response to the Pharisees who question Jesus' practice of sharing table fellowship with tax collectors and sinners. Overhearing their objections, Jesus says, "Those who are well do not need a physician, but the sick do. Go and learn the meaning of the words, 'I desire mercy, not sacrifice'" (9:12-13). The parallelism of the second half of the verse in Hosea—"and knowledge of God rather than holocausts"—makes it clear that the sacrifice referred to here is the temple offerings. Thus the citation is not a fulfillment citation but the invocation of a principle: Meeting a human need takes priority over the carrying out of ceremonial and purity laws.

The second instance, also quoting Hosea 6:6, is in Matthew 12:7, when some Pharisees complain to Jesus that his disciples' snacking on grain in the fields (a kind of harvesting) is a breach of the law forbidding work on the Sabbath: "If you knew what this meant, 'I desire mercy, not sacrifice,' you would not have condemned these innocent men."

The third time Matthew uses *eleos* is in chapter 23, in the series of woes against the scribes and Pharisees. Here Matthew appears to edit the Q form of the saying by replacing "justice and the love of God" (cf. Luke 11:42) with *"the weightier matters of the law: judgment and mercy [to eleos] and fidelity"* (23:23).

The biblical concept of (mainly divine) mercy has two main meanings: *pardon* granted to the guilty (e. g., Exodus 34:6-7) and *help* for those in need (Exodus 22:27). In what sense do the subjects of the fifth Matthean beatitude have this Godlike quality? Evidence points to forgiveness as the primary meaning here. And while the noun/verb forms for mercy are not frequent in Matthew, the way the concept is illustrated makes mercy a powerful theme in his gospel. Mercy, both as pardon and as help, is a quality of God the Father and of Jesus, and it is to be a characteristic of those who would follow Jesus. Five times people in physical need beg for merciful help from Jesus with a phrase that Christians have taken into their public worship down through the centuries—*Kyrie eleēson* ("Lord, have mercy!"). The phrase is spoken by two sets of blind men (9:27; 20:30, 31); by the Canaanite woman seeking help for her demonized daughter (15:22); and by the father of the demoniac (17:15). Each time Jesus responds with healing or deliverance from evil spirits. The call to imitate the divine mercy of forgiveness comes through loud and clear in Matthew's elaboration of the final petition of the Lord's Prayer:

"If you forgive others their transgressions, your heavenly Father will forgive you. But if you do not forgive others, neither will your Father forgive your transgressions." (Matthew 6:14-15)

However, the best commentary on the fifth beatitude in the Gospel of Matthew is the parable of the unforgiving servant (18:23-35). In this story a servant is forgiven an almost unthinkable debt—10,000 talents. A talent equaled about 6,000 days' wages; 10,000 talents would mean 60 million days' wages—over 164,000 years' worth! This servant soon happens upon a fellow servant who owes him 100 denarii (a mere 100 days' wages), and he has him put in debtors' prison. Hearing of this, the master confronts the unforgiving servant with the obvious paradox:

"You wicked servant! I forgave you your entire debt because you begged me to. Should you not have had pity [*eleēsai*] on your fellow servant, as I had pity [*eleēsa*] on you?" (Matthew 18:32-33)

Note that this story comes as an elaboration on Jesus' answer to a question from Peter about how many times he must forgive his brother. Peter asks, "As many as seven times?" and Jesus answers, "I say to you, not seven times but seventy-seven times" (18:21, 22).

As in the case of previous beatitudes, the passive voice of the promise—"They will be shown mercy"—is another divine passive, referring to a future act of God. But are we to understand the beatitude to say simply that those who forgive will be forgiven by God in the end? The parable of the unforgiving servant reminds us that there is more to the good news than that. Just as *finding* is the first act in the parable of the hidden treasure in Matthew 13:44, being forgiven is the first act here. The servant's obligation to forgive derives from the amazing largess of forgiveness he has received from his master. That is the situation of those congratulated in the fifth beatitude as well. Healed and in the presence of the Messiah who ushers in the beginning of the end times, Christian disciples know the unexpected forgiveness of the king. They are enabled to be *eleēmones* ("mercy givers") because they have first experienced the forgiveness of God as mediated by Jesus' healing and forgiving ministry. The passage in 1 John 4:10-11 expresses the same thought in terms of love: "In this is love: not that we have loved God, but that he loved us and sent his Son as an expiation for our sins. Beloved, if God so loved us, we also must love one another."

THE CLEAN OF HEART

5:8 "Blessed are the clean of heart [*katharoi tē kardia*], / for they will see God."

I would guess that most Christian readers spontaneously associate this beatitude with sexual morality, especially when the adjective *katharoi* is translated "pure" (as in the KJV, NIV, and NRSV; the Rheims and NAB 1986 have "clean"). English speakers tend to understand the clean or pure in heart to be those who steer clear of "impure or dirty thoughts." There is good reason for this spontaneous association, for the next mention of "heart" in this gospel occurs twenty verses later on in the Sermon: "But I say to you, everyone who looks at a woman with lust has already committed adultery with her in his heart" (5:28). To be sure, this is part of what the sixth beatitude means, but the Old Testament background and the rest of the Gospel of Matthew indicate that purity of heart is a much fuller image. The most obvious background for this beatitude is Psalm 24:

> Who shall go up to the mountain of the Lord?
>   And who shall stand in his holy place?
> The person innocent of hand and clean of heart [*katharos tē kardia*].
> Who has not raised his soul to vanity,
>   nor sworn deceitfully to his neighbor.
> He will receive a blessing from the Lord,
>   and mercy from God his savior.
> This is the generation of those who seek him,
>   who seek the face of the God of Jacob.
> (LXX Psalm 23 [24]:3-6, translation mine)

What connects the sixth beatitude most obviously with this psalm is the linking of *cleanness of heart* with the prospect of access to the *face of God* (which is conventional biblical language for *seeing* God).[25] This is an entrance psalm, composed in the voice of a pilgrim about to enter the Jerusalem temple area. The language about cleanness and purity, then, is to be understood in the cultic or ritual sense. But notice that the psalm participates in the prophetic tradition that interiorizes the cultic language. That is, it takes talk about "clean and unclean," which was traditionally used to designate spaces, times, persons, and things that were set aside and dedicated to God in a special way, and applies that language to the whole of the pilgrim's person and life.

The person who is fit to ascend the mountain of the Lord (note the coincidental resonance with the setting of the Sermon on the Mount) is one whose whole life—in external action, as represented by the hands, and internally, as represented by the *heart*—is dedicated to God (thus called "clean"). The clean-hearted pilgrim of this psalm, then, is a person whose whole being is fit for divine worship because the dedication is total. Indeed, the initial verse of the psalm appears to wipe out the notion of clean and unclean in creation, for it declares that *everything* is God's: "The earth is the Lord's and the fullness thereof, / the world and those who dwell therein; / for he has founded it upon the seas, / and prepared it upon the rivers" (the opening verse of LXX Psalm 23 [24]:1). The pure-hearted person is the one who has recognized this truth and so lives respectfully as a creature among fellow creatures. For us today, this has ecological implications.

This contrast between ritual purity and the higher purity of heart manifested in just and merciful behavior is a strong theme in the teaching of Jesus and a special interest of Matthew's. The contrast is evident in Matthew's addition of Hosea 6:6 ("I desire mercy, not sacrifice") at 9:13 and 12:7, as noted above regarding the beatitude on the merciful. In his treatment of the parable of the sower and its interpretation, Matthew highlights *heart* talk: He extends the reference to Isaiah 6 at 13:15 to include "Gross is the *heart* of this people. . . / lest they . . . *understand* with their *heart*," and he goes on to add those words to the interpretation that follows, so that bringing forth a fruitful harvest becomes a matter of receiving the word in the heart and understanding it (13:19, 23).

Again, in his rendition of Jesus' teaching on what truly renders a person "unclean," which he finds in Mark 7:14-23, Matthew heightens the connection between heart and external behavior by emphasizing *actions* in his list of what proceeds from the heart; he reduces to six Mark's list of twelve products of evil thoughts rooted in the heart and lists them in the order of their appearance in the Ten

Commandments: "But the things that *come out* of the mouth come from the heart, and they defile. For from the heart come evil thoughts: murder, adultery, unchastity, theft, false witness, blasphemy" (15:18-19). And in the parable of the unforgiving servant, the climax reads, "So will my heavenly Father do to you, unless each of you *forgives his brother from his heart*" (18:35).

As we will see shortly, the whole thrust of the six reinterpretations of the law in the Sermon on the Mount (5:21-48) is to move disciples from preoccupation with external actions to the interior source of those actions. The focus is on the heart, where one can nurse anger, foster lust, distinguish falsely between breakable and unbreakable oaths, calculate a balance of vengeance, and withhold love from the enemy. And yet the summons is to *action* rooted in a properly dedicated heart: actions of reconciliation, removing obstacles, saying a simple yes or no, turning the cheek, giving over the cloak, going the extra mile, and letting one's love expand to be as inclusive as the Father's sun and rain.

Both the OT background and the rest of Matthew's gospel, then, clarify the meaning of this sixth beatitude. To a gathered and healed end-time Israel (the church, as Matthew understands it), the Messiah congratulates those who respond to God's fresh initiative in his ministry by letting their whole lives and persons become dedicated (cleansed, set aside) to God. Already enjoying the presence of the risen Son, they shall, in the end, know the divine presence face-to-face. Indeed, the Christian community understands itself as the Messiah's new temple (see Matthew 16:18, the community imaged as something built by the Messiah, who was expected to build the end-time temple). So they have already begun to "see the face of God" in the presence of the risen Lord, whom they have come to know as Emmanuel ("God with us"), especially when two or three gather in his name (18:20). For St. Ignatius of Loyola, it was part of spiritual maturity for dedicated Christians to "find God in all things."[26]

THE PEACEMAKERS

^{5:9}"**Blessed are the peacemakers, / for they will be called children [literally, sons] of God.**"

This beatitude presents two stumbling blocks for some contemporary readers. First, when we read "peacemaker," we tend to project onto that word what we usually mean in our culture—antiwar activists, a legitimate contemporary application of the word, but not necessarily what peacemaking might have meant for Matthew, and before him, Jesus. Second, when we hear "sons of God," many of us understandably reach for more inclusive language like "children of God" (the choice of the KJV and the Rheims already in the seventeenth century, and also the modern versions of the NRSV and the NAB 1986; but see the NASB and the NIV for "sons of God"). However, "children of God"—on the face of it a more pastorally appropriate translation—has a downside. That translation loses the association with "Son (of God)" as applied to Jesus at 2:15; 3:17; 4:3, 6 and also with the clause "that you may be sons [literally translated] of your heavenly Father" at 5:45. A peacemaker, male or female, imitates the Son of God.

As for the first stumbling block, anachronism, we have some warrant for associating this beatitude with our sense of peacemakers, for the word "peacemaker" came into English in the first place by way of an early English-language translation of this beatitude; the *Oxford English Dictionary* cites Tyndale's translation of this beatitude in 1534 as the earliest instance of the word "peacemakers" in English. Given that history, all uses of the word in English, whether or not the user is conscious of it, are rooted in this beatitude.

In the full biblical context, however, "peace" means more than the absence of war. While the Hebrew Bible has no noun (or adjective) that we would translate as "peacemaker," the Hebrew word for "peace" is one that virtually every educated person knows—the Jewish greeting *shalom*, and *salaam*, its counterpart in Arabic. That Hebrew word for "peace"—and its normal Greek translation in the LXX, *eirēnē*—means not simply absence of conflict but much more: the fullness of life, abundance, right relationships all around. The classic image of the peace of *shalom* is a great feast such as that evoked in Isaiah 25:6-8. *Shalom* is mainly a gift of God, and if there is a peacemaker in the Old Testament, it is God. The most immediate background for our beatitude is the rabbinical *asah shalom*, which refers to the establishment of peace and concord between human beings.[27] And this, of course, entails human activity.

If we have been right in identifying the mountain of the beatitudes with end-time Zion, then we should note that the famous Zion text of Isaiah 2:2-5 contains one of the most powerful images in the Old Testament regarding peacemaking:

> In days to come,
> The mountain of the LORD's house
>   shall be established as the highest mountain
>   and raised above the hills.
> All nations shall stream toward it;
>   many peoples shall come and say:
> "Come, let us climb the LORD's mountain
>   to the house of the God of Jacob,
> That he may instruct us in his ways
>   and we may walk in his paths."
> For from Zion shall go forth instruction [torah]
>   and the word of the LORD from Jerusalem.
> He shall judge between the nations,
>   and impose terms on many peoples.
> They shall beat their swords into plowshares,
>   and their spears into pruning hooks.

One nation shall not raise the sword against another,
nor shall they train for war again.

O house of Jacob, come,
let us walk in the light of the LORD! (Isaiah 2:2-5)

Like the beatitude about the clean of heart, this one, too, has its home on Zion. And notice how fully the imagery is echoed in the setting and beginning of the Great Sermon: the ascent of the mountain, the gathering of many people, the presentation of instruction (new Torah), the evocation of justice and peace. And even if biblical *shalom* is about *more* than cessation of war, it does include the end of war-making as absolutely central.

Perhaps the most important clue to Matthew's understanding of this beatitude lies in the other stumbling block, the promise that "they shall be called sons of God." Our contemporary sensitivity to the apparently noninclusive nature of the phrase "sons of God" catches our attention. The more inclusive, generic term, *tekna* ("children"), was available to Matthew (indeed, it occurs fifteen times in this gospel).[28] But the author chooses here to use "sons of God"—a concept he will use only one other time in his gospel, a little later in this same speech. (In fact, the phrase "sons of God" occurs only one other time in any gospel, at Luke 20:36—"They are sons of God, being sons of the resurrection" [translating the Greek literally]. The same idea is expressed in a different phrase at Luke 6:35—"Love your enemies . . . ; then your reward will be great and you will be children [literally *sons*] *of the Most High*, for he himself is kind to the ungrateful and the wicked."[29] Matthew's choice of the phrase may well come from the fact that it echoes the title "Son of God" used so powerfully for Jesus in the early chapters of his gospel. Recall how the title "Son" occurred at 2:15 ("Out of Egypt I called my son"—Hosea 11:1); 3:17 (the divine affirmation at the baptism); and the trials in the desert (4:3, 6). Above all, "Son of God" in these episodes connotes Jesus' obedience to the Father. The natural association carried by the promise of the seventh beatitude, then, is that the peacemakers somehow participate in Jesus' obedient sonship and become part of the new Israel that he heads up (2:15).

The idea that the peacemakers *will be called* sons of God alerts us to the fact that this idea of sonship is different from the status of "sons of God" that Paul talks about, for example, in Romans 8:14. For Paul, as for John, a person is *adopted* as a son of God when he or she is baptized and receives the gift of the Holy Spirit. What this beatitude asserts is that one *will be called son of God* if one lives as a peacemaker. Exactly what kind of behavior this entails becomes evident in the other place where this gospel refers to becoming "sons of God"—at the climax of this chapter in the Sermon:

> "But I say to you: Love your enemies, and pray for those who persecute you, that you may be *sons* [*huioi*] of your Father in heaven. He causes his sun to rise on the evil and the good, and sends rain on the righteous and the unrighteous." (Matthew 5:44-45, NIV)

Ironically, what first appeared to be a noninclusive title (because of its sexist ring in our contemporary ears), namely, "sons of God," becomes a vehicle of Jesus' most radical call to *inclusive* love. We, men and women alike, are to become "sons of the Father" in our imitation of the Creator's universal benevolence, the kind of inclusive love symbolized in our nurturing God's prodigally showered gifts of sunshine and rain upon *all*. In the language of the Sermon, we become "sons" of God to the extent that we join in the Son of God's imitation of the Father's inclusive love.

THE PERSECUTED:
YES, YOU—INSULTED AND PERSECUTED

To help us hear the final beatitudes clearly, I include here Matthew's and Luke's versions in parallel format:

MATTHEW 5:10-12	LUKE 6:22-23
[10] Blessed: they who are *persecuted* for the sake of righteousness, for theirs is the kingdom of heaven.	
[11]Blessed are you [plural] when they insult you	[22]Blessed are you when people hate you, and when they exclude and insult you and denounce your name as evil
and *persecute* you and utter every kind of evil against you [falsely] because of me.	on account of the Son of Man.
[12]Rejoice and be glad, for your reward will be great in heaven.	[23]Rejoice and leap for joy on that day! Behold, your reward will be great in heaven.
Thus they *persecuted* the prophets who were before you.	For their ancestors treated the prophets in the same way.

As we noted earlier, this climactic beatitude is the one that explicitly links the beatitude with the following of Jesus. It also most explicitly addresses the audience in the second-person plural: "Blessed are *you* [a plural pronoun in Greek]." Further, it is the most developed of the beatitudes; where they parallel, both evangelists devote two verses to it, one verse elaborating the blessed situation (rejection), and the second verse elaborating the consequence (reward in heaven). The comparison also reveals several differences:

1. The language of rejection is intensified in Matthew with the repeated use of the word for "persecute" [*diōkō*] in verses 10, 11, and 12, suggesting that Luke's version may be earlier and therefore closer to the Q version; strong as Luke's language is ("hate," "exclude," and "denounce"), it is not as fierce as Matthew's *diōkō*, which elsewhere in his gospel entails physical abuse and parallels the final suffering of Jesus (10:16-24).

2. Both versions stress continuity with the persecution of the prophets of old, but whereas Luke speaks of the enemies' continuity with the former *persecutors* of the prophets, Matthew underscores the continuity of the disciples with the prophets of old ("thus they persecuted the prophets who were before you"—5:12).

3. Matthew anticipates the two-part Q version of the final beatitude by supplying an abbreviated version, his eighth beatitude (verse 10), folding the two Q verses into one, putting it into the third-person format of his first seven beatitudes, and using language that echoes his first and fourth beatitudes ("righteousness . . . for theirs is the kingdom of heaven"), creating a fitting conclusion to the list.[30]

The observation about the continuity of Jesus' followers with the prophets before them deserves further comment. Both Luke and

Matthew, in different ways, portray Jesus as a prophet. For example, Luke introduces Jesus in 4:18-19 with the quotation from Isaiah 61:1-2 and 58:6, which interprets his person and mission as prophetic; Matthew quotes another part of Isaiah (42:1-4 at Matthew 12:18-21) to make the same point. This can come as something of a surprise to today's Christians, since the idea of Jesus as prophet is not a major part of our tradition or our catechesis. The likely reason is that the Islamic tradition, since the seventh century, has honored Jesus as a prophet, but *only* as a prophet leading to their definitive prophet, Muhammad. Consequently, for many Christians it has seemed a denigration of Jesus' status to refer to him as prophet.

For the authors of the New Testament, this was not a problem. They could think of Jesus as the expected "prophet like Moses" in the sense that he truly was and is the definitive mediator of the word of God. That said, as Son of God and Lord, he is of course *more* than a prophet. But we do well to appreciate what the evangelists were communicating by including that model to portray Jesus' role in salvation history. As the word of God *in person*, Jesus of Nazareth fulfills the prophetic role supremely. When we use the categories of prophet, priest, and king at baptisms to speak of the baptized person's participation in the mission of Jesus, we are acknowledging both his and our role as mediators of the word of God. Like Jesus, we too are prophets—as evangelizers, tellers of the good news, and, when the situation calls for it, as critics of injustice.[31]

Matthew's eighth and ninth beatitudes, then, comprise the perfect climax to the entire set. As we have already noted, the eighth beatitude picks up the language of the first and fourth. It does a variation on the righteousness motif of the fourth by moving from the theme of righteousness as divine gift to the theme of righteousness as human task. By associating the addressees explicitly with the person of Jesus ("on my account"), the ninth beatitude (verses 11-12) expresses the grounds for congratulation: As followers of Jesus, they are already among the healed and empowered of messianic Israel. Sharing in Jesus' lot can only lead to sharing in the vindication of his resurrection. The promises of both the eighth and ninth macarisms ("Theirs *is* the kingdom of heaven" and "Your reward [is] great *in heaven*") embrace the complete time focus of the kingdom preaching: The apocalyptic blessing is grounded in a blessing already experienced through contact with the kingdom available through union with the risen Son of God in Christian community. The shift from the third-person mode of the first eight beatitudes to the second-person mode ("Blessed are *you*") facilitates the transition to the body of the Sermon. This is especially true for the "six antitheses" (verses 21-48), which climax in the challenge to "love your enemies, and pray for those who persecute you" (5:44).

CHAPTER 4

SALT, LIGHT, AND THE FULFILLMENT
OF THE LAW
(MATTHEW 5:13-20)

YOU ARE SALT AND LIGHT

5:13 "You are the salt of the earth. But if salt loses its taste, with what can it be seasoned? It is no longer good for anything but to be thrown out and trampled underfoot. 14You are the light of the world. A city set on a mountain cannot be hidden. 15Nor do they light a lamp and then put it under a bushel basket; it is set on a lampstand, where it gives light to all in the house. 16Just so, your light must shine before others, that they may see your good deeds and glorify your heavenly Father."

Having shifted in the ninth beatitude from the "they" form of address to the "you [plural]" form, Jesus continues to address the whole audience. Unlike Greek (and most other languages), contemporary English does not have a pair of pronouns that distinguishes between "you" in the singular and "you" in the plural. For example, if I address a roomful of people with the question "Are you still with me?" the audience does not know whether I am addressing that question to a drowsy student in the third row or checking with the group as a whole. I would have to give a physical cue (with a gesture or look) or clarify my intent verbally. This is not a problem in the southern parts of the U.S. where "y'all" usually signifies the plural (although I am told that "all y'all" is required when you want to make it perfectly clear that you mean the whole group).

It is important to notice that throughout the Sermon on the Mount, the pronoun "you" is usually the plural pronoun. Let that be your "default setting" as you read. I will point out the exceptional instances of "you" singular when they occur (usually in a concrete example). This point is crucial. I am convinced that it is the habit of most of us Western Anglophone readers to think of ourselves addressed *individually* when we read "you" in the Sermon. This is a product of both an accident of the English language and our cultural individualism. But Jesus is addressing a crowd—indeed, from Matthew's and Luke's post-Easter perspective, a community. It makes an important difference whether one hears the promises and challenges of the Sermon addressed to isolated individuals or to a healed community intent on following Jesus.

"You are the salt of the earth." What did it mean in Jesus' culture to use that metaphor? The evidence of other biblical texts and other Jewish writing shows that salt was used in a variety of ways and therefore connoted a variety of qualities. It is required for temple sacrifices (Ezekiel 43:24; Ezra 6:9). It is associated with the covenant (Numbers 18:19). Elisha uses salt to miraculously purify drinking water. It is of course a condiment (Job 6:6). It is a preservative (Ignatius, *To the Magnesians,* 10). It is an absolute necessity ("Chief of all needs for human life / are water and fire, iron and salt," Sirach 39:26). Eating salt with someone is a sign of loyalty (Ezra 4:14). Greek literature uses "salt" metaphorically to mean *wit* as the "spice" of conversation, which may be what underlies the advice of Paul in Colossians 4:6: "Let your speech always be gracious, seasoned with salt, so that you know how you should respond to each one."[32] Our contemporary awareness of salt's contribution to high blood pressure was not, of course, part of first-century thought.

Among these possibilities, salt as seasoning and salt as preservative seem to be the qualities that best lend themselves to metaphorical meaning. But there is yet another use of salt, apparently still little known among scholars, that illuminates some of Jesus' salt sayings quite powerfully. The ancient Semites, like today's Arabs, covered the bottom of their kilns and ovens with plates of salt to help activate the fire. Since Palestine is practically without wood or coal, peasants had to use dried camel and donkey dung as combustible material. Salt worked as a catalyst for burning the dung. After a while salt loses its catalytic power; instead of fostering the combustion, it arrests the flames. The catalyst turns into an anti-catalyst. "It is no longer good for anything but to be thrown out and trampled under foot" (Matthew 5:13b).[33]

Understood this way, "earth" in Matthew 5:13 has a double meaning. Joined with the phrase "light of the world," the saying refers first to the earth in the sense of *the human habitat* (as in Matthew 4:8 and 13:38). Second, it implies the image of the kiln or oven; disciples are to be catalysts for the fire that Jesus would bring to the oven of the world. The Hebrew word for "earth"—*eretz*—can also be translated "oven" or "kiln." It happens that the Arabic name for kiln is *artsa* (cognate with the Hebrew for *eretz*), which can mean "earth"— an apt name for a kiln when the kiln is made of clay.[34] Understood this way, Jesus' saying makes perfectly good sense: "You are the salt of the kiln. If salt loses its property (to catalyze the fire), with what shall it be salted? It is good for nothing but to be thrown out and to be trodden under foot, for it is good *neither for the kiln* [the earth] *nor for the dunghill*" (to use Luke's—more original?—phrasing of the saying at 14:35).[35] The disciple of Jesus is imaged as a catalytic agent, sent to facilitate the "fire" that Jesus intends to spread, as in Luke 12:49: "I have come to set the earth on fire, and how I wish it were already blazing."

Jesus then shifts from the metaphor of salt to the metaphor of light. "*You are the light of the world [to phōs tou kosmou].*" "The world" here carries the meaning of *to kosmos* at Matthew 4:8 and 18:7, meaning the whole of humanity. Is there any OT background for that idea of being "the light of everybody"? Several passages immediately spring to mind. In Isaiah 2:5, climaxing the oracle about the gathering of all nations for Torah on Mount Zion, the prophet says, "O house of Jacob, come, / let us walk in the light of the LORD!" Isaiah 42:6, regarding the Servant ("I formed you, and set you / as a covenant for the people, / a *light for the nations*"), is just two verses after the passage (42:2-4) that Matthew applies to Jesus at 12:18-21. Still another passage is Isaiah 49:6b ("I will make you a *light to the nations* / that my salvation may reach to the ends of the earth"), which is the climax of another Servant song. Fresh in the minds of both our author and his audience is the fulfillment citation (the seventh) that Matthew inserts in his gospel just prior to the Sermon on the Mount of Isaiah 8:23–9:1, illustrating Jesus' withdrawal to Galilee: "The people who sit in darkness / have seen a great *light,* / on those dwelling in a land overshadowed by death / *light has arisen*" (Matthew 4:16). Given this background, when Jesus says, "You are the light of the world," there could be no more direct way of assigning to the audience—the followers in the narrative and also the evangelist's audience—the role of continuing Jesus' mission. The image of Jesus as light will come to its simplest and fullest expression in the Fourth Gospel in one of its key "I AM" sayings: "I am the light of the world" (John 8:12 and 9:5).

A city set on a mountain cannot be hidden. This statement of obvious fact becomes a little similitude when the context suggests a comparison: If disciples are called "light," then the statement about the undeniable visibility of a mountaintop town suggests that the disciples are an object of scrutiny, like it or not. That image provides a context for the next assertion of the obvious: *Nor do they light a lamp and then put it under a bushel basket; it is set on a lampstand, where it gives light to all in the house.* As people who are used to electric lamps, we need to remind ourselves that Jesus and the evangelists were talking about a little terra-cotta lamp holding olive oil and a wick, and that such lamps were the only illumination in very dark interiors. Matthew seems to have taken this saying from Mark's gospel, where it sits in the middle of Mark's presentation of Jesus' speech about parables of growth (verse 21 within Mark 4:1-34). Matthew, however, omits the lamp saying in his version of the parables speech (Matthew 13) and places it here, where the implication for discipleship is more obvious: If the purpose of a lamp is to help people see in the dark, then you, since you are light, need to shine. Indeed, the next verse says exactly that: *Just so, your light must shine before others, that they may see your good deeds and glorify your heavenly Father.* If we were still "in the dark" regarding the meaning of the metaphor "disciples = light," here is the answer: For you to "shine" is to *perform visible good deeds*, so that those who see them may glorify God. (The words of a familiar African-American gospel song capture the point perfectly: "This little light of mine, / I'm gonna let it shine.")

For the person who knows the rest of Jesus' teaching—or just the rest of the Sermon—this particular teaching raises a problem. As the Sermon progresses, Jesus will say, "Take care not to perform righteous deeds [literally, "do righteousness"—*dikaiosynēn . . . poiein*] in order that people may see them; otherwise, you will have no recompense from your heavenly Father" (6:1). Or again, in his series of "woes" against the scribes and Pharisees in Matthew 23, Jesus says, "All their works are performed to be seen" (verse 5). These statements seem to fly in the face of the advice given in chapter 5, to let one's good deeds be seen. What makes those teachings of later chapters compatible with the teaching of 5:16 is the difference in the kind of deeds and in motivation.

In his critique of doing deeds for show, Jesus is speaking specifically of religious deeds—acts of piety like prayer, fasting, and almsgiving. In the teaching of 5:16 (Let it shine!), Jesus must be referring to the other parts of one's life and also to other eyes. In 5:16 the actions in question may be associated with being a follower of Jesus, which are the actions entailed in the six interpretations of the Torah about to be discussed in the rest of Matthew 5—the control of anger, reconciliation, marital fidelity, straight talk, non-retaliation, and love of enemies.

In addition, the motives are different. Jesus criticizes behavior done *simply* to be seen—to gain honor for oneself. On the other hand, the behavior Jesus praises is that done in public *to evoke the honor of God*. (For another expression of this same theme, see 1 Peter 2:12: "Maintain good conduct among the Gentiles, so that if they speak of you as evildoers, they may observe your good works and glorify God on the day of visitation.") The unity of the Christian community is to have the same effect (see John 17:20-23).

JESUS AND THE LAW: THE CALL TO A GREATER RIGHTEOUSNESS

[5:17]"Do not think that I have come to abolish the law or the prophets. I have come not to abolish but to fulfill. [18]Amen, I say to you, until heaven and earth pass away, not the smallest letter [*iōta*] or the smallest part of a letter will pass from the law, until all things have taken place. [19]Therefore, whoever breaks one of the least of these commandments and teaches others to do so will be called least in the kingdom of heaven. But whoever obeys and teaches these commandments will be called greatest in the kingdom of heaven. [20]I tell you, unless your righteousness surpasses that of the scribes and Pharisees, you will not enter into the kingdom of heaven."

For Matthew's audience, these words would come as something of a surprise. Nothing in the gospel up to this point described Jesus challenging the authority of the Torah or the prophets. Indeed, the narrative was punctuated by formula quotations claiming that events in Jesus' life "fulfilled what was written" in the prophets. And the only places where the law came up were Jesus' own citations of Deuteronomy in response to Satan's tests of him in the desert.[36] There Jesus fulfills what he quotes by acting as the obedient Son, as contrasted with disobedient Israel as described in Deuteronomy. The issues addressed in this passage (5:17-20) seem rather to be those of the post-Easter church. As such, this passage fits well the situation that Matthew faced within his faith community as Davies and Allison assess it:

Three different attitudes about the Mosaic law existed in first-century Jewish Christianity. There were first of all the so-called "Judaizers" who apparently expected Gentiles to become Jews and uphold the Torah (cf. Acts 15:1, 5; 21:21; Galatians 6:13; Justin, *Dial.* 47:3). There were, secondly, those who believed the law had been set aside so that neither Jew nor Gentile had to submit to its yoke (Stephen?; John's Gospel; Epistle of Barnabas). Then, thirdly, and somewhere between the two extremes, were those who recognized the relative freedom of the Gentiles and yet at the same time believed that those born as Jews should remain within the law and Jewish tradition (so James, and Cephas, and John according to Galatians 2; also probably Paul (see 1 Corinthians 7:18; 9:19-21; Galatians 5:3; cf. Justin, *Dial.* 47). Matthew, we should like to think, belonged to this third group. For him, the law was still to be observed by Jewish Christians (5:17-20; 23:3), but such was not necessary for the Gentiles. . . . It would, therefore, be no problem for the evangelist to affirm the perpetuity of the Torah and yet embrace the mission to the uncircumcision . . . And the Paul of Acts, who does not require circumcision for the salvation of the Gentiles and yet himself submits to Jewish tradition (Acts 16:3; 18:18; 21:23-26), might be a figure not altogether unlike Matthew.[37]

In addition to these three Jewish-Christian positions regarding the Torah, there was the position of the "outsiders," that majority of Jews who did not accept Jesus as the Christ, mostly because they saw in his person (a nonmilitary crucified failure) and in his followers (which included tax collectors and sinners) a challenge to the Torah and to the expected Messiah as they understood these things.

Building on the tradition handed to him, as evidenced in Luke 16:17 ("It is easier for heaven and earth to pass away than for the smallest part of a letter of the law to become invalid," paralleling Matthew 5:18), Matthew can be understood as drawing on the Jesus tradition to address three fronts: (1) the "Judaizing" Jewish Christians who wanted gentile converts to take on the whole Jewish law, including circumcision; (2) those Christians who felt that the Mosaic law could be jettisoned entirely; and (3) those *non*messianic Jews who denied that Jesus could be the authoritative interpreter of the Torah.

For Matthew, as for Jesus, the scrolls of the Jewish Scriptures (though not necessarily the oral traditions interpreting those texts) remained the authoritative word of God. But now, in the wake of the Roman destruction of the temple in A.D. 70, when the burning question was *how to be a Jew without the central national sanctuary*, the Christian answer was that "something greater than the temple is here" (12:6)—the Lord Jesus Messiah. He is now the authentic interpreter of the law. Indeed, while the incumbent leadership of the Jewish community is to be respected ("Do and observe all things whatsoever they tell you, but do not follow their example"—23:3), Jesus calls his followers to a greater "righteousness" (5:20). Clearly, here "righteousness" (the same *dikaiosynē* that we met in Matthew's dialogue in the Jordan baptism scene and in the fourth and eighth beatitudes) means *doing the right thing*, behaving in ways that are faithful to the covenant relationships. This is precisely what the next section of the Sermon, Matthew 5:21-48, is all about.

Is the question of Jesus' relationship to the law (Torah) simply an issue of the early days of Christianity, of no particular relevance to the life and mission of the church today? The six examples of Jesus' relationship to the Torah that follow in the remainder of Matthew 5 will give us occasion to pursue this question in some detail, but it is good to pause and contemplate the introductory verses that we have just reviewed. They do have a powerful pastoral pertinence even now, at the beginning of the third millennium of the Christian era.

As a Catholic priest, I have to acknowledge that my church was complicit in a centuries-long "teaching of contempt" regarding Jews and Judaism. There are reasons, all too human, for how this came about. Any minority group emerging from a larger majority—and this was the situation of the early church regarding its parent, second-temple Judaism—will emphasize its differences as it develops its sense of identity. Just as an adolescent says in various verbal and behavioral ways to his or her father or mother, "I am not you," so the early Christians, in "the parting of the ways" with the Israelite faith community, asserted its identity. We can see Paul do that with vigor in his Letter to the Galatians, only to reassert the continuity of Christian faith with the Torah in his more mature letter to the Romans. The Letter to the Hebrews also stresses difference. Similarly, the author of the Fourth Gospel casts *hoi Ioudaioi* [the Jews] as the chief opponents of Jesus in his narrative, whereas Luke is at pains to underscore continuities between Judaism and the emergent Christian community. And Matthew, as we will see, favors the language of fulfillment and what we might call a deepening of the law.

During the postbiblical centuries, the church tended to lean more toward the approach of the Paul of Galatians, the Gospel of John, and Hebrews. The Gospel of Matthew was read in that light as well. We have come to call this tendency, in its extreme form, *supersessionism,* the theory that the Christian revelation so transcends Judaism that, in effect, the New Testament *supersedes* the Old Testament. This position was already condemned as heresy in its early expression, the work of the second-century writer Marcion. Moreover, the church's use of the Hebrew Scriptures as its own Holy Book obviously validates the authenticity of the Old Testament. And yet some forms of supersessionism continued to prevail for centuries in Christian art, in liturgical expression, in European passion plays, in the creation of ghettoes, in catechesis, and in preaching. Only recently the Roman Catholic bishops of the world, assembled at the Second Vatican Council, recognized the need to confront supersessionism directly. They did so in the document *Nostra aetate* (1965), the declaration on the relation of the church to non-Christian religions. In the section on Judaism, they repudiated the charge of deicide and the interpretation of the statement of Matthew 27:25 as holding all Jews responsible for the death of Jesus.[38]

Christians can still rightly identify their mission as serving the world as communities of salt and light, but it is no longer useful—indeed, it is harmful—to emphasize discontinuity with the traditions of Israel. Remembering the roots we have in common with Judaism is not simply a matter of human decency; knowing and honoring those roots helps Christians better understand their faith in Jesus and the One who sent him in the power of the Holy Spirit.

CHAPTER 5

ANGER, LUST, DIVORCE, AND OATHS
(MATTHEW 5:21-37)

Matthew has introduced the spirit and vision of Jesus' teaching with the nine beatitudes, characterizing the Christian mission with the metaphors of salt and light. He has also introduced Jesus' relationship to the authority of the Torah as fulfillment and Jesus' teaching as a call to a greater righteousness. Matthew now begins the body of the Sermon (5:21–7:12), a spelling out of what that righteousness should look like in the life of Jesus' followers. The most challenging and best-known part is in 5:21-48, Jesus' teachings about Torah texts on murder, adultery, divorce, oath-taking, retaliation, and hating enemies. Put positively, they are teachings about anger management and reconciliation, curbing lust, sexual fidelity, straight talk, nonviolence, and love of enemies.

Because each of the six teachings begins with the formula "You have heard (or it was said) . . . But [*dè*] I say to you . . . ," it has become conventional to call these assertions "the six antitheses." While such a label is a convenient way of referring to this part of the Sermon, it is a bit misleading. Although the term "antithesis" can mean "contrasting proposition," its usual meaning in contemporary English is "direct opposite." In this passage, Jesus' assertions directly oppose the Old Testament teaching only on two topics, divorce and oaths. Mainly, his teachings *contrast* with the earlier teachings, usually by way of *deepening* or developing the teaching of the elder Scripture. Indeed, in the repeated formula "you have heard it said, but I tell you," the Greek conjunction translated by "but" is the relatively weak adversative *dè*, rather than the stronger conjunction *allá*.[39] For convenience, and with a nod to an established commentary tradition, I will sometimes refer to verses 21-48 as "the six antitheses," but always with the understanding that the term is misleading and does not apply to each teaching in the same way. As a reminder of that reality, I will occasionally enclose the words "antithesis" and "antitheses" in quotation marks.[40] Let us listen to the first one.

THE FIRST ANTITHESIS: FROM NOT KILLING TO ANGER MANAGEMENT AND RECONCILIATION

5:21"You have heard that it was said to your ancestors, 'You shall not kill; and whoever kills will be liable to judgment.' 22But [dè] I say to you, whoever is angry with his brother will be liable to judgment, and whoever says to his brother, 'Raqa,' will be answerable to the Sanhedrin, and whoever says, 'You fool,' will be liable to fiery Gehenna. 23Therefore, if you bring your gift to the altar, and there recall that your brother has anything against you, 24leave your gift there at the altar, go first and be reconciled with your brother, and then come and offer your gift. 25Settle with your opponent quickly while on the way to court with him. Otherwise your opponent will hand you over to the judge, and the judge will hand you over to the guard, and you will be thrown into prison. 26Amen, I say to you, you will not be released until you have paid the last penny."

Notice that there are four parts in this teaching:

1. *Citation of Scripture* (verse 21): A citation of the fifth commandment (Exodus 20:13; Deuteronomy 5:17).[41]

2. *"Antithesis"* (verse 22): Jesus' "antithesis" in the form of three "cases": being angry, calling someone "*raqa*," and calling someone "fool," accompanied by a (satirical?) escalation of judgment

venues: local court, then the Sanhedrin (the supreme court!), and then hellfire.

3. *An example of reconciliation* (verses 23-24): The case of being the object of someone else's resentment.

4. *A parable about reconciliation* (verses 25-26): The case of being litigated by a creditor (a parable in the form of advice).

The teaching begins with Jesus' citation of one of the Ten Commandments. The passive form of the phrase "it was said" is a Hebrew way of referring to an act of God. In this case, the act is God's communication to Israel through Moses, what we have come to call the fifth commandment, "You shall not kill." What follows—"will be liable to judgment"—is not part of the commandment but a reference to the procedure conveyed in the Torah legislation regarding one accused of murder, that is, trial by a local court. In this context, the word translated "judgment" (*krisis*) does not mean divine judgment but trial by the local tribunal at the city gates.

Jesus' revision of the commandment against murder to one about anger is startling, for two reasons. The first surprise is the move from a completely physical act back to its very beginnings in the human spirit, the emotion of anger. Already this is a leap. Second, Jesus presents the odd scenario of litigation over anger. Suppose you suspected that an acquaintance was angry with you; imagine further asking an attorney to prosecute that person. Your lawyer would surely ask, "Has he *done* anything against you?" You would have to admit that no hostile act has been performed. Your lawyer would surely say, "I'm sorry, but there is no matter for litigation here. We need an external action, something that could be witnessed. You have no case." An external action was also necessary for matters brought for judgment in ancient courts.

So Jesus' statement is a kind of "mind tease." Once the listener thinks this through, the point begins to dawn: Don't think that you have carried out the fifth commandment just because you have not killed anyone. Deal with what could *lead* to hostile action; manage your anger. It is as if Jesus had said, "I am challenging you to something beyond the reach of the law courts. Mind the habits of your heart. Deal with your anger before you are tempted to act it out."

But there is more to Jesus' teaching on anger: "Whoever says to his brother, 'Raqa,' will be answerable to the Sanhedrin. . . ." *Raqa* is an Aramaic insult term whose root meaning is "empty"—something like our "airhead" or "lame brain." With the mention of the Sanhedrin, the hyperbolic nature of Jesus' expression becomes even more humorous; we now have the external act of verbal abuse, but nothing close to physical violence, much less murder, and already the venue of judgment has become the highest court of the land! And Jesus does not stop there. The verse continues with "and whoever says, 'You fool,' will be liable to fiery Gehenna."[42]

With this last statement, the series of "cases" has moved from (a) being angry to (b) calling someone "airhead" to (c) calling someone "fool." Meanwhile, the accompanying venues of judgment have escalated from (a) the local court to (b) the supreme court to (c) now hellfire—while the offense has not progressed beyond "trash talk." There can be no doubt that Jesus is engaging in prophetic hyperbole here. The point made in the first example (I am challenging you to something the law does not reach) is driven home with the second and third expressions. Moreover, scholars have seen in the strained calibration of procedures a parody of the casuistry exercised by some religious leaders of Jesus' day.[43] Jesus is challenging his audience to get to the root issue of the commandment: Mind your anger!

What comes next is a set of short parables masquerading as legal counsel. In the form of what looks like straightforward advice, the discourse moves from third-person form to direct second-person (singular) address, taking up the case of attending to the anger of someone *else* against the person addressed. You are now not the agent but the object of another's anger, with the implication that you are somehow responsible for that person's anger. *"If you bring your gift to the altar, and there recall that your brother has anything against you, leave your gift there at the altar, go first and be reconciled with your brother, and then come and offer your gift"* (5:23-24). The scenario envisions that you are at the altar of sacrifice in the Jerusalem temple and suddenly recall that all is not right between you and your "brother." You are advised to drop the lamb right there and travel back to see your brother (presumably up in Galilee, the locale of most of Jesus' teaching), get reconciled, and *then* come back to the temple in Jerusalem to complete the offering. Here again we are encountering exaggerated behavior whose purpose is to drive home a familiar theme of the Hebrew prophets: If all is not right between you and your fellow human beings, especially your "brother" (or companion in the faith community), then your worship of God is empty. (See Jeremiah 7:1-15 or Micah 6:6-8 or a passage key to Matthew's thought, Hosea 6:6, which he inserts twice in his gospel, "I desire mercy, not sacrifice," quoted at Matthew 9:13 and 12:7.)

Even apart from the amazing interruption of ritual, there is the further nonliteral element in picturing an ordinary person presenting a sacrificial victim at the great altar of sacrifice in the court of the priests. Only priests did that, and nothing suggests that either Jesus or Matthew was addressing temple priests. This scenario makes more sense if the story of Cain and Abel (Genesis 4) is in the background.[44] This first antithesis and Genesis 4 have in common the mention of sacrifice, enmity between "brothers" (an echo lost in the inclusive translation of the NRSV, "you remember that your brother or sister has something against you"), and the link between anger and murder. The allusion carries a powerful suggestion: Remember where unresolved anger led Cain! The First Letter of John 3:11-12 makes a similar connection: "For this is the message you have heard from the beginning: we should love one another, unlike Cain who belonged to the evil one and slaughtered his brother." In the teaching of Jesus in the Sermon, presenting murder as the alternative to love may seem an extreme either/or option, but the point is clear: The distance between lack of reconciliation and killing may be shorter than you think.

The fourth part of this teaching, verses 25-26, at first looks like straightforward advice: Settle out of court! Even in our own litigious society, most people prefer to settle out of court. However, given what we have met in the verses leading up to this admonition, we should be open to the possibility that this scenario is meant as another little parable, the kind called a similitude, where a comparison is drawn between a common occurrence in human experience and a religious reality. "Settle out of court" is good advice any time, but this statement comes in a sermon that begins and ends with references to the ultimate consequences of one's actions. Framed in this way, it is natural to take the human judge as a reference to the ultimate Judge ("your Father" who sees in secret—6:4, 15, 18). Understood this way, the advice to "settle with your opponent quickly while on the way to court with him" (5:25) lends urgency to the mandate to reconcile given in the previous similitude about taking care of one's human-to-human relationships before worshiping God. Settle your interpersonal conflicts *as if your whole life were a trip to the court*—because your life *really is like that*: You are on your way to being judged by the returning Son of Man. This interpretation is confirmed by Luke's treatment of this Q material. Luke presents the similitude at the end of a series of parables about watchfulness and reading the signs of the times, all pointing to the second coming and judgment (Luke 12:35-53).

To return to the core of this section, Jesus' association of anger with murder raises a question: Is Jesus teaching that the spontaneous response of anger—the mere feeling of anger springing up in a threatening or hostile situation—is itself a sin? I know of no reputable moralist who has interpreted the saying in this way. A moment's reflection on one's own experience of spontaneous anger—say, someone gives you a kick in the shin—reveals that the surge of anger one feels in such a situation is simply a fact, not a choice. It is a spontaneous response of our entire person (emotional and physical) to a situation that calls for *some* kind of protective or assertive response to an injury. It is simply part of life for any healthy human being of any age. Such anger is virtually automatic and comes as a surprise over which we have no immediate control. Free choice enters when we are aware that we can choose where to go with the energy of that anger—to act it out in mindless hostility or to take other more rational measures in response.

Almost everyone knows what it means to harbor resentment. We can choose to indulge resentment by dwelling on the hurt, especially if it is unjust and unacknowledged by the offender. Freedom enters the picture when we choose to spend time either focusing on reprisal and revenge or simply feeling sorry for ourselves. The Mosaic law addresses this reality in Leviticus 19:18a. Christians are quite familiar with the second part of this verse, 18b ("You shall love your neighbor as yourself"), but the first part, 18a, is also important, and speaks directly to this issue of inner disposition: "Take no revenge and *cherish no grudge against your fellow countrymen.*" And this simply reinforces the previous verse: "You shall not bear hatred for your brother in your heart" (19:17a). There is still more to explore here, which is better addressed when we come to the Lord's Prayer and its petition regarding forgiveness in Matthew 6. It is sufficient now to recognize that what Jesus critiques in this passage is not the *emotion* of anger, but how one uses one's freedom in response to that emotion. It is what modern parlance calls "anger management." At the same time, the examples illustrate that Jesus is calling for more than management of an emotion. The examples or parables of verses 23-26 show that he is challenging his audience toward active reconciliation.

As will become apparent, thinking through the antithesis on murder has prepared us to hear more clearly the teaching on the sixth commandment, the one on adultery.

THE SECOND ANTITHESIS: FROM MARITAL FIDELITY TO CURBING LUST

5:27"You have heard that it was said, 'You shall not commit adultery.' 28But I say to you, everyone who looks at a woman with lust [*pros to epithymēsai autēn*] has already committed adultery with her in his heart 29If your right eye causes you to sin, tear it out and throw it away. It is better for you to lose one of your members than to have your whole body thrown into Gehenna. 30And if your right hand causes you to sin, cut it off and throw it away. It is better for you to lose one of your members than to have your whole body go into Gehenna."

This passage repeats the pattern we met in the teaching on murder; Jesus first cites a commandment, gives his response, and then follows with some startling advice regarding concrete actions. Jesus' response to the commandment on adultery deserves a very close reading. When we first read verse 28, we may think the statement refers directly to sexual desire, much as the first antithesis referred to anger. But this is not exactly what Jesus is saying. The phrasing of the second clause in the NAB translation, which we are using—"everyone who looks at a woman with lust"—is valid, but the compact translation "looks . . . with lust" can be heard as a reference to the spontaneous feeling of sexual desire. Such an understanding, however, misses an important element in the Greek original. The phrase "with lust" renders the fuller Greek phrase that is noted in the brackets in the passage quoted above. Literally, it means "*with the purpose of desiring.*" The phrase spells out the *intent* of the looking: to foster the desire. The context of the passage, the sixth commandment forbidding adultery, makes it clear that the acting out of the sexual desire would violate right order in the covenant community, someone else's marital relationship. So the focus of the statement is first on the act of looking with the intention of fostering illicit desire. The element of purpose is caught in some translations; KJV and Rheims both have "to lust after her." NASB has "to lust for her." But the NAB ("looks . . . with lust"), the NIV ("looks . . . lustfully") and NRSV ("looks . . . with lust") miss that element of *deliberate intention* to foster illicit desire.

It is as if the phrasing of Matthew's Greek anticipates the question raised by the antithesis about anger. Is Jesus saying that the spontaneous feeling of sexual desire (for another's wife) is sinful? No. As in the case of anger, the initial feeling is spontaneous and natural. Freedom (and sin) enters the picture in the decision regarding where one "goes" with the initial feeling. In this case, the focus on the act of *looking* with the purpose of fostering an illicit desire makes clear that Jesus' statement is about this free, and misdirected, act. The use of the verb *epithymeō* adds to the power of the statement. It is a rare word in the gospels (occurring twice in Matthew and four times in Luke). In the Greek version of the Torah, it turns up only a dozen times, but four of those occur in the ninth and tenth commandments of the Decalogue forbidding the desiring of the neighbor's wife and the neighbor's house and property (LXX Exodus 20:17; Deuteronomy 5:21). Thus Matthew's audience heard Jesus saying, in effect, "If you use your eyes to indulge in an illicit sexual desire, you have already committed adultery in your heart *and* disobeyed the ninth commandment of the Decalogue about 'coveting' your neighbor's wife."

Now come the two startling mandates to *get rid* of the offending eye or hand if one or the other occasions sin. The examples in the teaching about murder and anger (interrupt your temple worship to reconcile, and settle on the way to court) have prepared us to expect hyperbole that lends itself to analogy. Is that pedagogy operating here? The reader familiar with Mark, of course, is not surprised. Mark 9:43-48 has already conveyed these sayings about removing the "scandalizing" hand, foot, or eye. And Matthew employs them not once but twice; the other place is at the beginning of the discourse on church order, Matthew 18:8-9, where the wording and context is much the same as Mark's. Here, in the context of the Sermon on the Mount, Matthew changes Mark's hand-foot-eye sequence and begins, naturally, with the statement about the scandalizing eye because it follows Jesus' statement about covetous looking.

If we wonder how this statement can be rescued from a bloody literalism, the clue may be Matthew's specification of the *right* eye as the offending member. It is possible that the choice may be to prepare for the comparative statement that is it is better to lose *one* of your members than to have your *whole body* thrown into Gehenna, but the phrasing raises the humorous notion that *one* eye could be lustful— and the other eye *innocent*. The advice surely looks like hyperbole. Yet if we are not meant to take the saying literally, we are still meant to take it seriously. And there *is* a clear message: Just as on the physical level, one willingly sacrifices part of the body to save the whole (a routine albeit painful decision in modern surgery), so when it comes to habits of the heart, one should take the necessary means—tough as they may be—to ensure what the sixth beatitude calls cleanness of heart. In this case, the intent is obvious: If you are visually sexually attracted to your neighbor's spouse, then do not use your eyes to *intentionally* foster an illicit desire. This is not a surprising challenge in ordinary social life.

At a time when we are rightly sensitive to gendered language, one cannot help but notice that this passage is addressed to men only. Does it not also apply to women? Of course it does. But the normal venue of Jesus' teaching is typically a public setting out of doors. The evangelists are faithful to the social setting of first-century rural Palestine when they portray Jesus speaking mainly to groups of men.

In this patriarchal culture, it simply was not "a woman's place" to congregate in crowds to listen to itinerant teachers or preachers. That accounts for Matthew's presentation of Jesus speaking specifically to men. More to the point here, the commandment regarding adultery, to which Jesus is responding, is cast in male terms. In the context of Mosaic law, adultery was the taking of another man's most important property, his wife. The sixth commandment was a law concerning the behavior of men. The Torah, of course, is clear that a woman who cooperates is guilty of the same capital crime as the man and receives the same punishment—death by stoning (Deuteronomy 22:22). As we will see below, there is evidence to suggest that capital punishment in this case was already commuted to divorce by the time of Jesus.

The Third Antithesis:
From Legal Divorce to Committed Monogamy

[5:31]"It was also said, 'Whoever divorces his wife must give her a bill of divorce' [Deuteronomy 24:1]. [32]But I say to you, whoever divorces his wife (unless the marriage is unlawful [*parektos logou porneias*]) causes her to commit adultery, and whoever marries a divorced woman commits adultery."

If we take the point of view of a first-time reader of (or listener to) this passage, several things are immediately apparent. First, unlike the two previous antitheses, each of which begins with a reference to one of the Ten Commandments, this third one begins with reference to a law from the covenant code in a later section of Deuteronomy, the divorce protocol (Deuteronomy 24:1-4). When we read that law in full, we discover that the statement in Matthew 5:31 is actually a paraphrase of a "when" clause beginning a four-verse sentence; 5:31 turns the "when" clause into a command. Second, Jesus' response, verse 32, consists of two startling statements: He asserts that the divorce procedure that Deuteronomy allows results in a situation that forces the divorced woman to become an adulteress, and he equates marriage to a divorced woman with adultery.

Jesus actually elaborates further on the Deuteronomy protocol later in the Gospel of Matthew, in the dispute with the Pharisees on this subject at 19:3-12. We will be better able to understand Jesus' teaching about divorce in the Sermon if we first turn to this passage. And since this passage is a rewrite of Mark's version, we do well to hear Mark's rendition first (10:2-12), the better to appreciate the emphases of Matthew's redaction.[45]

As Mark tells it, the discussion begins with the Pharisees asking Jesus, "Is it lawful for a man to divorce his wife?" (10:2). Against the background of the Old Testament teaching, this seems to be a strange question, for the main passage about divorce in the Mosaic law (Deuteronomy 24:1-4, the passage to which Jesus refers in the Sermon) presumes that the practice of divorce is a fact of social life, and its legality is presumed in the code. It is instructive to read the text:

> When a man, after marrying a woman and having relations with her, is later displeased with her because he finds in her **something indecent** [*'erwat dabar*], and therefore he writes out a bill of divorce and hands it to her, thus dismissing her from his house: if on leaving his house she goes and becomes the wife of another man, and the second husband, too, comes to dislike her and dismisses her from his house by handing her a written bill of divorce; or if this second man who has married her, dies; **then her former husband, who dismissed her, may not again take her as his wife after she has become defiled.** That would be an abomination before the LORD, and you shall not bring such guilt upon the land which the LORD, your God, is giving you as a heritage. (Deuteronomy 24:1-4)

I have bolded the second clause in verse 4 to highlight the point of the law, which might be paraphrased in this way: "Be careful before you decide to divorce your wife; you won't be permitted to marry her again if she marries and then is divorced from another man." Notice that the legality of divorce is presumed; the focus is on a possible outcome—the case of a man who wants to remarry the wife he divorced if she is divorced from that second husband. The law forbids such remarriage. The apparent intent of the law is to forestall frivolous divorces. I have also bolded a phrase in the first verse—"something indecent"—to highlight the vagueness of the language referring to the *grounds* for divorce, something that would inevitably give rise to debate among the rabbis. Most famously, the Mishnah (the late second-century-written compendium of oral tradition) records this summary of the debate:

The School of Shammai says: A man may not divorce his wife unless he has found unchastity in her, for it is written, *Because he hath found in her **indecency** in anything*. And the School of Hillel says: [He may divorce her] even if she spoiled a dish for him, for it is written, *Because he hath found in her indecency in anything*. R. Akiba says: Even if he found another fairer than she, for it is written, *And it shall be if she find no favour in his eyes*. . . . (*m. Gittin* 9:5)[46]

Given that the schools of Shammai and Hillel flourished in Jesus' time, the Pharisees might be expected to ask Jesus what he considered to be the *grounds* of divorce, not whether the law of Moses *allowed* divorce (to which the obvious answer would seem to be a simple yes). There is, however, more to the background. Evidence from the Dead Sea Scrolls found in the caves around Qumran—specifically the *Temple Scroll* (11QTemple 57:7-19) and the *Damascus Document* (CD 4:19-21)—reveals that at least one group in first-century

Palestine, the Essenes, held that fidelity to the Mosaic covenant prohibited divorce. The passage from the *Temple Scroll* expands the law
regarding the king's monogamous marriage in Deuteronomy 17:17 to
say that "only she will be with him all the days of her life." And what
was required of the king was required of his people. The *Damascus
Document*, describing the net of "unchastity" [*zenut*] in two ways,
says first that *zenut* includes "the taking of two wives in their lives"—
"their" understood as referring to the lifetimes of both partners in
the couple; the phrase can be understood as prohibiting both polyg-
amy and marriage after divorce. The second way *zenut* is explained
is incest, "taking the daughter of his brother, and the daughter of his
sister" (seen as a violation of Leviticus 18:13).[47]

A third witness to the Jewish practice of the divorce protocol at
the time of Jesus is contained in the Gospel of Matthew itself, in the
account of Joseph's dilemma when he learns of Mary's pregnancy
(1:18-19). Since betrothal in that culture constituted permanent commitment, sexual activity of a betrothed woman with another man
was an act of adultery. Since Joseph is described as *dikaios* ("righteous" in the sense of Torah-keeping) and has decided to divorce
Mary because she, his betrothed, has been discovered to be preg-
nant by someone other than her husband, the implication is that
the Mosaic law regarding an adulterous woman required that the
husband divorce her. Deuteronomy 22:20-21 mandated death by
stoning for a woman found to have been adulterous. Joseph's plan
to "divorce her quietly" (verse 19) implies that death by stoning as
punishment for adultery has by this time been commuted to man-
datory divorce.[48]

Given that fuller background, let us examine that controversy
about divorce between the Pharisees and Jesus, first according to
Mark 10:2-12. When the Pharisees ask Jesus if it is lawful for a man to
divorce his wife, their question can be understood as challenging Jesus
to take a stand regarding a current controversy: Do you side with

the Essenes (no divorce permitted) or with us Pharisees (divorce permitted on some grounds)? When Jesus asks them what Moses taught on this matter, they paraphrase Deuteronomy 24:1 (quoted on page 108). Jesus then interprets the Mosaic divorce protocol as a concession to their hardness of heart [*sklērokardia,* a word that appears in the NT only here and in the Matthean parallel; think "cardiosclerosis"], which compromised the Creator's original intention regarding the permanence of male-female union. Jesus drives home his point by alluding to both of the Genesis creation accounts:

"But from the beginning of creation, 'God made them male and female [Genesis 1:27c]. For this reason a man shall leave his father and mother [and be joined to his wife], and the two shall become one flesh' [Genesis 2:24]. So they are no longer two but one flesh. Therefore what God has joined together, no human being must separate." In the house the disciples again questioned him about this. He said to them, "Whoever divorces his wife and marries another commits adultery against her; and if she divorces her husband and marries another, she commits adultery." (Mark 10:6-12)

In one sense, Jesus is again *deepening* the law of Moses in that he is moving from a rule that says, "*Re*-marriage to a woman you have divorced is forbidden" to denying the presumption behind the divorce protocol, namely, that divorce *is permitted* when the husband is displeased by "something indecent." Jesus reinterprets Deuteronomy 24 in the light of the creation accounts of the male-female relationship and maintains that the Genesis creation accounts trump Deuteronomy 24. He forbids divorce followed by remarriage and does it with the startling assertion that divorce followed by remarriage is tantamount to breaking the commandment against *adultery*: "Whoever divorces his wife and marries another commits adultery against her" (Mark

10:11). (To paraphrase: "What you thought was legal is really a sin against the sixth commandment.") And the phrasing has an extra edge to it. Divorce is not simply adultery (which is usually understood as an offense against the woman's husband, such as the stealing of his property); it is adultery *against her*. In other words, divorce and replacing the wife by another woman is tantamount to stealing what is rightfully hers, her relationship with you!

Verse 12 adds a further surprise: Jesus applies the same principle to women ("And if *she* divorces her *husband* and marries another, *she* commits adultery"). What is surprising here is that the Torah divorce protocol pertained only to men; women could not divorce either in ancient Israel or in first-century Palestine. For this reason, scholars see this verse as being derived from the post-Easter life of the church in regions outside of Palestine, where Greek and Roman law permitted a woman to divorce her husband. This verse appears only in Mark, not in the Gospel of Matthew.

Matthew's version of this controversy (19:3-9) makes seven redactional changes:

1. He phrases the Pharisees' question in a way that appears to press Jesus further than they did in Mark: "Is it lawful for a man to divorce his wife *for any cause whatever*?" (19:3).
2. He reverses the order in which Jesus comments on the two Torah texts, addressing Genesis 1–2 first and Deuteronomy 24 second, thereby more directly juxtaposing the teaching of Moses ("Moses allowed," verses 4-6) with the teaching of Jesus ("I say to you," verses 7-8).
3. He changes Jesus' audience from the disciples alone ("in the house" in Mark 10:11-12) to the whole crowd, including the Pharisees, heightening Jesus' authority as he counters the Pharisees directly.

4. He omits Mark 10:12 (forbidding a woman to divorce her husband), presumably because it would not apply in Matthew's setting.

5. He introduces the climactic teaching with the phrase "And *I* say to you . . ." (19:9). Coming as it does immediately after the statement about *Moses'* teaching, the concession to their hardness of heart, the phrase echoes the antithesis of the teaching on divorce in the Sermon on the Mount: "It was also said [by Moses] . . . But *I* say to you . . ." (Matthew 5:31, 32).

6. He omits Mark's phrase "against her"—perhaps because he has already underscored the plight of the divorced wife in the Sermon at 5:32.

7. And finally, he includes the famous exception clause—*mē epi porneia* (literally "except for *porneia*"—which the NAB renders "unless the marriage was unlawful").

Having read Matthew's account of this fuller treatment of Jesus' teaching on divorce in the dispute with the Pharisees in Matthew 19, it is now reasonable to see the treatment of this topic in the Sermon as a kind of abbreviation of Jesus' teaching on the subject. Let us return, then, to 5:32.

Since the more original version of this saying (Mark's) comes without the exception clause, and since the exception clause is unique to Matthew's versions, two questions arise: What did Jesus mean by forbidding divorce absolutely (or teaching what we have come to call the "indissolubility" of marriage)? And what did Matthew mean by including the exception clause in his two versions of the teaching in his gospel?

Let us consider the question of Jesus' meaning first. If we take Matthew 5:32, minus the exception, as the more original version (since it is also simpler, like his omission of reference to remarriage on the part of the divorcing man), we get the likely form of Jesus' original teaching. It has two parts: (1) "Whoever divorces his wife . . . causes her to commit adultery"; (2) "Whoever marries a divorced woman commits adultery." Notice that in his comment on the protocol of Deuteronomy 24, a law dealing with the action of the husband, Jesus has placed the emphasis not on the act of the husband but on the act's consequences for the wife (mirroring "commits adultery *against her*" in Mark 10:11). Just how does his divorcing her *cause her to commit adultery*? In first-century Palestine, a woman who was not embedded in a family had no resources to survive.[49] Thus, unless her father's family took her back, a divorced woman was simply cast adrift and therefore was compelled to attach herself to another male. In calling this new union "adultery," Jesus is denying that the first union was in fact dissolved. In this case Jesus is going beyond the situation described in Deuteronomy 24. He is taking a prophetic stance against the abuse of women that typically resulted from the divorce protocol of Deuteronomy 24 as practiced in his day.

The second statement—"Whoever marries a divorced woman commits adultery"—simply gives a further consequence of the first statement: Marrying a divorced woman is violating the "ownership" of another husband, a bond that ought not to have been dissolved in the first place, in view of Jesus' teaching about permanent marriage as grounded in the original order of creation. Rather than introducing a new legal burden, Jesus is taking a prophetic stand against the abuse of the woman in the first case and in favor of the seriousness and permanence of the bond in the second case.

If this is the likely meaning of Jesus' original statements, what is the point of the exception clause that Matthew (or the tradition he had inherited) introduces into the saying of Jesus at 5:32 and 19:9? Although worded slightly differently in each case—*parektos logou porneias* at 5:32 and *mē epi porneia* at 19:9—the meaning, commentators generally agree, is the same: "except in the case of *porneia*." What has remained unsettled is the meaning of *porneia*. Lexicographers agree that *porneia* always refers in some way to illicit sexual activity; only context can illuminate what kind of illicit sexual activity is meant—prostitution, fornication, adultery, or unions with close relatives (such as the unions forbidden in Leviticus 18, incestuous and otherwise). Adultery and incest are the main meanings suggested today for *porneia* in Matthew 5:32 and 19:9. The variety of English translations of Matthew's exception phrase reflects the range of meanings that scholars have offered for *porneia*:

KJV 1611: saving for the cause of fornication
Rheims: excepting for the cause of fornication
NASB: except for the cause of fornication
JB 1966: except for the case of fornication
Good News Translation: for any cause except for her unfaithfulness
NIV: except for marital unfaithfulness
NRSV: except for the ground of unchastity
NAB 1986: unless the marriage is unlawful
NJB 1989: except for the case of an illicit marriage

Late twentieth-century discussions of the meaning of *porneia* have discovered a plausible first-century scenario. One of the key passages where *porneia* occurs elsewhere in the New Testament is in the apostolic decree summarizing the deliberations of the Council of Jerusalem in Acts 15:20, 29; 21:25. Gathered to decide whether gentiles needed to be circumcised when they became Christians, the assembly determined that circumcision was an unnecessary burden to place on gentile converts; the assembly asked, rather, that such converts simply comply with what had been traditionally required of "resident aliens" living among Jews, namely, that the newcomers "avoid pollution from idols, *porneia*, meat of strangled animals, and blood" (Acts 15:20). Leviticus 17–18, in its treatment of what was forbidden to foreigners who lived among Israelites, includes sexual unions within close degrees of consanguinity and affinity (blood relatives and in-laws) along with blood and meat of strangled animals. This same cluster of concerns also appears in the apostolic decree summarized in Acts 15:28-29 and 21:25, so the legislative context has led some commentators to interpret *porneia* as a reference to the close-kinship marriages forbidden in Leviticus 18.

This fits a scenario that the early church faced: what to do when gentiles in such marriages (say, with a cousin), which were permitted by Greek and Roman law, joined the Christian community. What was permissible among the gentiles in this case was unlawful among Jewish Christians. Therefore, such unions were dissolved. It is easy to see why Matthew would include the exception of *porneia* understood in this sense. Jewish Christians could view this separation as a kind of annulment, since in their understanding such incestuous unions were invalid in the first place. This understanding of *porneia* gained further support in the passage from the *Damascus Document* discussion on page 110, where the Hebrew word *zenut*, which the Greek Old Testament sometimes translates as *porneia*, is applied to the relationships prohibited in Leviticus 18.

Thus for Matthew, the insertion of "except for *porneia*" into Jesus' statements on divorce in 5:32 and 19:9 was not a dilution of Jesus' teaching but an application of that teaching to the circumstances of the community for which he was writing, a situation that did not exist during Jesus' ministry. This interpretation of *porneia* is reflected in the English translations of the exception clause in the NAB 1986 and the NJB, quoted on page 115.

Well, you might say, it is all very well to try to get at the meaning of the teaching on marriage and divorce in the original context of the historical Jesus and also in the context of the Gospel of Matthew; but what does this examination of Matthew 5:31-32 contribute to our approach to marriage within the life and mission of the church today, given that many Catholic marriages end in civil divorce? I submit the following considerations.

The Roman Catholic teaching about the indissolubility of marriage of baptized Christians is well grounded in Jesus' teaching as we meet it in Matthew's gospel. The gospel teaching highlights the union and mutual benefit of the spouses as a fundamental purpose of the male-female union. Our tradition had long treated that purpose as secondary to the goal of the procreation and education of children, but the Vatican II document *Gaudium et spes* restored mutual love and support of the spouses to an importance equal to the begetting and raising of offspring. Matthew's presentation of Jesus' teaching in the Sermon, understood in the light of the account of Matthew 19:1-10, powerfully supports this renewed emphasis.

In a patriarchal society, Jesus showed a special concern for women in the male-female relationship. At a time when domestic violence remains an issue, Jesus' special concern for the treatment of women provides a helpful reminder.

When Jesus describes the permanent union of male and female sexual commitment that he finds in the original order of creation, he locates the primary block to living that permanent commitment in what he calls "hardness of heart" (Matthew 19:8; par. Mark 10:5). This is no mere put-down of his adversaries. That rare word—*sklērokardia*—used only in these two places in the New Testament, occurs only three times in the Greek Old Testament: (1) LXX Deuteronomy 10:16, in a summary of Israel's call to love and serve the Lord God with heart and soul ("Therefore, you shall circumcise your *sklērokardia* . . ."); (2) LXX Jeremiah 4:4, in a similar image, here referring to conversion and repentance ("Circumcise yourselves to your God, men of Judah and inhabitants of Jerusalem . . ."); and (3) LXX Sirach 16:10, referring to Israelites rebelling against Moses in the wilderness ("the six hundred thousand footmen, who were gathered together in their *sklērokardia* . . ."). That

117

this image of the hard heart becomes a classic image for rebellion against the will of God becomes evident in Psalm 95:8: "Do not harden your hearts as at Meribah, / as on the day of Massah in the desert." Conversely, God's remedy of that rebellion is powerfully described as the divine reversal of that cardiac hardness in Ezekiel 36:26: "A new heart I will give you, and a new spirit I will put within you; and I will remove from your body the heart of stone and give you a heart of flesh" (NRSV).

Given this biblical tradition in regard to hardness of heart, it is significant that Matthew is careful to apply it only to Jesus' adversaries and to omit the application of that image where Mark has applied it to the disciples. For example, Mark says at the end of the account of Jesus' walking on the water, "They had not understood the incident of the loaves. On the contrary, their hearts were hardened" (6:52). But Matthew omits this description and instead portrays them as worshiping and acknowledging him as Son of God (14:33). And in the discussion about bread and leaven in Mark 8:14-21, Jesus says, "Are your hearts hardened? Do you have eyes and not see, and ears and not hear?" (8:17c-18a). Matthew omits that scolding and instead describes the disciples as understanding Jesus' instruction just fine. My point in comparing Mark's description of the disciples as hard of heart with Matthew's portrayal of them is to suggest that for Matthew, hardness of heart and discipleship are simply incompatible. In other words, for him, Christian conversion entails a removal of the heart of stone; the disciple is one who is blessed with Ezekiel's cleanness of heart expressed in the sixth beatitude and is thereby *enabled* to live the greater righteousness expressed in the antitheses. It would follow that for the members of this community of disciples, lifelong monogamy is expected and sustainable.

It is helpful at this point to recall Jesus' words about what really defiles a person (Mark 7:1-23; par. Matthew 15:1-20). There he argues that true personal uncleanness comes not from failing to wash one's hands but in the disorientation of the heart, which is the source of all sinning. In support of this truth, he quotes Isaiah 29:13 ("This people honors me with their lips / but their heart is far from me"—Mark 7:6b; Matthew 15:8). At the end of this section, Matthew, even more than Mark, emphasizes the heart as the source of human evil: "Do you not realize that everything that enters the mouth passes into the stomach and is expelled into the latrine? But the things that come out of the mouth come *from the heart*, and they defile. For *from the heart* come evil thoughts, murder, adultery, unchastity [*porneiai*], theft, false witness, blasphemy" (15:17-19).

The primary support for facing the challenges to sustainable marriage today is in the life of the community of Christian disciples, the presupposition of the Sermon on the Mount.

THE FOURTH ANTITHESIS:
FROM OATH-TAKING TO CONSISTENT TRUTH-TELLING

5:33 "Again you have heard that it was said to your ancestors, 'Do not take a false oath [*ouk epiorkēseis*], but make good to the Lord all that you vow [*tous horkous sou*]. 34But I say to you, do not swear at all; not by heaven, for it is God's throne; 35nor by the earth, for it is his footstool; nor by Jerusalem, for it is the city of the great King. 36Do not swear by your head, for you cannot make a single hair white or black. 37Let your 'Yes' mean 'Yes' and your 'No' mean 'No.' Anything more is from the evil one."

Verse 33 describes what was said to the ancestors in two mandates: first, "Do not take a false oath," and second, "Make good to the Lord all that you vow." The "swearing" here refers to oath-taking—calling upon God to witness either (a) to the truth of one's statement or (b) to the promise one is making. Consequently, the verb for false swearing— *epiorkeō,* used only here in the New Testament—can mean either (a) to perjure oneself or (b) to fail to do what one has promised under oath. The commands referenced in verse 33 summarize several laws of the Torah—for example, Exodus 20:7 (the second commandment of the Decalogue); Numbers 30:3 and Deuteronomy 23:22-24 (on keeping vows or pledges); Psalm 50:14; Zechariah 8:17; and Wisdom 14:28. The phrasing comes close to Leviticus 19:12 ("You shall not swear falsely in my name, thus profaning the name of your God").

Jesus' imperative, "But I say to you [plural], do not swear at all," appears to prohibit all oath-taking. The three examples that follow—by heaven, by earth, by Jerusalem—are all dismissed because of their relationship to God: "neither by heaven, *for it is God's throne;* nor by earth, *for it is his footstool;* nor by Jerusalem, *for it is the city of the great King* [meaning God]." What is the point here? Is Jesus saying, "Don't think that you are lightening the moral weight of your oath (circumventing its binding force) by invoking heaven, earth, or Jerusalem as a substitute for the name of God; each of these things, after all, is intimately linked to the Creator"? This is one way of making sense of verses 34b-35.

The next verse, "Do not swear by your head, for you cannot make a single hair white or black," is a variation on that theme, in the sense that a human being cannot directly control the effects of aging. Hair dye, a possibility even in the first century, does not seem to be in view here. Like the statement about the human inability to add "a single moment to your life-span [or a cubit to your stature]" (6:27), the point seems to be that even the hair on your head, which seems to be under your control, is part of an organic process that is ultimately a gift of the Creator. See, too, the reference to the fact that "even all the hairs of your head are counted [by God, implied by the context]" at Matthew 10:30.

The final part of this teaching on oaths moves from prohibition to a positive mandate: "Let your 'Yes' mean 'Yes' and your 'No' mean 'No.' Anything more is from the evil one." A more literal translation of the first part would be "Let your word be 'yes yes, no no [*nai nai, ou ou*].'" Given that oath-taking is well established in the Torah and has functioned as a serviceable institution in many cultures, what is Jesus' purpose in prohibiting it? How does invoking the divine name become devilish? Is he simply insisting on simplicity of speech? Commentators suggest that insisting on a distinction between the assertions of ordinary human exchange and oath-taking implies that there are times when lying and breaking promises are permitted and other times when you "really mean" what you are saying. Against such presumption and practice, Jesus urges the higher righteousness of *always* telling the truth and *always* keeping your promises, thereby rendering oath-taking unnecessary.

Oath-Taking Elsewhere in Matthew

Matthew has a special interest in the issue of oaths and oath-taking. Talk of oaths and oath-taking is rare in the other gospels—just one passage each in Mark (at 6:22-26, regarding Herod Antipas during his deadly birthday party) and in Luke (at 1:73, in the Benedictus: "the oath he [God] swore to Abraham"). Matthew, however, uses the word for "oath" (*horkos*) four times (5:33; 14:7, 9 [Herod, during the party]; and 26:72 [Peter in the high priest's yard]). He uses the verb for swearing (*omnyō*) thirteen times, here in 5:34, 36 and thereafter in two significant places: in his account of Peter's denial of his Master in the high priest's courtyard, and in the third "woe" in the series of seven woes against the scribes and Pharisees in chapter 23.

Matthew edits Mark's account of the exchanges between Peter and a maid in Caiaphas' courtyard. According to Mark, the maid says to the bystanders, "This man is one of them," and Mark writes that Peter denied this again (14:69-70). In Matthew, the maid says, "This man was with Jesus the Nazorean," and Matthew writes, "Again he denied it *with an oath, 'I do not know the man!'*" (26:72). Thus Peter becomes a prime example of how oath-taking can be "from the evil one." It definitely refers to perjury here.

That this emphasis is deliberate finds support in Matthew's redaction of the exchange between Caiaphas and Jesus just eight verses prior to the exchange between Peter and the maid. Where Mark records that Caiaphas simply asks Jesus, "Are you the Messiah, the son of the Blessed One?" and Jesus says, "I am" (Mark 14:61, 62), Matthew turns the high priest's question into a command that Jesus speak under oath: "I *order you to tell us under oath* [*exorkizō*] *before the living God*, whether you are the Messiah, the Son of God" (26:63). And Jesus refuses to do that, saying, "You have said so." Matthew's redaction underscores the fact that Peter swears falsely by denying "with an oath" that he was with Jesus (26:72). Just when Jesus refuses to take an oath at all, Peter swears falsely.

Finally, Matthew gives the matter of swearing oaths special attention in the middle of chapter 23, the denunciation of the scribes and Pharisees in the form of seven woes. The third woe focuses on the Pharisees' teaching on oath-taking:

> "Woe to you, blind guides, who say, 'If one swears by the temple, it means nothing, but if one swears by the gold of the temple, one is obligated.' Blind fools, which is greater, the gold, or the temple that made the gold sacred? And you say, 'If one swears by the altar, it means nothing, but if one swears by the gift on the altar, one is obligated.' You blind ones, which is greater, the gift, or the altar that makes the gifts sacred? One who swears by the altar swears by it and all that is upon it; one who swears by the temple swears by it and by him who dwells in it; one who swears by heaven swears by the throne of God and by him who is seated on it." (Matthew 23:16-22)

At first it would seem that Jesus here grants what he denies in the Sermon's teaching on oath-taking. He appears to presume that, correctly understood and properly done, oath-taking has its place. But a closer reading reveals that the validity of oath-taking is not the issue here; instead, the focus of this woe is the illogical nature of the scribes' and Pharisees' empty distinctions between which oaths bind and which do not. The point is that the authorities' distinctions have things upside down; they have become "blind" (a quality mentioned three times) to the reality that the things of the temple (the temple gold and the altar gifts) take their value from the holiness of the temple and the altar. Moreover, the temple and even heaven are holy only in relation to the Holy One. The Pharisees are blind guides because they do not see this truth.

That Jesus came to remedy blindness, physical but especially spiritual, is an important theme for all four evangelists, especially John in his account of the man born blind (John 9). But among the synoptic evangelists, Matthew makes the most of blindness, both physical and spiritual, the latter especially with respect to the teachers, the scribes, and the Pharisees. Five times in the "woes" passages (chapter 23), Jesus calls the teachers "blind" (verses 16, 17, 19, 24, and 26). In the same way and for a similar reason, in his redaction of Mark's account of the controversy with the Pharisees and scribes about what makes for cleanness and uncleanness (Mark 7; Matthew 15), in which Jesus upbraids the religious leaders for making the practice of supporting the temple greater than the obligation to support one's parents, Matthew inserts a similar excoriation of those leaders as blind guides:

[Jesus] said in reply, "Every plant that my heavenly Father has not planted will be uprooted. Let them [the Pharisees] alone; they are blind guides [of the blind]. If a blind person leads a blind person, both will fall into a pit." (Matthew 15:13-14)

And what constitutes their blindness in the matter of oath-taking? Their failure to perceive the universal presence of God with respect to all creatures, a presence that requires truth-telling and promise-keeping always, not simply on special occasions.

To return to our consideration of the teaching on oaths in the Great Sermon, what, practically, is a Christian to do? Has the Master prohibited all oath-taking for all time? Some Christians have understood Jesus to mean exactly that. Quakers and Mennonites ask to be excused from oath-taking in court. Roman Catholic tradition, however, has interpreted this passage as not excluding swearing in a court of law. The *Catechism of the Catholic Church,* citing the precedent of St. Paul's oath in Galatians 1:20 ("Before God, I am not lying"), says, "Following St. Paul, the tradition of the Church has understood Jesus' words as not excluding oaths made for grave and right reasons (for example, in court)." The same principle is expressed negatively in the Code of Canon Law and is cited in the Catechism: "An oath, that is the invocation of the divine name as a witness to truth, cannot be taken unless in truth, in judgment, and in justice" (2154).

A neglected passage in the *Spiritual Exercises* of St. Ignatius provides a fascinating example of how Jesus' teaching could be understood in the sixteenth century in a way that can still speak to us today. Among the considerations organized under what Ignatius calls "The First Week" (of four) of the *Exercises,* Ignatius includes instructions on the General Examination of Conscience. In his analysis of sins under the three classic headings of thoughts, words, and deeds, when he deals with the category of sinning by words, Ignatius treats first and spends the most time on oath-taking. On that topic, he deals with how one sins in "swearing" (or oath-taking) in a single clear sentence: "It is not permissible to swear, either by God or by a creature, unless it is done with truth, necessity, and reverence" (§ 38.1). The remainder of his discussion of oaths is devoted to who is most likely to swear correctly and how. The passage is worth quoting in full because of the way Ignatius manages to capture the point of Jesus' teaching on oaths in both the Sermon passage and in the third woe in Matthew 23.

In an unnecessary oath, it is a more serious sin to swear by the Creator than by a creature. However, we should note, it is harder to swear by a creature with the proper truth, necessity, and reverence than to swear by the Creator, for the following reasons:

The first. When we desire to swear by a creature, our very desire to name a creature makes us less careful and cautious about speaking the truth or affirming it with necessity than is the case when our urge is to name the Lord and Creator of all things.

The second. When we swear by a creature, it is not as easy to maintain reverence and respect for the Creator as it is when we swear by the name of the Creator and Lord himself. For our very desire to name God our Lord carries with it greater respect and reverence than desire to name a creature. Consequently, to swear by a creature is more permissible for persons spiritually far advanced [*los perfectos*]. *The perfect, through constant contemplation and enlightenment of their understanding, more readily consider, meditate, and contemplate God our Lord as being present in every creature by his essence, presence, and power* [my italics]. Thus when they swear by a creature they are more able and better disposed that the imperfect to render respect and reverence to their Creator and Lord.

The third. To swear continually by a creature brings a risk of idolatry that is greater in the imperfect than in the perfect. (*Spiritual Exercises*, 39)[50]

Strange as all this may sound to our twenty-first-century ears, it is clear that the "bottom line" for Ignatius is the same as it was for Jesus and Matthew, namely, that for a follower of Jesus, a proper use of the gift of speech entails profound reverence for God and for God's creatures and a cultivated awareness of God's presence in and with all creatures in all times and places. Incidentally, Ignatius provides specific instructions on a practice for cultivating that sense of God's presence in the last part of his *Exercises*, "The Contemplation to Attain Love" (230–237).

CHAPTER 6

THE FIFTH ANTITHESIS:
FROM BALANCED RETALIATION TO
CREATIVE NONVIOLENCE
(MATTHEW 5:38-42)

5:38 "You have heard that it was said, 'An eye for an eye and a tooth for a tooth.' 39But I say to you, offer no resistance to one who is evil [*mē antistēnai tō ponērō*]. When someone strikes you on [your] right cheek, turn the other one to him as well. 40If anyone wants to go to law with you over your tunic, hand him your cloak as well. 41Should anyone press you into service for one mile, go with him for two miles. 42Give to the one who asks of you, and do not turn your back on one who wants to borrow."

"AN EYE FOR AN EYE": A CURB ON VIOLENCE?

To our twenty-first-century ears, "an eye for an eye"—occurring three times in the Torah (Exodus 21:23-24; Leviticus 24:19-20; and Deuteronomy 19:21)—sounds like a harsh law. In fact, in its original context, it was a careful curbing of vengeance. If we try to imagine what it was like to live in the world of migratory clans and tribes, it is easy to think of scenarios of unbridled vengeance ("You hurt my brother's eye; I'm going to get the rest of my brothers, and we are going to take out both of yours"). In such situations, "an eye for an eye" *limits* retaliation.

A recent newspaper report of a case from Tehran illustrates some of the issues around a strictly reciprocal *lex talionis*—in this case literally a matter of an "eye for an eye"! Several men had asked for the hand of Ameneh Bahrami, 31, in marriage. The hazel-eyed electrical technician had refused them all. One of the spurned suitors poured a bucket of sulfuric acid over her head, leaving her blind and disfigured. An Iranian court ordered that five drops of the same chemical be placed in each eye of her attacker, acceding to Ms. Bahrami's demand that he be punished according to a principle in Islamic jurisprudence that allows a victim to seek retribution for a crime. The sentence had not yet been carried out at the time of the report. Such retaliatory corporal punishments allowed under Islamic law have provoked controversy within Islam itself.

Bahrami defends her demand for the blinding of her attacker as a necessary deterrent against such "honor" attacks, which she claims are on the rise in Iran. "I am doing this because I don't want this to happen to any other women," she said. A Tehran human rights journalist, Asieh Amini, expressed doubt that the sentence against Bahrami's attacker would reverse the trend: "Social violence will not be cured with more violence." Bahrami's attacker, Majid Movahedi, showed no remorse when the court ruled on the case. When the judge asked whether he was ready for his punishment, Movahedi said that he still loved Bahrami but that if she asked for his eyes to be taken out, he would seek the same punishment for her. "They must also completely empty out her eyes, since I'm not sure that she cannot secretly see," he said. "The newspapers have made this a huge case, but I haven't done anything bad."[51]

This contemporary example illustrates several things. *Lex talionis*, or the law of proportionate reprisal, is still part of contemporary law in parts of our world, and the argument that the dramatic nature of the *lex talionis* carried out as corporal punishment works as a deterrent still carries weight with some. The fact that no one has murdered anyone in this case suggests that the literal eye-for-eye punishment has forestalled disproportionate vengeance. However, the attacker's insistence that he would demand the reprisal of complete eye gouging of his victim if his sight is destroyed shows that the eye-for-an-eye principle does not necessarily stop the cycle of violence. That the attacker can say "I have done nothing wrong" implies that he considers his action somehow sanctioned by the prevalence of such honor attacks in his culture. And if this is true, his thinking indicates that this expression of *lex talionis* is not deterring, at least among those who think and act as he does.

History shows that Israelite practice moved from a literal implementation of this law to legally enforced payment for physical damage—a reasonable solution, one might think. But Jesus moves beyond this careful fairness to *mē antistēnai tō ponērō*. I leave this phrase in the Greek for the moment to remind us that we have a translation challenge. Here is a sampling of English translations of 5:39a:

KJV: But I say unto you, *That* ye *resist not evil*:
Rheims: But I say to you *not to resist evil*:
NASB: But I say to you, *do not resist him who is evil*;
NIV: But I tell you, *Do not resist an evil person.*
NAB: But I say to you, *offer no resistance to one who is evil.*
NRSV: But I say to you, *Do not resist an evildoer.*
NJB: But I say this to you: *offer no resistance to the wicked.*
Christian Community Bible: But I tell you this: *do not oppose evil with evil*;
Good News Translation: But now I tell you: *do not take revenge on someone who wrongs you.*

Several insights emerge from a comparison of these English versions. The translators have generally favored "resist" as the basic meaning of the verb, accurately reflecting the essential dictionary meaning. But that version is open to misunderstanding, as we will see shortly. The KJV's and Rheims' rendering of *tō ponērō* as "evil" gives the impression of urging the listener/reader simply to "go limp" in the face of evil generally. Heard or read by itself, "Resist not evil" sounds like "Give in to evil," a reading that is open to the famous caveat "All that is necessary for evil to triumph is that good people do nothing." And that is surely not what Jesus' teaching and behavior indicate. It is interesting, however, that both KJV and Rheims place a colon after this sentence, thereby alerting the reader that this assertion is to be understood in the light of what follows. And what follows in the text is a set of scenarios that provide a clarifying context for the meaning of verse 39a. The last two translations, the Christian Community Bible and the Good News Translation, offer paraphrases that interpret the verb and its object in the context of the clarifying examples in verses 39b-42.

These examples portray human adversaries, not evil in the abstract or "the evil one" in the sense of the devil. The scenarios present a series of human offenders—striking a cheek, litigating unjustly, pressing into service, and importuning with begging or borrowing. And the behavior that Jesus mandates for the "victim" in these scenarios is more than simply nonresistance; in each case Jesus calls for a surprising positive *action*. Let us look at each of the four scenarios. They will help us understand the meaning of verse 39a.

FOUR EXAMPLES OF CREATIVE NONVIOLENCE

"When someone strikes you on [your] right cheek, turn the other one to him as well" (5:39b). When we read this statement in today's North American context, we picture someone starting a fight. Viewed within the first-century Palestinian framework, a different situation emerges. There the action is not so much a matter of inflicting pain as assaulting a person's honor. In such a culture, as in many others, the left hand is reserved for such unclean or unhygienic tasks as toilet activity. One simply dishonors oneself if one dares to use one's left hand in a social activity of any kind—such as eating, greeting, or even in a hostile contact like slapping. Thus, a slap across the *right* cheek—necessarily

delivered by the right hand—would be a backhanded slap. And a back-handed slap is a gesture of insult or dishonor. This, then, is the scenario evoked by Jesus' first example: One has been the recipient of an insult slap. The cultural expectation is that the one thus insulted will restore the balance by a countergesture. But Jesus' advice is something else alto-gether: *"Turn the other to him as well."* In other words, surprise the offender by presenting your other cheek—thus showing that you are not so easily insulted. What is more, you have caught him in a bind: In order to repeat the backhanded slap on your *left* cheek, the offender would have to use his left hand, thereby dishonoring himself! You have caught the insulter off guard and interrupted the violence.

The second example takes us into a trial scene, or rather the threat thereof. *"If anyone wants to go to law with you over your tunic* [chitōna], *hand him your cloak* [himation] *as well"* (5:40). Picture a tough creditor confronting a debtor who is so poor that he literally possesses only the clothes on his back—his woolen cloak and his linen undergarment—and the creditor demands one of these (the under-garment, in this case!) as earnest money to ensure payment of the debt. A law in Exodus envisions this extreme case: "If you take your neighbor's cloak [*himation* in the Greek translation] as a pledge, you shall return it to him before sunset; for this cloak of his is the only covering he has for his body. What else has he to sleep in? If he cries out to me, I will hear him; for I am compassionate" (Exodus 22:25-26). Jesus' example alludes to such a case. If your creditor threatens to take legal possession of one of your garments, Jesus says, give him the other. Yes, that would render you naked. Your oppressor would be left standing there with your cloak in one hand and your tunic in the other, and you stark naked! That, of course, would shock peo-ple—and expose the creditor for the oppressor that he is.

The third example takes us to the roadway. *"Should anyone press you into service* [angareusei] *for one mile, go with him for two miles"* (5:41). This is a very specific scenario; the Greek verb is a Persian loan word left over from the days of the Persian occupation of Judah and that came to be used in Latin and Greek to refer to the requisitioning of provincials by the occupying militia, mainly to carry burdens. The two other places it turns up are Matthew 27:32 and Mark 15:21, where the verb describes the Romans' impressment of Simon of Cyrene to carry Jesus' cross. Scholars find that Roman law allowed occupying forces to coerce a provincial to carry, say, a backpack, but only for a mile. Jesus' strategy of carrying it a second mile would surprise the soldier, catch him off guard, and possibly get him into trouble with his military superior.

Each of these three examples shows an oppressor taking advantage of a poor person—the kind of person who is typically a target of a put-down or cruel lending practice or forced service—and in each case Jesus recommends an assertive action that is neither flight nor fight. Instead, in each case a nonviolent action saves the dignity of the one oppressed and exposes the oppressor in a public way. Together the examples help us perceive the intent of the statement that they exemplify: *mē antistēnai tō ponērō*. However lexically correct the NAB translation may be, "Offer no resistance to the one who is evil" does not capture what is going on in the examples. In the examples, Jesus urges his audience to do much more than not resist; they are to make a creative move—turn a cheek, hand over a garment, tote an extra mile. One translation that captures the meaning of verse 39a in context is "Do not counter evil in kind."[52]

The fourth saying (verse 5:42)—*Give to the one who asks of you and do not turn your back on one who wants to borrow*—is of a slightly different character than the preceding three cases. Here one is not confronted by an oppressor; one is simply approached by a person in need. Correspondingly, what is called for is not creative nonviolence but a nonpossessive generosity. Note that lending presumes a hope for return; as we will see, Luke's version of this saying (6:30) is more demanding.

A Translation Crux: "Resist Not Evil" or "Do Not Counter Evil in Kind"?

Now that we have studied the examples that illustrate verse 39a ("offer no resistance"—*mē antistēnai*—"to the one who is evil"), we are in a better position to understand what this Greek verb means. It is important that we do our homework to get it straight, since how we understand this saying affects how we, as followers of Jesus, deal with questions of crime and punishment, war and peace.

The particle *mē* is a negative signal, "not," and *antistēnai* is an infinitive form of the verb *anthistēmi*, whose root sense is "set against" (from *histēmi* = "stand" or "set" and *anti* = "against"). The word occurs fourteen times in the New Testament. The standard English lexicon for NT Greek gives these meanings for those occurrences in the New Testament: (1a) to be in opposition to a person, *to set oneself against, oppose* (as in Matthew 5:39, the sole use in Matthew); (1b) *to oppose a thing;* and (2) to be resistant to power; *resist.*[53] But those thirteen NT instances beyond our passage do little to clarify the kind of resistance forbidden in Matthew 5:39a. The Greek version of the Old Testament, however, is quite helpful. In the Septuagint, *anthistēmi* is used mainly as a *military term*, 44 out of 71 times. Walter Wink summarizes his research on the classical and Old Testament meaning of the word this way:

In short, *antistenai* means more in Matthew 5:39a than simply to "stand against" or "resist." It means to resist *violently*, to revolt or rebel, to engage in an insurrection. Jesus is not encouraging submission to evil; that would run counter to everything he did and said. He is, rather, warning against responding to evil in kind by letting the oppressor set the terms of our opposition. Perhaps most importantly, he cautions us against being made over into the very evil we oppose by adopting its methods and spirit. He is saying, in effect, Do not mirror evil; do not become the very thing you hate.[54]

In the end, Wink's preferred rendering of 5:39a is "Do not counter evil in kind."[55] Although not a *literal* translation of the Greek (it is more specific than the Greek verb), his translation offers the kind of "dynamic equivalence" required by the context provided by the three examples that follow. They demonstrate a kind of *nonviolent* resistance that is neither tit-for-tat retaliation nor nonresistant pacifism—that is, neither fight nor flight. Indeed, it is what Wink calls "Jesus' third way"—what can be termed *assertive nonviolence*. This understanding of 5:39-41 inspired the strategies of Mahatma Gandhi and Martin Luther King, Jr.

NONVIOLENT RESPONSE ELSEWHERE IN MATTHEW

Where else does Matthew's gospel illuminate this passage? The obvious place to look is his account of the passion of Jesus. Like his predecessor Mark, Matthew tells of Jesus' knowledge of Judas' planned betrayal; despite this knowledge, Jesus proceeds with the evening as planned, celebrating the Passover supper with his disciples and moving on to the Mount of Olives, to Gethsemane. After his prayer he can announce that his betrayer is "at hand" (26:46), and yet he does nothing to avoid the encounter. Facing this threat, he does not flee—when escape was a real possibility, given that Jerusalem was crowded with pilgrims and the wilderness was just over the hill. In fact, Jesus does not flee. This may be stating the obvious, but it is an important fact to note when we are considering Jesus' own response to hostility.

When Judas arrives with the "large crowd, with swords and clubs" (Matthew 26:47) and identifies Jesus with a kiss, "one of those who accompanied Jesus"—the Fourth Gospel identifies him as

Peter—stretches out his hand and draws his sword and strikes the slave of the high priest, cutting off his ear (26:51). All four evangelists mention the cutting off of the ear of the high priest's slave. Mark's Jesus makes no comment. In Luke, Jesus says, "Stop, no more of this!" and touches the ear to heal it (22:51). In John, Jesus is even more assertive about stopping the swordplay: He tells Peter, "Put your sword into its scabbard. Shall I not drink the cup that the Father gave me?" (18:11). But in the Gospel of Matthew, Jesus' response not only halts the violence but famously transcends the moment with a general condemnation of sword fighting:

> "Put your sword back into its sheath, for all who take the sword will perish by the sword. Do you think that I cannot call upon my Father and he will not provide me at this moment with more than twelve legions of angels?" (Matthew 26:52-53)

Here Jesus clearly acts in the spirit of his teaching in the Sermon regarding a nonviolent response to adversaries.

During the hearing before the Sanhedrin, after they judge Jesus worthy of death, Matthew describes their physical abuse much as Mark does, but Matthew adds these words: "Some slapped [*erapisan*] him" (26:67). Since this verb—*rapizō*—occurs only twice in the NT, the other place being Matthew 5:39, it would seem that Matthew is making a deliberate link between this passage and the mention of slapping in the Sermon. Some commentators have observed that since Matthew does not say that Jesus turned the other cheek, Jesus is not acting in conformity with his teaching. However, given that the situation also involves spitting and striking, the slapping in question is not a matter of mere insult but the more aggressive abuse that was customarily visited upon persons convicted of capital offenses. Matthew's point in making the verbal link may be to help the reader appreciate that suffering such maltreatment places a disciple in solidarity with the Lord Jesus.

If the language of slapping and turning one's cheek evokes not only the passion of Jesus but also the Servant tradition of Isaiah, such an association may be deliberate on Matthew's part. It has been noted that seven of the words that appear in Matthew 5:37-42 occur in the third Servant Song of Greek Isaiah (see especially LXX Isaiah 50:4-9); the seven are the Greek words for "offer resistance," "give," "cheek," "slap," "turn," "go to court," and "cloak."[56] It is possible that Jesus himself may have made the association between these acts and the Servant tradition, but given that only three of the seven correlations appear in Luke's parallel (6:29), and given Matthew's bent toward applying the language of Isaiah to the story of Jesus, it is likely that the association of the Servant language with Jesus' teaching is Matthew's work. This fits well with the ninth beatitude and Matthew's theme that the follower of Jesus will imitate the Master's living out of the role of Isaiah's Servant of the Lord (see the last beatitude, Matthew 5:11-12).

Since the sixth antithesis regarding love of enemies is so closely connected to the fifth, and Luke's treatment of both together in his Sermon on the Plain has a power of its own, I will move on immediately to the teaching on loving our enemies. An extended discussion of the postbiblical reception and application of this teaching on nonviolence can be found in the last chapter.

CHAPTER 7

LOVE OF ENEMIES
CLIMACTIC IN MATTHEW, CENTRAL IN LUKE
(MATTHEW 5:43-48 AND LUKE 6:27-36)

5:43 "You have heard that it was said, 'You shall love your neigh-bor and hate your enemy.' 44But I say to you, love your enemies, and pray for those who persecute you, 45that you may be chil-dren [*huioi*, literally "sons"] of your heavenly Father, for he makes his sun rise on the bad and the good, and causes rain to fall on the just and the unjust. 46For if you love those who love you, what recompense [*misthos*] will you have? Do not the tax collectors do the same? 47And if you greet [*aspasēsthe*] your brothers only, what is unusual [*perrison*] about that? Do not the pagans [*ethnikoi*, also "gentiles"] do the same? 48So be per-fect [*teleioi*] just as your heavenly Father is perfect [*teleios*]."

THE LIKELY BACKGROUND OF MATTHEW'S PRESENTATION
(AND JESUS' TEACHING)

If the fifth antithesis advocates a number of practical actions, this sixth and final one focuses on the attitude that can motivate and *enable* such practical strategies of nonviolence. The attitude is summa-rized in "Love your enemy" and in a very particular spiritual practice: "Pray for those who persecute you" (5:44). Verses 45-47 offer motiva-tion for cultivating the interior posture implied in verse 44, and verse 48 climaxes the passage (and the whole section on the six antitheses) with the stunning mandate: *Be perfect, like God!*

This language invites some careful thinking.

We have no trouble recognizing the Torah passage Jesus has in mind when he cites the first part of his reference: "You shall love your neighbor. . . ." This is from Leviticus 19:18b, a passage that Jesus invokes a number of times in his teaching and *three* times in Matthew—here, again at 19:19, and once more at 22:39. In his redaction of Mark's account of the dispute about the "greatest" commandment (12:28-34), Matthew repeats Mark's quotation from the *Shema* ("You shall love the LORD, your God, with all your heart," Deuteronomy 6:5) and the "second" commandment from Leviticus 19:18b to love one's neighbor (22:34-39). Following this statement, each evangelist has a distinct way of underscoring the importance of these two commandments. Mark reports the enquiring scribe repeating Jesus' answer and then *adding* that love of God and neighbor "is worth more than all burnt offerings and sacrifices" (12:33). Love of God and neighbor trumps the temple liturgy! Matthew, on the other hand, stresses the importance of the two by saying, "The whole law and the prophets depend on these two commandments" (22:40). This comprehensive way of referring to the law and the prophets echoes two similar references in the Sermon on the Mount—Matthew 5:17 ("Do not think that I have come to abolish the law or the prophets"), and 7:12 (characterizing the Golden Rule: "Do to others whatever you [plural] would have them do to you. This is the law and the prophets"). Thus, for Matthew, the commands to love God and neighbor and the Golden Rule are essentially alternative ways of saying the same thing. Both summarize the law and the prophets.

The other place where Matthew highlights the importance of Leviticus 19:18b is in his rendition of Jesus' encounter with the rich young man (Matthew 19:16-22; par. Mark 10:13-16). Where Jesus recites five commandments of the Decalogue to illustrate what the young man needs to do to enter eternal life, Matthew *adds* to Mark's account, "And you shall love your neighbor as yourself" (19:19), as if to make sure that all the bases are covered. And while we have this page of Matthew's gospel open, we do well to note a further insertion of Matthew's into Mark's narrative. Where Mark has Jesus say to the man, "You are lacking in one thing. Go, sell what you have, and give to [the] poor and you will have treasure in heaven; then come, follow me" (Mark 10:21), Matthew presents a man who *knows* that he lacks something: "All of these I have observed. What do I still lack?" (19:20). Jesus says to him, "*If you wish to be perfect* [*teleios*], go, sell what you have, and give to [the] poor, and you will have treasure in heaven. Then come, follow me" (19:21). Those italicized words indicating Matthew's redaction have a special bearing on our understanding of the passage we are examining in the Sermon, which is the other place in Matthew where *teleios* occurs. We shall return to this in a moment.

The second part of what Jesus refers to when he says "You have heard that it was said" contains a surprise: ". . . and hate your enemy." While the Old Testament provides language that *implies* hatred of enemies (especially in some of the psalms, for example Psalm 137:9), the literal mandate "Hate your enemy" is nowhere to be found in the Hebrew Bible. Moreover, the Old Testament itself sometimes points beyond a narrow understanding of love of neighbor. It is true that the parallelism of Leviticus 19:18b ("You shall love your neighbor as yourself. I am the LORD") with the first part of the verse ("Take no revenge and cherish no grudge against your fellow countrymen") indicates that the first meaning of "neighbor" here is the ordinary one of a person who lives nearby. But the same passage, a few verses later, stretches the call to love to include the resident alien: "You shall treat the alien who resides with you no differently than the natives born among you: have the same love for him as for yourself; for you too were once aliens in the land of Egypt. I, the LORD, am your God" (Leviticus 19:34). Notice that in both cases, verse 18b and verse 34, the assertion of the identity of the LORD God is attached to the command to love both neighbor and resident alien ("I am the LORD," "I, the LORD, am your God"). This is a reminder that God is the "third person" who is present in every relationship of a member of the covenant people. Jesus takes this another step further, to the heretic (as modeled by the Samaritan in Luke 10:29-37) and to the enemy. These considerations should keep us from assuming too narrow an understanding of the Old Testament's teaching on love of neighbor.

Jesus' reference to a teaching of contempt may point to tradition outside the Scriptures. The biblical text is not the only Jewish tradition to which his peers were exposed. Some would surely have been acquainted with the teaching and practices of the Essene communities, as revealed in the Dead Sea Scrolls. One of those documents, *The Rule of the Community*, states that a person joining the community must pledge to "love all the sons of light, each one according to his lot in God's plan, *and to detest all the sons of darkness, each one in accordance with his blame in God's vindication*" (1QS 1:9-11).[57]

Whether Jesus, or Matthew, was explicitly alluding to this Essene teaching, the comparison and contrast with Jesus' teaching is illuminating. Whereas the Essene *Rule of the Community* divides humanity into the *us* of "the sons of light" and the *them* of "the sons of darkness," Jesus speaks of being "children [sons] of your heavenly Father" (5:45; or "children [sons] of the Most High" in Luke 6:35), who is loving to all people in that he "makes his sun rise on the bad and the good, and causes rain to fall on the just and unjust" (or "is kind to the ungrateful and the wicked" in Luke 6:35). Thus, where the Essene community rule uses sonship language to divide, Jesus' uses sonship language to speak of human solidarity under the one Father who is creator of all. A verse from the prophet Malachi comes to mind: "Have we not all the one Father? / Has not the one God created us?" (2:10). But while the prophet addresses the fractured solidarity within the covenant community, Jesus speaks of the solidarity of the whole human family—neighbors and enemies alike.

In citing the passage above, I called attention to the fact that the word underlying "children" in the translation is *huioi* (literally, "sons"). The point is not to deny the value of an inclusive translation but to highlight some likely associations on the part of Matthew (and Jesus?), associations not transmitted by the more generic word "children." First, there is the possibility of the intended contrast with this Essene teaching, the division of the humanity between "the sons of light" and "the sons of darkness." Second, and even more likely, is the link with the seventh, eighth, and ninth beatitudes. The seventh beatitude declares that it is peacemakers who will be called "sons of God" (5:9), and surely love of enemy and imitation of the inclusive love of the Creator are necessary for peacemaking. Further, those three final beatitudes speak specifically of persecution, and "those who persecute you" are precisely the enemies that Jesus calls his audience to pray for in verse 45. Their prayers for their enemies make them "sons of God." Third, "sons of your heavenly Father" echoes the Son title used for Jesus at four key moments up to this point in the Gospel of Matthew—2:15 (the application of Hosea 11:1); 3:17 (heavenly voice at the baptism); and 4:3, 9 (the taunt of the devil during the testing). Thus, calling those imitating the Creator in his inclusive love "sons of your heavenly Father," Matthew reminds his readers that they are also acting as imitators of the Father's son, Jesus. The enemies may not act like sons of God, but Jesus' followers—male and female alike—are to act as fellow "sons" of God with respect to enemies.

What "enemies" are in view here? For Jesus' immediate listeners, "your enemies" likely evoked the hated Romans, with their irreverent ways and heavy taxes. For Matthew's audience, "your enemies" no doubt entailed those who persecuted them as Christians, both gentiles and hostile Israelites—precisely the people Jesus says to pray for in verse 45b.

"For if you love those who love you, what recompense [misthos] *will you have? Do not the tax collectors do the same?"* (5:46). The mention of "recompense" or "reward" in talk about love sounds strange

to our ears. Shouldn't true love be entirely focused on the good of the other and not on what one will "get out of it"? But Jesus' point is that all of our human relationships have as their ultimate framework our relationship with the Father. The feedback that counts is the divine one, not the human one. Jesus had already referred to heavenly reward early in the Sermon, in the elaboration of the eighth beatitude: "Rejoice and be glad, for your reward [misthos] will be great in heaven" (5:12). This ensures that Christian love never, ultimately, goes unrequited. Heavenly (as opposed to earthly) reward becomes a primary theme in the first half of the next chapter (6:1, 2, 5, and 17).

This reminds me of an anecdote from an unexpected source. A Jesuit colleague speaks of his experience of Muslim hospitality during a sojourn of teaching in a Turkish university. Soon after he moved into a rented apartment in a working-class neighborhood, he discovered that while he was away during the day teaching, his place was being cleaned and meals were being provided by a group of neighborhood women. When he was getting ready to leave the country, his next-door neighbor asked if there was anything he needed before he left. He said, "Well, I would surely like to meet and thank those women who took such wonderful care of me during my stay." "Oh," the neighbor said. "You don't have to thank them. They didn't do it for you. They did it for God."

If that sounds strange to North American ears, it may be that this way of thinking and behaving is closer to the framework of Jesus' teaching than to our own culture. It is of course a deeply human thing to desire appreciation and "positive feedback." The human psyche, and therefore most of society, is structured accordingly. The only way we can be liberated from the dark side of the need to be appreciated is to trust that God stands ready to give us all the appreciation we need.

"And if you greet your brothers only, what is unusual [perisson] *about that? Do not the pagans* [ethnikoi] *do the same?" (5:47).* The

context implied here is the mandate given in verse 20, where Jesus had said that his followers must strive for a righteousness that "surpasses [exceeds, *perisseusē*] that of the scribes and Pharisees." That *something more* pertains even to such conventional behavior as greetings. The openness that the Creator shows in the universal distribution of sunshine and rain should be evident in the readiness to greet strangers, not just members of the community ("your brothers [and sisters]"). Is this mandate to share greetings beyond "the brotherhood" a special emphasis on Matthew's part? One might recall another statement of Jesus: "Greet no one along the way" (Luke 10:4); but that statement is unique to the Third Gospel, where it appears in Jesus' address on the occasion of the commissioning of the seventy-two disciples. In that context, the point seems to be the urgency of keeping focused on the mission, not dallying along the way with spontaneous visiting, as was customary in the Middle East among travelers.

There are plenty of references and encouragements to hospitable greeting in the rest of the New Testament. The word for "to greet" [*aspazomai*] is sometimes used to mean "to visit" in references to Paul's visits with various local churches (Acts 18:22; 20:2; 21:7, 19). And he uses the verb no less than twenty-one times in Romans 16 to send greetings to the numerous mobile friends that currently belong to the Christian community in Rome. But Matthew 5:47 urges the listeners to go beyond just greetings in their openness to others. The same theme is evident in the mission discourse to the twelve disciples in Matthew 10. There, in contrast to both Mark and Luke, Matthew writes, "As you enter the house [or "household"], *greet* it" (10:12 in the more literal NRSV). The NAB translation ("As you enter a house, wish it peace") presumes the Jewish greeting of "*Shalom*" ("Peace!"), a presumption supported by the next verse: "If the house is worthy, let your peace come upon it; if not, let your peace return to you." The implication: The Christian missionary meets strangers with complete benevolence and openness; the ball is in the others' court as to how the strangers will respond to this benevolence. What the disciples bring, after all, is nothing less than the good news and healing of the kingdom of heaven (10:7).

Finally, we come to the stunning mandate that climaxes not only this sixth antithesis but the last thirty-three verses—"*So be perfect, just as your heavenly Father is perfect*" (5:48). Apart from its immediate context, this sounds like a call to some kind of absolute flawlessness. But "perfect" here has less to do with being error free than with fullness and completeness. "As your heavenly Father is perfect" refers to the qualities of the Creator evidenced precisely in what has just been described—the inclusive bestowal of sunshine and rain upon everyone—"the bad and the good . . . the just and the unjust." Inclusiveness of love, then, not flawlessness, is the focus. Luke's parallel to this verse is "Be merciful [or "compassionate"—Jerusalem Bible], just as [also] your Father is merciful" (Luke 6:36). The word used by Luke here is *oiktirmōn*, occurring in the New Testament only here and at James 5:11 ("The Lord is compassionate and *merciful*," alluding to Exodus 34:6 and Psalm 103:8). Which wording is more likely to go back to Jesus? Exegetes give the nod to Luke's version, seeing that Matthew has introduced the word for "perfect" (*teleios*) in his version of the call of the rich young man, where he inserts the saying, "If you wish to be perfect [*teleios*] . . ." (Matthew 19:21). Notice that the context is about following Jesus and also about having treasure in heaven, as in the "recompense" of 5:46 in the Sermon. Matthew's use of "perfect" at 5:48 is also a fitting conclusion to a passage that spells out the greater (or more complete) righteousness urged in verse 20.

LOVE OF ENEMY AND NONVIOLENCE IN
LUKE'S SERMON ON THE PLAIN

If Matthew's presentation of Jesus' teaching on nonviolence and love of enemies is the climax of the six "antitheses," Luke's handling of that material constitutes the very core of his Sermon on the Plain. It is instructive, therefore, to read Luke 6:27-36 on its own terms. How much of the wording and design of this passage goes back to the tradition Luke inherited (Q), and how much derives from his redaction of that tradition—these are questions whose answers we can only guess at. But the process of comparing Luke's version with Matthew's is so illuminating that is it worth the effort. We shall move straight through Luke's version a few verses at a time.

6:27a"But to you who hear, I say . . . "

Following immediately after the four "woes" addressed to the rich, filled, laughing, and well-thought-of, "you [plural] who hear" obviously addresses their opposites: those who are blessed because they are poor, hungry, weeping, and hated, excluded, insulted, and denounced. The fact that they are those who "hear" obviously refers to more than the health of their auditory nerves. Throughout his gospel, Luke makes a point of the fact that true disciples are such because they *have heard the word of God* deeply and taken it to heart, in the sense of responsive hearing expressed in Israel's daily prayer, the *Shema*—"*Hear*, O Israel!" For example, Luke changes Mark's version of Jesus' word on hearing: "Take care what you hear" (Mark 4:24) becomes "Take care, then, *how* you hear" (Luke 8:18). A few verses later, in the passage about the true family of Jesus, Luke redacts Mark's form of Jesus' statement: "Whoever does the will of God is my brother and sister and mother" (Mark 3:35) becomes "My mother and my brothers are *those who hear the word of God and act on it*" (Luke 8:21). Luke makes the same point about hearing deeply when a woman on the street praises Mary for bearing and raising such a son as Jesus. Jesus says that she is even more to be praised for *hearing*: "Rather, blessed are those who hear the word of God and observe it" (11:28).[58] Indeed, it takes a special readiness to hear what Jesus is about to say:

6:27b-d"I say, love your enemies, do good to those who hate you, [28]bless those who curse you, pray for those who mistreat you."

What Matthew made the *climax* of his "antitheses" in chapter 5 is in Luke the *first* thing out of Jesus' mouth after the beatitudes and woes—Love your enemies!—without skipping a beat. And this love of enemies is specified with three parallel statements, as if to help "those who hear" take in the implications:

Do good to those who hate you.
Bless those who curse you.
Pray for those who mistreat you.

The third mandate parallels Matthew 5:44b, but the first two are special to Luke. He continues:

6:29"To the person who strikes you on one cheek, offer the other one as well, and from the person who takes your cloak, do not withhold even your tunic. [30]Give to everyone who asks of you, and from the one who takes what is yours do not demand it back."

Having begun with what is the core of Matthew's sixth antithesis, love of enemies, Luke now moves to the examples with which Matthew illustrates his fifth antithesis, the call to respond nonviolently to hostility. Thus, the Sermon on the Plain does not address the issue of retaliation ("eye for an eye"); rather, the examples of nonviolence directly illustrate the love of enemies. Note, however, that Luke's version of those examples lacks Matthew's variety of scenarios—the insult slap, the intent to litigate, the roadside requisition by occupying militia. Instead, Luke seems to envision a mugging: physical attack, snatching the cloak, grabbing one's possessions.

[6:31]"Do to others as you [plural] would have them do to you."

This is a version of the Golden Rule, which works in Matthew's Sermon as a kind of summary of the speech's teaching—indeed, he calls it "the law and the prophets"—toward the end of the speech at Matthew 7:12. Whether Luke deliberately moves it to this place in his Sermon or found it here in his source, the *effect* of the placement should not be lost on us. In Luke's context, the saying provides startling motivation for loving enemies and nonretaliation. In effect, he presents Jesus as asking a very unusual thing: Put yourself in your oppressor's shoes! This surely goes against human instinct, but its enactment may be the quickest way to halt a given cycle of violence. It is in fact part of the program of the restorative justice movement, which also entails helping the offender put himself in the shoes of his victim and helping the victim understand the situation of the offender.

[6:32]"For if you love those who love you, *what credit is that to you?* Even sinners love those who love them. [33]And if you do good to those who do good to you, *what credit is that to you?* Even sinners do the same. [34]If you lend money to those from whom you expect repayment, *what credit [is] that to you?* Even sinners lend to sinners, and get back the same amount."

Where Matthew's parallel to these sayings presents just two examples of the usual reciprocity of the world—loving those who love you and greeting your own people—Luke's version gives three, including the prime example of precise *quid pro quo* reciprocity, lending money. Notice, too, that whereas Matthew names examples of the usual way of the world that would appeal to his mainly Jewish audience, namely, those worldly *tax collectors* and *gentiles*, Luke, who has a mainly gentile audience, simply refers to those "others" as *sinners*.

[6:35]"But rather, love your enemies and do good to them, and lend expecting nothing back; then your reward [*misthos*] will be great and you will be children [*huioi*] of the Most High, for he himself is kind [*chrēstos*] to the ungrateful and the wicked. [36]Be merciful just as [also] your Father is merciful."

Luke *repeats* here the mandate to love and be good to enemies with which he began this section at verse 27, thereby forming an *inclusio*, a frame that highlights this passage as the core of the Sermon on the Plain. For Luke, love of enemies is the heart of the matter. Though his wording emphasizes "expecting nothing back,"[59] like Matthew he does not shy away from underscoring that those who act with no concern for human reciprocity can expect reward from the ultimate benefactor, the Father. As in Matthew, the note of *imitatio Dei* is here, with the divine qualities put succinctly as "kind" and "merciful." We have already considered the relationship between Luke's "merciful" and Matthew's "perfect."

LUKE'S TREATMENT OF NONVIOLENCE ELSEWHERE

Two Lukan episodes reflect Jesus' nonviolent response to hostility in ways little noticed in Christian writing on violence, war, and peace—Jesus' response to Samaritan inhospitality in Luke 9:51-55, and the Jerusalem Christian community's response to the hostility of the Sanhedrin in Acts 4:23-31.

Samaritan Inhospitality

Students of Luke have long noted that Luke 9:51-55 marks a key turning point in the Third Gospel. The identity of Jesus has been well established through the infancy narratives, key speeches, healings, the transfiguration, and two predictions of his coming passion.

With verse 51 he begins the nine-chapter journey toward his final week and Jerusalem.

> When the days for his being taken up were fulfilled, he resolutely determined to journey to Jerusalem, and he sent messengers ahead of him. On the way they entered a Samaritan village to prepare for his reception there, but they would not welcome him because the destination of his journey was Jerusalem. When the disciples James and John saw this they asked, "Lord, do you want us to call down fire from heaven to consume them?" Jesus turned and rebuked them, and they journeyed to another village. (Luke 9:51-55)

Why should the Samaritans have refused to welcome Jesus because he was heading toward Jerusalem? Luke obviously expects his readers to know the connection between Jesus' destination and their hostility. What Luke does not say, and what his audience would know, is that the ancient cause of hostility between Samaritans and Jews was their difference over the proper place to worship God. It is the very thing that the Samaritan woman at the well brings up to Jesus in the Gospel of John: "Our ancestors worshiped on this mountain [Gerizim]; but you people say that the place to worship is in Jerusalem" (John 4:20).

I once heard a Samaritan scholar address a mainly Jewish audience in Omaha, and he said: "We Samaritans and you Jews are both exponents of the Israelite tradition. But we have the authentic tradition. You say that the proper place to worship God is in Jerusalem. We know that the right place is on Mount Gerizim. Nowhere in the Torah does it say to worship in Jerusalem. God says in Deuteronomy, 'You will worship me in the place I will cause my name to dwell.' We know that Deuteronomy is referring to Mount Gerizim; that is where Joshua worshiped when he entered the promised land. That has been the proper place ever since." The audience received this assertion with surprising calmness. They knew that Jews and Samaritans have had this disagreement for some twenty-six centuries. So it was already an old quarrel at the time of Jesus. Luke clearly expects his readers to know about it.

Against such a background, Luke's account of Jesus' response to the Samaritan village's inhospitality is pointed. When the "sons of thunder" ask Jesus if he wants them to "call down fire from heaven to consume [the Samaritans]," Jesus simply rebukes them, and they move on. Jesus is able to put himself in the sandals of the Samaritans and see that, from their point of view, he and his disciples are "heretical" Jews from Galilee, acting out their heresy by going up to Jerusalem to worship, and they are not going to support that misguided pilgrimage with any hospitality. Rather than provoke further hostility, Jesus simply moves on. This is a wonderful example of Jesus' practice of nonviolence.

Finessing the Sanhedrin's Hostility

The other neglected example of Jesus' approach to hostility shows that the disciples have learned their master's lesson. It occurs in Acts 4. Shortly after the first Pentecost, after the chief priests and elders of the Sanhedrin have ordered Peter and John to cease teaching in the name of Jesus, the two leaders return to their community. Luke's description of what follows takes the form of a spontaneous prayer that they speak together. The author wants us to hear this prayer either as a miracle of choral speaking (some five thousand voices improvising the same text together), or as Luke's composition of a speech portraying the community's understanding of itself as a people continuing the mission of Jesus. Since it is cut from the same cloth as the other speeches in Acts—a commentary applying Scripture to Jesus and the church—the latter interpretation is more likely the correct one.

The power of the prayer that Luke puts into their collective mouth becomes more evident when we attend to the full context of the psalm they quote. After addressing God as creator of all, they cite the opening verses of Psalm 2. When we turn to that place in the Old Testament, we read:

Why do the nations protest
    and the peoples grumble in vain?
Kings of the earth rise up,
    and the princes plot together
    against the LORD and his anointed:
"Let us break their shackles
    and cast off their chains!" (Psalm 2:1-3)

Scholars conjecture that this was a hymn used in the temple ritual for the accession of an Israelite king. It imagines the gentiles raging in jealousy at the privileged scenario of a Hebrew king raised up to kingship by the King of the universe himself, the Lord God. The psalm proceeds with a script that first attributes some verses to the Lord God:

The one enthroned in heaven laughs;
    the LORD derides them.
Then he speaks to them in anger,
    terrifies them in wrath:
"I myself have installed my king
    on Zion, my holy mountain." (2:4-6)

Then the newly anointed king is given some lines to say:

I will proclaim the decree of the LORD,
    who said to me, "You are my son;
    today I am your father.

Only ask it of me,
    and I will make your inheritance the nations,
    your possession the ends of the earth.
With an iron rod you shall shepherd them,
    like a clay pot you will shatter them." (2:7-9)

There is also a fourth stanza, but this is enough to get the flavor of the psalm. Notice that it is robustly nationalistic and bellicose, and does not shy away from violent language ("like a clay pot you will shatter them"). Now we turn back to the community prayer of Acts 4. Watch how the prayer changes the tone of the psalm in its application to Jesus and the Christian mission:

"'Why did the Gentiles rage
    and the peoples entertain folly?
The kings of the earth took their stand
    and the princes gathered together
        against the Lord and against his anointed.'
Indeed they *gathered* in this city *against* your holy servant Jesus whom you *anointed,* Herod [a *king*] and Pontius Pilate [a kind of *prince*], *together* with the *Gentiles* [Romans] and the *peoples* of Israel, to do what your hand and [your] will had long ago planned to take place." (Acts 4:25b-28)

I have italicized the words of Psalm 2 that Luke applies to the recent happenings in Jerusalem. This is a form of writing called a *pesher*, in which an ancient writing is interpreted as being fulfilled in a current (or recent) event. Notice that the verbs of the psalm are cast in the past tense, reflecting the Greek version of Psalm 2, which Luke is using. At this point one might expect the prayer to go the way of the psalm and call down God's wrath. Instead, this is how the prayer in Acts continues:

"And now, Lord, take note of their threats, and enable your servants to speak your word with all boldness, as you stretch forth [your] hand to heal, and signs and wonders are done through the name of your holy servant Jesus." As they prayed, the place where they were gathered shook, and they were all filled with the holy Spirit and continued to speak the word of God with boldness. (Acts 4:29-31)

Since this is the sole New Testament portrayal of the Christian community at prayer that includes the content of the prayer, Luke surely means it to be understood as a kind of paradigm or model. The implications are powerful:

1. The community prays in the tradition of the psalms, addressing the Lord God as creator of all.
2. They pray from a text of Scripture (Psalm 2).
3. They understand the ancient text as fulfilled both in the events of Jesus' life, death, and resurrection and also in their own continuation of his mission.
4. While they do not exactly pray for those who persecute them, neither do they pray that their enemies be punished. Rather, they parallel their lot with the rejection that Jesus suffered. It is a stunning example of a prayerful, nonviolent response to hostility.
5. They understand their mission as the same as Jesus'—preaching the word of God and healing by the power of the Holy Spirit.
6. The summary description of community life that follows in verses 32-35—being one "in heart and mind," spontaneously meeting one another's material needs, and bearing witness to the resurrection of the Lord Jesus—is presented as part of the Pentecostal grace that flows from their common prayer.[60]

That Jesus' teaching regarding love of enemies is not simply a "sound bite" occurring in the Sermon on the Mount/Plain is demonstrated by its presence in other parts of the New Testament. Jesus' prayer that the Father forgive his killers (Luke 23:34) is paralleled by Stephen's similar prayer *to* Jesus in Acts 7:60 as he undergoes an extralegal execution by stoning, witnessed by Saul of Tarsus. Later the converted Saul himself shows how well he has learned his lesson by his words to the Christian community in Rome:

> Bless those who persecute [you]; bless and do not curse them. . . . Do not repay anyone evil for evil; be concerned for what is noble in the sight of all. If possible, on your part, live at peace with all. Beloved, do not look for revenge but leave room for the wrath; for it is written, "Vengeance is mine, I will repay, says the Lord." (Romans 12:14, 17–19)

If Paul dares to cite Proverbs 25:21-22, to the effect that doing good to your enemy will result in his getting burning coals heaped upon his head (Romans 12:20), his point is that the Christian should leave "payback" to God (he does not deal here with the pastoral question this metaphor raises regarding one's image of God). To the Corinthian Christians, Paul can write, "When ridiculed, we bless; when persecuted, we endure; when slandered, we respond gently" (1 Corinthians 4:12-13).

The New Testament authors are realistic enough to acknowledge that one may be challenged by "enemy" behavior even *within* the Christian community. As Paul exhorts the Thessalonians about living the life of Christian community toward the end of his first letter to them, he says, "See that no one returns evil for evil; rather, always seek what is good [both] for each other and for all" (5:15). If Paul never refers to the Sermon on the Mount as such, his writing shows that he surely "got" the teaching. Similarly, the author of the First Letter of Peter writes to the scattered Christian communities of Asia

Minor: "Be of one mind, sympathetic, loving *toward one another*, compassionate, humble. Do not return evil for evil, or insult for insult; but, on the contrary, a blessing, because to this you were called, that you might inherit a blessing" (3:8-9). As in Matthew 5, this admonition carries the promise of divine reward.

A further witness to the centrality of Jesus' teaching on nonviolence and love of enemies is the early document called *The Didache: The Teaching of the Lord to the Gentiles by the Twelve Apostles*. The following is a translation of the opening verses of that work:

There are two ways, one of life and one of death, and there is a great difference between these two ways. Now this is the way of life: First, you shall love God, who made you. Second, **you shall love your neighbor as yourself; but whatever you do not wish to happen to you, do not do to another.** *The teaching of these words is this*: **Bless those who curse you, and pray for your enemies, and fast for those who persecute you. For what credit is it if you love those who love you? Do not even the Gentiles do the same? But you must love those who hate you, and you will not have any enemy.** Abstain from fleshly and bodily cravings. **If someone gives you a blow on your right cheek, turn to him the other as well and you will be perfect. If someone forces you to go one mile, go with him two miles; if someone takes your cloak, give him your tunic also; if someone takes from you what belongs to you, do not demand it back, for you cannot do so. Give to everyone who asks you, and do not demand it back, for the Father wants something from his own gifts to be given to everyone** [italics and bolding added].[61]

What is fascinating about this expression of Jesus' teaching is that the verses about love of enemies and nonviolence (paralleling the format of Luke's Sermon but reflecting some of the wording of Matthew) are presented here as the very *meaning* of the commandments to love God and neighbor and of the Golden Rule (see the italicized clause and what follows).

A UNIQUE TEACHING?

Is Jesus unique among Israelites in advocating love of enemies? I once heard a rabbi criticize a fellow Jew for defending the human rights of Palestinians, saying, "We do not belong to the religion that teaches love of enemies." I was shocked—in two ways. First, I was shocked by the recognition that I do belong to the religion that teaches love of enemies and so felt challenged to act according to my Master's teaching. Second, I was shocked by the denial that Judaism has indeed taught love of enemies in aspects of its rich tradition.

For example, consider this passage from Exodus: "When you come upon your enemy's ox or ass going astray, see to it that it is returned to him. When you notice the ass of one who hates you lying prostrate under its burden, by no means desert him; help him, rather, raise it up" (23:4-5). Then there is the example of David, who refuses to kill Saul when he has the chance, at the very time when Saul is seeking to kill him. When Saul discovers what David has done, he says, "Great is the generosity you showed me today, when the LORD delivered me into your grasp and you did not kill me. For if a man meets his enemy, does he send him away unharmed? May the LORD reward you generously for what you have done this day" (1 Samuel 24:19-20). This incident illustrates both the usual Israelite (and generally human) attitude toward enemies and also presents David as an example of what, in the light of Jesus' teaching, we have learned to call "creative nonviolence." Or consider how the book of Jonah portrays the Lord chiding the prophet for being disappointed that the enemy Ninevites escaped divine wrath by repenting:

"You are concerned over the plant which cost you no labor and which you did not raise. . . . And should I not be concerned over Nineveh, the great city, in which there are more than a hundred and twenty thousand persons who cannot distinguish their right hand from their left, not to mention the many cattle?" (Jonah 4:10-11)

Other similar examples could be adduced, but these three illustrate the folly of generalizations about love of enemies being absent from the Old Testament. At the same time, it is true to say that Jesus makes that concern for "the other" and nonviolence a central part of his teaching. And Matthew and Luke are at pains to communicate that centrality by placing nonviolence and love of enemies at the heart of Jesus' first extended teaching in their respective gospels; the *Didachē* is another witness to that understanding. In chapter 12, I have considered this topic further, examining the postbiblical response to Jesus' teaching on nonviolence and including a brief history of the developing tradition.

CHAPTER 8

FOR HIS EYES ONLY:
ALMSGIVING, PRAYER, AND FASTING
(MATTHEW 6:1-18 AND LUKE 11:2-8)

6:1 "[But] take care not to perform righteous deeds [*tēn dikaiosynēn hymōn*, literally "your righteousness"] in order that people may see them; otherwise, you [plural] will have no recompense [*misthon*] from your heavenly Father."

Matthew 6:1-18 is unified and balanced in a variety of ways. It deals with three key practices of Jewish, and now also Christian, piety—almsgiving, prayer, and fasting. The first verse introduces the treatment of these topics with a thematic statement that is developed through the next seventeen verses: Do these practices mainly for God, expecting approval from God, not from people. Those who do these things for show are characterized, in each case, as hypocrites. The treatment of each practice is carefully structured and balanced with the other two; even the word count in Greek comes out virtually the same: sixty-four words devoted to almsgiving, sixty-four words devoted to prayer (skipping verses 6-15, the Lord's Prayer, which is Jesus' example of how to pray and a careful insertion that interrupts the patterned treatment of the three topics), and sixty-three words devoted to fasting. Accordingly, we will first discuss the teaching on the three practices. Then we will take up the Lord's Prayer, which is the centerpiece not just of this three-fold teaching but of the whole Sermon.

ALMSGIVING

6:2 "When you [singular] give alms, do not blow a trumpet before you, as the hypocrites do in the synagogues and in the streets to win the praise of others. Amen, I say to you [plural], they have received their reward [*misthon*]. ³But when you [singular] give alms, do not let your left hand know what your right is doing, ⁴so that your [singular] almsgiving may be secret. And your Father who sees in secret will repay you [singular]."

"Take care not to perform righteous deeds" paraphrases a mandate whose literal translation is "Take care not to do your righteousness [*tēn dikaiosynēn hymōn poien*]," where "righteousness" refers to specific pious practices fulfilling one's covenant relationships to God and fellow human beings. It is helpful here to note that this is the fifth of seven instances of this thematic word in Matthew (3:15; 5:6, 10, 20; 6:1, 33; 21:32). In the broad sense, righteousness (*dikaiosynē*) refers to fulfillment of covenant relationships. From God's side, it refers to the fulfillment of God's promises to rescue, sustain, and judge; from the human side, it refers to righteous behavior. In the Sermon we have seen two beatitudes refer to righteousness: one about hungering and thirsting for righteousness and another about suffering persecution for righteousness' sake (5:6, 10). The passage that acted as a bridge between the beatitudes and the six "antitheses" and introduced those six examples (5:21-48) used language about a "righteousness" that *surpasses* that of the scribes and Pharisees (6:20). The six antitheses illustrate that greater righteousness. Now chapter 6 moves from these major illustrations of living the life of the "empire of the heavens" and zooms in on three traditional Jewish religious practices that continue to be part of the Christian way of living out the covenant relationships—almsgiving, prayer, and fasting.[62]

If we wonder how to take the word "hypocrite," the best commentary may well be the passage that Matthew inherits from Mark, where that evangelist makes his sole use of the word. It is the passage where Jesus discourses on the only "cleanness" that counts—true moral authenticity and transparency with God. After chiding the Pharisees and scribes for caring more about temple donations than about the commandment to honor father and mother, he says:

> "Hypocrites, well did Isaiah prophesy about you when he said:
>   'This people honors me with their lips,
>   but their hearts are far from me;
>   in vain do they worship me,
>   teaching as doctrines human precepts.'" (Matthew 15:7-9;
>   par. Mark 7:6-7; LXX Isaiah 29:13)

As is true of the whole Sermon, the issue for Jesus is "Where is your heart? Do what you do from a heart that is informed by the beatitudes."

It is likely that the words "hypocrite" and "hypocrisy" made their way into English through their use in the New Testament, especially in the Gospel of Matthew. One of the earliest examples in the *Oxford English Dictionary* comes from the Wycliffe translation of Matthew in the fourteenth century. In extrabiblical texts, *hypocritēs* usually means an actor in the theater. In the NT it is always used in the metaphorical sense of a pretender or dissembler. The fact that archeology has discovered a magnificent theater dating to the first century after Christ in the remnant of the town of Sepphoris, not far from Nazareth—indeed, it is not impossible that Joseph and Jesus, as local craftsmen, worked on its construction—has led some commentators to speculate that Jesus may have known and used this Greek word for "play actor" to make his point.[63]

An obvious challenge that this teaching on secret almsgiving addresses to contemporary Christians is the publicity sometimes given benefactors. Obviously, the various ways that benefactors are publicly honored have their place in the secular culture. We name buildings after donors; the urban center of ancient Greece and Rome encouraged the rich and powerful to accrue honor by endowing the city with monumental structures. In our day, programs for plays and concerts typically list sponsors, individual and corporate, in various categories according to the size of their benefactions. There is a place for these innocent and beneficial honorific customs in any human culture. The issue in this teaching is specifically almsgiving, that is, making contributions to help the needy both within and outside the faith community. The teaching does not in any way challenge the act of almsgiving. It spotlights motivation. Are you doing this to avoid the embarrassment of being seen as stingy? Are you making the contribution in a way that calls attention to yourself?

PRAYER

6:5 "When you [plural] pray, do not be like the hypocrites, who love to stand and pray in the synagogues and on street corners so that others may see them. Amen, I say to you, they have received their reward. 6But when you [singular] pray, go to your inner room [*tameion*], close the door, and pray to your Father in secret. And your Father who sees in secret will repay you."

When we, in our individualistic twenty-first-century North American culture, hear reference to prayer, we spontaneously think of a solitary and silent activity. For us, prayer is first of all private and mental. Communal liturgical prayer is for us a secondary, perhaps once-a-week activity, most often at weekend Eucharist. It was just the opposite for Jesus and his peers. Prayer for them was oral and usually communal; recall that most of the written prayers in the Bible are found in the psalms, the book of common prayer that was used, probably in song, when people gathered in the precincts of the Jerusalem temple around the time of the daily sacrifices, or on Sabbath evenings in the village synagogues. In that context Jesus' practice of going off by himself to pray may have been unusual. (See Matthew 14:23, when, after the feeding of the five thousand, Jesus stays behind and goes up on the mountain by himself to pray, and 26:36-46, the prayer in Gethsemane, where Matthew underscores the fact that Jesus withdraws three times from his disciples to pray alone.) Luke makes a point of Jesus' solitary prayer by multiplying such instances: 3:21 (after the baptism); 5:16 (withdrawing to deserted places to pray); 6:12 (spending the night in prayer to God, before the selection of the twelve); 9:18 (praying in solitude); 9:29 (before the transfiguration); and 11:1 (on the road, before teaching the disciples the Our Father).

Given his practice of private prayer, is Jesus' teaching here denigrating the traditional communal prayer of traditional Jewish culture? That would not seem to be the case. When he prepares for the distribution of bread and fish, he says the traditional blessing before meals (14:19 and 15:36). When he performs his prophetic action in the Jerusalem temple, the texts he cites ("'My house shall be a house of prayer [Isaiah 56:7]', / but you are making it a den of thieves [Jeremiah 7:11]," 21:13) indicate that his objection is against the sins of the leadership, not against the practice of temple worship and public prayer. And the reference we saw regarding the authentic practice of temple sacrifice at 5:24 (be reconciled first, and only then offer your gift) was not a denigration of public worship but an assertion of the importance of reconciliation if one's worship is to be worthy. So when Jesus speaks of "the hypocrites, who love to stand and pray in the synagogues," this is not to be heard as a Christian put-down of Jewish common prayer but the words of a Jew speaking prophetically about certain peers who pray ostentatiously with the false motive of looking good in the eyes of their fellow congregants. The obvious application for Christians is to make sure they are showing up in church on Sunday for the right reasons. Given that an "inner room" (*tameion*) in the Mediterranean world was sometimes a place of special hospitality with privileged friends, the practice advocated in verse 6 may point to offering special attention to the divine presence available even to the individual.[64]

FASTING

6:16"When you fast, do not look gloomy like the hypocrites. They neglect their appearance, so that they may appear to others to be fasting. Amen, I say to you, they have received their reward. 17But when you fast, anoint your head and wash your face, 18so that you may not appear to be fasting, except to your Father who is hidden. And your Father who sees what is hidden will repay you."

As in the case of prayer, when we read about fasting in the New Testament, we may mistakenly hear this as a reference to the kind of fasting contemporary Catholics do in Lent, especially on Ash Wednesday and Good Friday. When it comes to the discipline regarding eating, in Catholic experience there is *abstinence*, which is the avoidance of meat; and then there is *fasting*, understood simply as eating less, so that in a three-meal pattern, the two small meals, typically breakfast and lunch, do not together equal the quantity eaten at the main meal, supper. Biblical fasting is something else; the fasting mandated on the one fast day in Mosaic law, the Day of Atonement, is abstention from all food and drink from sunrise to sunset. It is what Muslims do every day during the month of Ramadan—nothing in the mouth, not even water, during daylight. (I have a pleasant memory of riding an Arab bus in Jerusalem during the month of Ramadan late in the afternoon, when suddenly bread and other food appeared and was passed joyfully to everyone, including me; it was sunset and therefore time for breakfast.) These days, most Jews also observe a fast on Tisha B'Av (the Ninth of Av), which commemorates the two destructions of the Jerusalem temple—by the Babylonians in the sixth century B.C. and by the Romans in A.D. 70, both traditionally understood as occurring on the same day of the year.

In Jesus' day, apart from this formally mandated fasting, some people fasted more often, some even twice a week. The parable of the Pharisee and the tax collector (Luke 18:9-14) exemplifies this practice when the Pharisee says, "I fast twice a week, and I pay tithes on my whole income" (verse 12). All three synoptic gospels witness to this practice of "extra" fasting in the passage called the "Question about Fasting" at Mark 2:18-22, Matthew 9:14-17, and Luke 5:33-39. As Matthew tells it, the disciples of John the Baptist raise the question in verse 14: "Why do we and the Pharisees fast [much], but your disciples do not fast?" (This likely refers to something like that twice-a-week fasting as apparently expected from those who wish to show special devotion. Thus they wonder that Jesus does not demand this special discipline of his disciples.) Then Jesus responds, "Can the wedding guests mourn as long as the bridegroom is with them?" (Matthew has "mourn" where Mark has "fast" because mourning was a primary motive for fasting. In this response Jesus draws on the tradition of the Messianic times as a kind of wedding feast celebrating the union between God and his people, and he implies that he functions as the bridegroom.) Jesus continues, "The days will come when the bridegroom is taken away from them, and then they will fast" (verse 15). This reflects the time—the time of Matthew's church—when Jesus is no longer visibly present, and they fast in commemoration of his crucifixion.

The *Didache* refers to the later Christian practice of fasting with language that provides a direct commentary on Matthew 6:16. This early Christian manual prescribes fasting for "the one baptizing and the one to be baptized," and says further, apparently referring to regular practice, "But do not let your fasts coincide with those of the hypocrites. They fast on Monday and Thursday, so you must fast on Wednesday and Friday" (*Didache* 8:1).

Given this background, Jesus' words at Matthew 6:16-18 fit either of two settings: (1) Stage One (his public ministry) but addressed to Jews who were not yet his disciples, since Matthew 9:14-15 says that his disciples did not fast during his earthly life; or (2) Stage Two or Three (the time of the apostolic preaching or the time of the writing of the gospels), when his disciples would have reason to commemorate his crucifixion with some regularity.

The reading of this gospel passage on Ash Wednesday carries a certain irony in our day. It can seem odd to read, *"Anoint your head and wash your face, so that you may not appear to be fasting"* on the very day we fast and bear the public mark of ashes on our foreheads. Obviously, what can save us from Jesus' charge of hypocrisy is the proper motivation and the realization that in our culture, this bearing of the ash smudge provides the opportunity to be a "light to the world" when someone outside our faith community asks us to explain the meaning of that mark.

An alert reader is likely to notice an apparent tension between the call, early in the Sermon, to let one's light *"shine before others, that they may see your good deeds and glorify your heavenly Father"* (5:16) and the three *warnings* against practicing almsgiving, prayer, and fasting to be seen by others in chapter 6. One way of sorting out this contradiction is to observe that the image of being light for the world has to do with the *external* effect of the community on the world around it, whereas the teaching on almsgiving, prayer, and fasting is *internal*, concerned with Christians doing these things to impress fellow Christians. The first is extramural; the second is intramural. Moreover, the light-for-the-world image is more immediately illustrated by the behavior advocated in the examples illustrating the antitheses—managing one's anger and lust, being sexually faithful, speaking simply and honestly, practicing nonviolence, and loving ene-mies—actions and attitudes one is unlikely to fake for show. On the other hand, the warnings against almsgiving, public prayer, and fast-ing for show have to do with religious practices, the very things that members of a faith community may be tempted to perform conspic-uously in order to impress their co-religionists.

The Lord's Prayer: Keystone of the Sermon

Whereas Luke conveys the tradition of the Lord's Prayer as some-thing Jesus teaches on the road to Jerusalem (Luke 11), Matthew inserts it right here, as an illustration of the teaching on prayer. Its placement here makes it the centerpiece of the Sermon, a deliber-ate choice on Matthew's part, and therefore something to be taken seriously in our interpretation of the whole Sermon on the Mount. Matthew frames the Our Father with a brief introduction (verses 7-9) and then a brief commentary on the final petition (verses 14-15).

6:7 **"In praying, do not babble [*mē battalogēsete*] like the pagans [*ethnikoi*], who think that they will be heard because of their many words [*polylogía*]. 8Do not be like them. Your Father knows what you need before you ask him. 9aThis is how you are to pray** [verbs and pronouns all plural]:

The rare word translated "babble" (compare "heap up empty phrases," RSV)—occurring only here in the Bible and rare elsewhere in ancient literature—is best explained by the second half of the verse. It seems to be a matter of multiplying words. The fact that such a way of praying is ascribed to the "ethnics," a Jewish way of referring to non-Jews, indicates that the statement has an intra-Jewish setting. And since prayer is not a matter of communicating fresh information to the Father, simplicity is the point, and the model that is about to be given—the Our Father—is meant to be understood as an example of that simplicity.

6:9b "Our Father in heaven, / . . . "

This way of addressing God as "Father" may well go back to Jesus' own way of praying to *Abba* (Mark 14:36), an Aramaic term of endearment taken over by Greek-speaking Christians as a liturgical formula (see Galatians 4:6 and Romans 8:15). We may best access Matthew's understanding of the term's import by his use of "Father" at 12:49-50: "And stretching out his hand toward his disciples, he said, 'Here are my mother and my brothers. For whoever does the will of my heavenly Father is my brother, and sister, and mother.'" And see Jesus' prohibition of titles of deference in the community of disciples at 23:9: "Call no one on earth your father; you have but one Father in heaven." Whether praying alone or with others, this way of addressing God as "our Father" presumes Jesus' vision of his community of disciples (all Christians) as a family of brothers and sisters whose kinship is rooted in knowing God as the father of their brother Jesus, precisely in the way implied in these passages.

6:9c "hallowed be your name, / . . . "

It might seem enough to understand this first petition simply as an utterance of praise, as in "Praised be your name!" Yet there is a likely biblical background that provides this language with a further powerful meaning. The place in the Bible where talk of the hallowing of God's name figures importantly is the oracle of the Lord in Ezekiel 36:16-37. This is one of a series of prophetic visions proclaiming the future restoration of Israel. The first part of chapter 36 speaks of the regeneration of the land, and the first vision of chapter 37 is the vision of the dry bones, imaging the regeneration of the people.

Ezekiel 36:16-37, sitting between those two visions, is another vision of God's regeneration of the people. The vision begins with the Lord explaining that the exile of the house of Israel was a matter of his scattering them among the nations as punishment for their idolatry. One sorry effect of this scattering is that it has given the Lord a *bad name* among the nations: "But when they came among the nations [wherever they came], they served to profane my holy name, because it was said of them: 'These are the people of the LORD, yet they had to leave their land'" (36:20). He goes on to say:

> Therefore say to the house of Israel: Thus says the Lord GOD: Not for your sakes do I act, house of Israel, but *for the sake of my holy name*, which you profaned among the nations to which you came. I will *prove the holiness of my great name*, profaned among the nations. . . . Thus the nations shall know that I am the LORD, says the Lord GOD, when in their sight I prove my holiness through you. For I will take you away from among the nations, gather you from all the foreign lands, and bring you back to your own land. I will sprinkle clean water upon you to cleanse you from all your impurities, and from all your idols I will cleanse you. I will give you a new heart and place a new spirit within you, taking from your bodies your stony hearts and giving you natural hearts. I will put my spirit within you and make you live by my statutes, careful to observe my decrees. You shall live in the land I gave your fathers; you shall be my people, and I will be your God. (Ezekiel 36:22-28)

When we pray the petition "Hallowed be your name" with that background in mind, it becomes the community's plea for *rescue from spiritual exile, a plea for total renewal, for the gift of God's Spirit and transformation of our hearts.* Indeed, we pray that we may become light for the world—and everything that is implied by that term.

[6:10a]"your kingdom come, / . . . "

This petition asks God to exert his *reign* or empire, whose immi-nence the Baptist and Jesus announced (3:2; 4:17, 23), whose possession by the poor in spirit and those persecuted for the sake of righteousness Jesus acknowledges in the first and eighth beatitudes (5:3, 10) and in the childlike (19:14), whose presence Jesus manifests in his ministry (12:28; 21:31) and in the life of the church (16:19, 28; 26:29), and whose fullness is yet to come (8:11; 13:24-43, 47-50; 18:23; 19:23-24; 21:43; 24:34). The petition acknowledges that the coming of God's reign is both the work of the Father and also the fruit of human response to God's initiative. The aspect of human response derives not from this petition directly but from what has been com-municated elsewhere in this gospel. For example, the explanation of the parable of the sower (13:18-23) implies that the *understand-ing* of the word makes for a fruitful response in the kingdom and requires that people persevere despite tribulation and persecution and resist worldly anxiety and the lure of riches. And the parables about the buying of the field with the treasure and purchasing the pearl of great price (13:44-46) imply a profound "investment" or commit-ment. One really needs to know the whole Gospel of Matthew to pray the second petition of the Lord's Prayer with an awareness of its full meaning. One prays that the Father continues to do his part in advancing the reign inaugurated through Jesus, and one prays as well that human beings, in increasing number, continue to respond to that divine initiative.

[6:10bc]"your will be done, / on earth as it is in heaven / . . . "

In a sense, this is a repetition of the previous petition. The coming of the kingdom is surely the exercise of the divine will and also the doing of this will by responsive people. Is it, then, a simple redundancy to pray this third petition after praying the second? Are these two petitions in "synonymous parallelism" like parallel verses in a Hebrew psalm? This third petition is an *unpacking* of "your kingdom come." The human doing of the divine will is a manifestation of God's reign. God's desire and human desires merge to create "peace on earth." The strongest Jewish challenge to Christians has always been this one: "If the Messiah has truly come in the person of Jesus of Nazareth, where is the peace and justice that was supposed to come about through the Messiah?" The only Christian answer is that we believe that the reign of peace and justice has indeed been *inaugurated* through Jesus' life, death, resurrection, and the outpouring of the Spirit of God; it continues to come to the extent that human beings cooperate. We continue to pray for, work for, and wait for the fullness of the coming of the messianic kingdom.

Matthew recognizes that Mark's account of Jesus' prayer in Gethsemane illustrates powerfully the profound cost of yielding to the will of the Father. Besides passing on Jesus' prayer to the Father (*Abba*, in Mark)—"My Father, if it is possible, let this cup pass from me; yet, not as I will, but as you will" (26:39; par. Mark 14:36)—Matthew reinforces the resonance with the Lord's Prayer by repeating the contents of Jesus' prayer a second time at verse 42: "My Father, if it is not possible that this cup pass without my drinking it, *your will be done [genēthētō to thelēma sou]!*" This is precisely the wording of the petition in the Lord's Prayer at 6:10b. Further, where Mark simply implies that Jesus prayed a third time, Matthew says explicitly, "He left them and withdrew again and prayed a third time, saying the same thing again" (verse 44; no explicit parallel in Mark).

As we shall see, the final seven verses of this Sermon make it clear that it is precisely in *doing* the will of Jesus' Father, who is in the heavens, that enables a person to *enter* the empire of the heavens (7:21). Jesus further explains what that means three verses later: "Everyone who listens to these words of mine and acts on them will be like a wise man who built his house on rock" (7:24). In other words, the way of life spelled out in the Sermon on the Mount, these words of Jesus, *are* the will of the Father.

It is doing the will of the Father as learned through the life and teaching of Jesus that creates disciples, the new family of Jesus. Mark had already communicated this truth with powerful brevity in his account of the true family of Jesus:

> "Who are my mother and [my] brothers?" And looking around at those seated in the circle he said, "Here are my mother and my brothers. [For] whoever does the will of God is my brother and sister and mother." (Mark 3:33-35)

Matthew nuances Mark's language when he tells this story in order to highlight its meaning of the church:

> "Who is my mother? Who are my brothers?" *And stretching out his hand toward his disciples,* he said. "Here are my mother and my brothers. For whoever does *the will of my heavenly Father* [*to thelēma tou patros mou tou en ouranois,* literally "the will of my Father in [the] heavens," echoing 7:21] is my brother, and sister, and mother." (Matthew 12:48-50)

Matthew's delicate adjustment of Mark's "those seated around him" to "his disciples" and his editing of Mark's "the will of God" to "the will of my heavenly Father" clarify that the followers of Jesus, the post-Easter church, are indeed disciples who have come to know God as the Father of Jesus who teaches them to do the Father's will and so become part of the family of Jesus, the Son of God. When we pray "thy will be done" in the Lord's Prayer, we are asking to be enabled to live the life described in the Sermon.

6:11 "Give us today our daily bread; / . . . "

This petition is so familiar and simple that most people spontaneously supply a straightforward meaning—something like "Please give us what we need today," taking "bread" as a kind of metonymy, naming a part (bread, as a basic food) to refer to a whole (all that we need for sustenance). This understanding is reflected in the Good News Translation: "Give us today the food we need." What keeps this petition from being all that simple is the fact that nobody knows for sure the meaning of the word usually translated "daily"—*epiousios*. The problem is that this adjective appears only once in all of Greek literature, right here in the Lord's Prayer (Matthew 6:11 and Luke 11:3). The only other instances occur in texts that refer to this unique instance. With nothing else to go on, lexicographers have had to resort to educated guesses based on possible etymologies and the context of the prayer itself. The standard New Testament lexicon summarizes the various interpretations for the word as the following four: "necessary for existence"; "for the current day"; "for the following day"; and "coming."[65] The Good News Translation acknowledges some of these alternative interpretations with a note, "*or* for today, *or* for tomorrow," and the NRSV has the note "our bread for tomorrow." The Rheims translation has for this verse "Give us this day our supersubstantial bread," reflecting the Latin of Jerome's Vulgate, *panis supersubstantialis,* a phrase that lends itself to a Eucharistic interpretation.

What is a Christian to do with this linguistic state of affairs? It may be a good thing that this simple prayer for bread is somewhat open-ended in its expression. That makes it easy to pray the verse as a humble acknowledgment of dependence on our creating God. Even though Genesis 3:19 reminds us of our human lot to work hard for bread ("By the sweat of your face / shall you get bread to eat, / Until you return to the ground, / from which you were taken"), we know that everything that sustains us with seeds or animal flesh is first of all a gift of our Creator and Sustainer. Human beings dig, plant, harvest, and bake, but they do not make seeds or the soil in which seeds grow nor do the human creatures provide the rain and sunlight that are required for that growth. Some commentators rightly hear an allusion to Exodus 16 regarding the manna in the wilderness, "bread from heaven" (16:4)—which is all about sustenance for the day supplied by God (and see the reflection on this episode in Psalm 78:17-25). The memory of that story helps us get in touch with the sense of trust in divine providence embodied in the petition. If *epiousios* has the sense of "tomorrow" or "coming," that can be taken as a reference to the messianic banquet. Then the petition becomes a plea for a taste now of what is to come in fullness later, and this has long been a traditional understanding of the Eucharist. However one takes that unique modifier, the prayer for bread today is never empty of rich meaning.

6:12"and forgive us our debts, / as we forgive our debtors; . . . "

As in the parable of the two debtors that Jesus tells at Simon the Pharisee's dinner party to illustrate the woman's gratitude for the forgiveness of her sins (Luke 7:41-43), debt can be used as a metaphor for sin. Sin, as it were, puts one in debt to God. Given that Luke's parallel at 11:4 has "sins" and "everyone in debt to us" where Matthew's version has "debts" and "debtors," the debts in this petition are best understood as sins. The same meaning is evident in the parable about the forgiveness of debts in the dramatic parable that Matthew includes in the final part of the fourth major speech in his gospel, the speech on church life (18:1-35). Like the Sermon on the Mount, this speech, constructed of parables and sayings of Jesus, is powerfully organized. The core of the speech is the escalating protocol for dealing with an erring member of the community: First, speak to the individual one-on-one; if that fails, take a witness and try again; and if that also fails, take the issue to the community (verses 15-18). To ensure that this rational protocol—parallels for which you can find in most policy manuals in the U.S. today—is carried out in a Christian spirit, Matthew surrounds it, before and after, with the parable of the shepherd and the lost sheep (verses 10-14) and sayings about communal prayer, the presence of the risen Lord where two or three are gathered in his name, and the need to forgive "seventy-seven times" (verses 19-22).

Matthew's arrangement rounds out this teaching with the parable of the unforgiving servant at the end (verses 23-35). A servant is forgiven a debt of "ten thousand talents"—a huge amount, something like the tribute the Roman Empire would exact from the province of Judea—and then, fresh from that forgiveness, has the audacity to violently force the immediate payment of a relatively small debt (100 denari, a hundred days' labor) owed him by a fellow servant. When his master hears about it, he summons the servant and says, "You wicked servant! I forgave you your entire debt because you begged me to. Should you not have had pity on your fellow servant, as I had pity on you?" (verses 32-33). In anger, the king punishes the unforgiving servant. Just in case anyone misses the point, Jesus says, "So will my heavenly Father do to you, unless each of you forgives his brother from his heart" (verse 35).

That this story about debt forgiveness (or lack thereof) is a parable about forgiving sins is clear, because the story is prompted by Peter's question, "Lord, if my brother sins against me, how often must I forgive him?" (verse 21). That the parable expresses the vision of the Lord's Prayer is evident from the language of "heavenly Father" and the idea of forgiving as one is forgiven. Forgiving *from the heart* captures an emphasis of the Sermon generally. The translation "Should you not have *had pity* on your fellow servant, as I *had pity* on you?" (verse 33) obscures the fact that "to have pity on" translates the verb also used in the fifth beatitude (*eleéō*), "Blessed are the merciful [*hoi eleēmones*], for they will be shown mercy [*autoi eleēthēsontai*]" (5:7). The parable gives an image for what happens when one goes counter to the spirit of the fifth beatitude. The beatitude summarizes the bright side of the parable. The specification of forgiving one's *brother* maintains the speech's focus on the internal life of the community. Regarding the harm inflicted by outsiders, Jesus asks that one prays for them and even loves them (not in the sense of affection but of wishing them good); talk of forgiveness addresses the more intimate matter of reconciliation within the community.

⁶:¹³"and do not subject us to the final test [*eis peirasmon*], / but deliver us from the evil one."

The phrasing of the first clause of this final petition in this NAB translation will come as a surprise to those used to the more familiar rendering, "And lead us not into temptation" (KJV, Rheims, NIV, RSV). The word *peirarmos* means, primarily, "an attempt to learn the nature or character of something; *test, trial.*" Secondarily it can mean "an attempt to make one do something wrong; *temptation, enticement.*"⁶⁶ The consensus of scholarship is that the secondary meaning, temptation, is not the correct one in this sentence. It contradicts the basic religious intuition that God is not an agent of temptation, something stated explicitly in James 1:13: "No one experiencing temptation should say, 'I am being tempted by God'; for God is not subject to temptation to evil, and he himself tempts no one." What, then, is the trial or testing from which one prays to be delivered? It was part of the end-time picture of first-century Judaism that messianic times would entail severe testing and tribulation. Jesus saw this testing as imminent, and the early church as actual. Is it, then, a petition to escape an inevitable element of the end times? Given Jesus' emphasis on the narrow gate, the rough road, "my yoke," and predictions of betrayal and rejection, a prayer for exemption from the inevitable hardly seems likely. The point of the petition clarifies when we attend to the second half of the verse, *"but deliver us from the evil one (or from evil)* [*alla rhysai hēmas apo tou ponērou*]*."* This is traditional biblical language for divine rescue from evil; and that salvation can take a variety of forms—healing, sparing, sustaining through difficulty—whatever is needed at the time.

The theme of the fifth petition—for being forgiven as we forgive—is so important for Matthew that he paraphrases here a saying of Jesus that he finds at Mark 11:25 (from Jesus' words on the day after the temple action) in order to drive the point home:

6:14"**If you forgive others their transgressions, your heavenly Father will forgive you. 15But if you do not forgive others, neither will your Father forgive your transgressions."**

We have seen Matthew's appreciation of this theme of forgiveness of sins in his inclusion of the parable of the unforgiving servant in the speech on church life (chapter 18). This interest is also evident in a number of other places in his gospel: the statement of the angel of the Lord that Jesus will "save his people from their sins" (1:21— the empowerment to forgive others may be part of how this saving happens); the response of the crowd to Jesus' healing *and forgiveness* of the paralytic (9:8—"When the crowds saw this they were struck with awe and glorified God *who had given such authority to human beings*"); and Matthew's addition to the word over the cup, that the blood of the covenant will be poured out for many *"for the forgiveness of sins"* (26:28). We usually limit the reference of these passages to divine forgiveness of human sinfulness, and this is surely the primary sense; but might they not also be understood as implying the empowerment of people to forgive others (especially 9:8)?

On this topic of empowerment to forgive, an experience of some Jesuit colleagues comes to mind. During the time of our theology studies, two of my brothers were serving a kind of ministerial internship at a mental health clinic. Their supervisor suggested that they begin by simply getting to know the patients. They soon discovered that many of the patients were in the clinic because they seemed to be stuck in resentment. Understandably, the seminarians tried to talk the people into forgiving those they resented. Equally understandably, the patients said that they were unable to forgive. It finally occurred to my brothers that they might try to get the people to pray for the gift of being able to forgive. So they began to approach those stuck in resentment by saying something like the following: "I understand you feel paralyzed by this resentment and unable to forgive on your own. But if God gave you the *gift* of being able to forgive, would you be willing to accept and act on that grace?" Many said yes to the invitation, and the seminarians began to join them in prayer for the gift of being enabled to forgive those against whom they felt such paralyzing resentment. Most of them eventually experienced the ability to forgive, and for many this grace marked the beginning of their recovery from mental illness.

The Lord's Prayer in the Gospel of Luke

Luke has his own version of the *Pater Noster* and places it in a different setting, linking it to a unique parable. Because of its importance to Christians as the prayer Jesus taught his disciples, the two versions have invited much comparison and speculation and have generated abundant scholarship. Let me share what I consider some important observations and insights:

1. The fact that this prayer comes to us in two versions in two gospels and is placed in a different setting in each gospel is instructive. The two quite similar versions provide a first-class example of

what scholars mean by Q material, a sayings-tradition that does not appear in Mark but does appear in Matthew and Luke, in similar wording but in different contexts. There are many other examples, but the Lord's Prayer is especially helpful because it is already familiar in Matthew's version as most Christians learn it by heart and recite it at worship. Our familiarity with one version makes us alert to the differences in Luke's version.

2. That this prayer appears in two gospels in different settings alerts us to the fact that each evangelist has placed it in a particular setting for a reason: Matthew, as the keystone of his Sermon; Luke, as a key teaching for the disciples following Jesus on the road to Jerusalem.

3. The absence in Luke's version of two clauses that occur in Matthew's version—"your will be done" and "but deliver us from evil"—helps us see that each of these petitions is an elaboration of the one just before it and therefore likely Matthew's redaction (perhaps to make it a more balanced expression for liturgical use).

4. Luke's phrasing of the "bread" petition—*didou hēmin to kath'hēmeron* (literally, "keep giving us each day") as compared to Matthew's *dos hēmin sēmeron* ("give us today")—suggests more clearly a focus on the need for material sustenance than Matthew's language, which is more open to the eucharistic and end-time possibilities of the meaning of bread.

References to technical discussions about variant readings in the manuscript tradition normally have no place in a pastoral commentary such as this one. But there is a fascinating variant for "thy kingdom come" that has rich pastoral, historical, and pedagogical significance; one NT manuscript and several patristic writings witness to a version of the Lord's Prayer that instead of "thy kingdom come," has *"Thy Holy Spirit come upon us and cleanse us."* It appears in an eleventh-century manuscript and, more important, in writings by Gregory of Nyssa in Cappadocia and Maximus the Confessor. Those quotations witness to the existence of this form of the Our Father in the fourth and fifth centuries. Regarding which petition is the more original, scholars have no doubt that "thy kingdom come" is the more original.[67] The value of the variant is that it testifies to an early Christian understanding of what it *meant* to pray "thy king-dom come." It understands the petition in terms of the very same prophetic text that we claimed on page 168 stands behind the peti-tion "hallowed be thy name"—that is, Ezekiel 36:16-37, the passage that speaks of the Lord's intention to hallow his name by reviving his people through the outpouring of his spirit, which Christian writers also took as a way of talking about the coming of his kingdom. It has been observed that St. Paul understood the outpouring of the Holy Spirit as a manifestation of the kingdom of God. That same under-standing is evident in this early Holy Spirit variant for the kingdom petition in the early church.

Luke's Parable of the Friend at Midnight

To his account of Jesus teaching his disciples how to pray, Luke joins a parable unique to his gospel, the similitude of the friend at midnight (11:5-8). Usually interpreted as a parable about persistence, a culturally sensitive case can be made that it is really a parable of assurance, in the spirit of the sayings that follow it (verses 9-13). The cultural elements that illuminate this story are the following:

1. In the ancient Near East, it was taken for granted that one offered food to a visitor.

2. A reputation for hospitality was a matter of honor for the whole village, not only for individuals and families.
3. Bread—as a dining "tool" (for eating from a common dish) as well as part of the menu—was an absolute essential for hospitality.
4. Since baking was done outdoors, at a common oven, neighbors knew who had baked bread on any given day.
5. In that setting, one woke up a sleeping neighbor by (a familiar) *voice*, not by a (startling, anonymous) knock.

So Jesus' similitude presents a common scenario. A friend of yours makes a surprise visit at night, and so of course you need to give him something to eat. Finding no bread in your house, you go to get some from your friend next door. You wake him up, explain your situation, ask to borrow three loaves, and he says, "Do not bother me; the door has already been locked and my children and I are already in bed. I cannot get up to give you anything" (Luke 11:7). Well, isn't it true that even if the old grouch won't get up because of his friendship with you (the needy host), he will get up and give what you need because of his *anaideia*. Grammatically, the quality mentioned in the Greek word goes more naturally with the sleepy neighbor than with the would-be host. And the word can be translated "avoidance of shame." This fits the scenario: You can be sure that neighbor is going to provide the bread to save the reputation of the village for hospitality.[68]

The point is, just as you know your grouchy neighbor-friend will come through with the bread, all the more can you expect your heavenly Father to provide what you need. Jesus teaches persistence in prayer quite clearly in another parable, that of the persistent widow in Luke 18. Here the point is assurance. The sayings that follow in Luke 11 drive this point home with other imagery: Even a "wicked" human father will give his child what the kid needs—an egg, say, or a fish. "If you then, who are wicked, know how to give good gifts to your children, how much more will the Father in heaven give *the holy*

Spirit to those who ask him?" (11:13). Luke's mention of "the holy Spirit" in this context (where Matthew's parallel has simply "good things," 7:11) makes it even more plausible that for Luke, as for others, the gift of the Holy Spirit lies in the background of the first two petitions of the Lord's Prayer, reflecting the association of the hallowing of God's name with the gift of his spirit in Ezekiel 36.

Our consideration of Matthew's and Luke's presentations of the Lord's Prayer turns out to be more than a scholarly look at alternate traditions. Matthew's presentation in the middle of his Sermon on the Mount reminds us that the community that lives according to the moral vision of the Sermon is a community that expresses in prayer its dependency on the Father of Jesus, who enables such a way of living together with his loving care. Matthew's emphasis on forgiveness reminds us of the absolute requirement of mutual forgiveness for such a way of life. And Luke's presentation of the Lord's Prayer helps us appreciate that praying to the Father as Jesus did is an essential part of following Jesus on the way to Jerusalem—the site of death, resurrection, and the movement into a mission that serves the entire world.

CHAPTER 9

TREASURE, EYE, MASTER, AND YOUR FATHER'S CARE

(MATTHEW 6:19-34 AND LUKE 12:13-34)

This section of the Sermon is all about priorities. It begins with three sayings about habits of the heart (Matthew 6:19-24) and continues with encouragement to trust your heavenly Father (6:25-34). As we will see, Luke also deals with these issues, not in Jesus' Sermon on the Plain, but later in his gospel.

Where is your treasure? How is your eye? Who is your master? Matthew follows the treatment of the three classic religious practices of almsgiving, prayer, and fasting with a set of images that provoke reflection on one's essential commitments. These three questions are a way of catching the drift of those images.

WHERE IS YOUR TREASURE?

6:19 "Do not store up for yourselves treasures [*mē thēsaurizete hymin thēsaurous*] on earth, where moth and decay destroy, and thieves break in and steal. 20But store up treasures in heaven, where neither moth nor decay destroys, nor thieves break in and steal. 21For where your treasure is, there also will your heart be."

A more literal translation—"Do not *treasure up treasures* for your-selves"—captures the repetition of the root in the Greek noun and verb in verse 19a; the swollen diction gives away the fact that the warning is against hoarding, not against normal provisions of prudence, such as the extra loaf in the cupboard or, in our setting, a backup roll of toilet paper or the carrying of health insurance. The Letter of James gives this teaching an ironic spin when he warns rich landowners that the wages they have held back from their harvesters will come back to bite them: "You have stored up treasure for the last days," for "the cries of the harvesters have reached the ears of the Lord of hosts," and "you have fattened your hearts for the day of slaughter" (James 5:3-5). This basic insight regarding the passing nature of material possessions is, of course, a common notion, available to any reflective human being. But when Matthew 6:20 repeats the phrase, it is applied metaphorically on the level of faith regarding an enduring relationship with the heavenly Father (being "rich in what matters to God," as Luke 12:21 puts it). Jesus here affirms a conviction in an image already available in his Jewish tradition, as for example in Tobit 4:8-9.

Verse 21 drives the point home with language that unites this passage with a theme that undergirds the whole Sermon from the beatitudes forward and what a contemporary book has called "the habits of the heart": *"For where your treasure is, there also will your heart be."*

"Heart" Theme in Matthew

This is a good place to pause and consider how "heart" language functions in the Gospel of Matthew. In Scripture generally, "heart"— *kardía* in Greek—never refers simply to the cardiac muscle; at least I have not encountered a biblical reference to "heart" that is anatomical. The Bible uses *kardía* for that key interior physical organ as a metaphor for the "seat of physical, spiritual, and mental life, . . . of moral decisions, vices and virtues, . . . of the emotions, wishes, desires, . . . dispositions."[69] Key examples from the Old Testament are important for New Testament writers, especially Matthew. One is the *Shema* (Deuteronomy 6:4-6, "Hear, O Israel! The LORD is our God, the LORD alone! Therefore, you shall love the LORD, your God, with all your *heart*, and with all your soul, and with all your strength. Take to *heart* these words which I enjoin on you today"; see Matthew 22:37). Another is the word of the Lord to Isaiah of Jerusalem on the occasion of his call ("You are to make the *heart* of this people sluggish, / to dull their ears and close their eyes; / Else their eyes will see, their ears hear, / their *heart* understand, / and they will turn and be healed"—Isaiah 6:10; see Matthew 13:15). A third example, based on Isaiah 29:13, is cited by Matthew in 15:8: "This people honors me with their lips, / but their *hearts* are far from me; / in vain do they worship me, / teaching as doctrines human precepts." Although the word *kardía* occurs only three times in the Sermon on the Mount (5:8, 28; 6:21), these references punctuate major parts of the Sermon—the beatitudes, the antitheses, and the three religious practices—and the focus throughout is on what goes on in the human heart and, consequently, what gets expressed in action. We saw that the sixth beatitude (on the clean of heart) has its home base in Psalm 24:3-4: "Who may go up the mountain of the LORD? / . . . The clean of hand and pure of *heart*, / who are not devoted to idols, / who have not sworn falsely."

Luke has his own way of stressing that love of enemies, nonviolence, and refraining from judgment of others are matters of the heart by saying toward the end of his Sermon on the Plain, "A good person out of the store of goodness in his *heart* produces good, but an evil person out of a store of evil produces evil; for from the fullness of the *heart* the mouth speaks" (Luke 6:45; paralleling a Q saying in Matthew 12:34b-35).

"Why do you think evil in your *kardiais?*" Jesus asks the scribes on the occasion of the healing of the paralytic (Matthew 9:4, NRSV; par. Mark 2:8 and Luke 5:22). Matthew's unique account of Jesus' self-description at 11:28-30 ("Come to me . . . Take my yoke upon you and learn from me, for I am meek and *humble of heart*") helps us understand that the third beatitude (and therefore perhaps all the beatitudes) is also a description of Jesus.

Matthew is emphatic that *speech* is, for good or for evil, a particularly important manifestation of the heart. When he conveys the Q saying "From the fullness of the *heart* the mouth speaks" (12:34; par. Luke 6:45), it follows his expansion of the "good tree/good fruit, bad tree/bad fruit" sayings, which he repeats from the Sermon (7:16-20) and then uniquely adds a judgment, saying, "I tell you, on the day of judgment people will render an account for every careless word they speak. By your words you will be acquitted, and by your words you will be condemned" (12:36-37). This emphasis is very much in tune with Matthew's inclusion of the antithesis on oath-taking in the Sermon.

The way Matthew develops the heart theme in chapter 13 in his retelling of the parable of the sower from Mark 4, with the reference to Isaiah 6 and the explanation of the parable, is revealing. Matthew's expanded quotation of Isaiah 6:9-10 in the parables speech includes the prophet's verses about not seeing and hearing and understanding because of dullness of *heart*: "You shall indeed hear but never understand, / you shall indeed look but never see. / Gross is the heart of this people, / they will hardly hear with their ears, they have closed their eyes, lest they see with their eyes / and hear with their ears / and *understand with their heart* and be converted" (13:14b-15). When Matthew proceeds with the interpretation of the sower parable, he uses language that precisely echoes Isaiah's language: "The seed sown on the path is the one who hears the word of the kingdom *without understanding it,* and the evil one comes and steals away what was sown *in his heart*" (13:19); here, understanding seems to be a free act on the part of the recipient, and the loss is a consequence of failure to understand. This note is struck again in the explanation of the seed sown on good soil: "But the seed sown on rich soil is the one who hears the word *and understands it* [Mark 4:20 has "accept it"; Luke 8:15 says, "Embrace it with a generous and good heart"], who indeed bears fruit and yields a hundred or sixty or thirtyfold" (13:23).

Matthew's use of LXX Isaiah 29:13 at 15:8 and Mark 7:6 ("Their hearts are far from me") again locates sin in the heart. He reinforces this idea at 15:18-19 (par. Mark 7:20–21): "But the things that come out of the *mouth* come from the *heart* [see Matthew 12:36!], and they defile. For from the *heart* come evil thoughts. . . ." Matthew uses heart twice here, where Mark has it once.

Maybe Matthew's interest in mouth sins is what leads him to include *pseudomartyría* ("false witness," 15:19) in the list of sins that come from the heart. This word does not appear in the LXX, but the verb form, *pseudomartyreō*, does twice—in Exodus 20 and in Deuteronomy 5 in the eighth commandment: "Thou shalt not bear false witness against thy neighbor."[70]

How Is Your Eye?

6:22 **"The lamp of the body is the eye. If your [singular] eye is sound [*haplous*, "healthy" or "generous"], your whole body will be filled with light; 23but if your eye is bad [*ponēros*, also "evil"], your whole body will be in darkness. And if the light in you [singular] is darkness, how great will the darkness be."**

On the plain-sense level, this passage appears to be stating the obvious. The eye functions like an oil lamp in that the faculty of vision enables us to find our way. If our eye is "bad" in the sense of being unhealthy and malfunctioning, we see poorly or not at all. We are truly "in the dark." Verses 22-23a can be read in this way, but then the saying is simply a truism (if your eyes are poor, you are in the dark), hardly worth preserving as a piece of wisdom. What signals that this passage has a parabolic meaning is the final sentence: *"And if the light in you is darkness, how great will the darkness be."* That mysterious saying contributes nothing to the description of physical vision and forces the listener or reader to search for another sense of "light" and "darkness."

For a person familiar with Mediterranean cultures, another sense of *ophthalmos ponēros* ("bad eye") is available—*evil eye*. Even today there are cultures that foster a conviction that an envious person develops an "evil eye" whose gaze causes harm. Specific artifacts and strategies—amulets, gestures, the color blue—are understood to ward off the effects of the evil eye.[71]

The phrase "evil eye" can even be used as a synonym for envy. For example, the saying of Jesus at Mark 7:22 lists twelve bad things that can come from a person's heart, of which the ninth item is *ophthalmos ponēros* (literally, "evil eye"). This is so odd and poorly understood that it is usually translated, reasonably, "envy." Matthew omits the phrase from his parallel list of six (external sins following the Decalogue order) at 15:19. But Matthew does include a reference to the evil eye in another place, the parable of the workers in the vineyard at 20:15b, where the landowner asks one of the full-day workers who complains that those hired at the eleventh hour receive a full day's pay: "Is your eye evil because I am good?" (KJV).[72] It is possible, then, that the phrase at 6:23 (par. Luke 11:34c)—"if your eye is bad" [*ean de ho ophthalmos sou ponēros*]—refers to envy. That fits well Matthew's (and possibly Jesus') context in the Sermon, where he has just warned against hoarding possessions and is just about to address the choice of God over mammon. If this interpretation is correct, the apparent truism about the importance of eyes for seeing becomes a parable warning against the possessive "looking" of envy. Finally, the mysterious saying about light and darkness becomes clear: To paraphrase, if the focus of your heart gets seduced into envious desire, then what is supposed to be your light (the attentiveness of your spirit) becomes a source of darkness. The "evil eye"—the coveting gaze—really does do harm.

When we allow the larger context of Matthew's narrative to resonate with this passage, the evangelist's other references to "light" suggest even fuller meaning for verse 22b: *"If your eye is sound, your whole body will be filled with light.*" Matthew linked his account of Jesus' move from Nazareth to Capernaum with his citation of Isaiah 9:1—"The people who sit in darkness / have seen a *great light,* / on those dwelling in a land overshadowed by death / *light has arisen*" (Matthew 4:16). Then, shortly after, we hear Jesus say to his disciples, "You are the light of the world" (5:14) and "Your light must shine before others, that they may see your good deeds and glorify your heavenly Father" (5:16). Heard within that rather immediate context, the eye imagery of verses 22-23 helps the would-be disciple understand that having the generous eye (liberated from envy) enables one to join Jesus' mission of being light for the world.

WHO (OR WHAT) IS YOUR MASTER?

6:24"No one can serve two masters. He will either hate one and love the other, or be devoted to one and despise the other. You [plural] cannot serve God and mammon."

The word "mammon" came into the English language precisely from this gospel passage (and its parallel in Luke 16:13; and see Luke 16:11, "unrighteous mammon," or "dishonest wealth" in the NAB; the traditional phrase "mammon of iniquity" comes from the Rheims version of Luke 16:9). In Greek it appears as *mamōna,* which in turn is simply the transliteration of the Aramaic word. Even people with no knowledge of Jesus' mother tongue can make a connection here: *mamōna* is built on the same root as the *Amen* we say at the end of prayers. Amen is an expression of faith: *Let it be! Truly!* In Aramaic, as in Hebrew, verbs often become nouns by prefixing an *m* (the Semitic *mu*). Mammon, in its root sense, means what is trustworthy. And because human beings, at least in good times, tend to place trust in their wealth, mammon became a name for wealth or money. Thus, some English versions (such as KJB, Rheims, NAB) have "mammon" in this verse; but NIV, NJB, and Good News have "money," and the NRSV has "wealth" (with a note citing the Greek, "mammon"). One reason to keep the translation *mammon* is that it sounds like the name of an idol, something that actually competes with God, which of course is the point of the saying. It was a matter of wisdom and wit that someone chose to have U.S. paper currency bear the legend "In God We Trust." For those who know the etymology, the text serves as a good reminder that we are *not* to place ultimate trust in our mammon but in God. The wisdom of the motto on our currency is that it acknowledges God as the master we serve. The power of the phrasing of Matthew 6:24 is that it acknowledges that wealth can indeed become an idol and is exactly that for many, as indeed it has been in almost any culture.

Does Matthew have a special take on wealth, such as Luke does in his version of the beatitudes, with a "woe" addressed to the rich balancing the congratulation addressed to the poor? Though Matthew does not have a special theme of "rich and poor," his two references to wealthy persons are noteworthy. We have already considered the plight of the rich young man: Because he was attached to his many possessions, he went away sad when Jesus told him, *"If you wish to be perfect,* go, sell what you have and give to [the] poor, and you will have treasure in heaven. Then come, follow me" (19:21). As in the case of Luke, Matthew then proceeds to pass on the conversation that follows regarding the difficulty of the rich entering the kingdom:

> Then Jesus said to his disciples, "Amen, I say to you, it will be hard for one who is rich [*plousios*] to enter the kingdom of heaven. Again I say to you, it is easier for a camel to pass through the eye of a needle than for one who is rich [*plousion*] to enter the kingdom of God." When the disciples heard this, they were greatly astonished and said, "Who then can be saved?"

Jesus looked at them and said, "For human beings this is impossible, but for God all things are possible." (Matthew 19:23-26)

There is no doubt that this exchange dramatizes the danger wealth can be to one's spiritual health. Such was this man's attachment to his possessions that he needed to sell them all. That Matthew did not understand this need to sell all our possessions as a universal mandate is evident in the other reference to a rich man in his gospel, Joseph of Arimathea. Whereas Mark introduces Joseph as "a distinguished member of the council, who was himself awaiting the kingdom of God" (15:43), Matthew calls him "*a rich man* from Arimathea" and "a disciple of Jesus" (27:57). The note of wealth is stressed by mention of the fact that he laid Jesus' body "in *his* new tomb that he had hewn in the rock" (27:60). And so Matthew presents two men called "rich" in his gospel. One fails to become a disciple because he is attached to his possessions and refuses to let go. As far as we can tell, he chooses to serve mammon. The other rich man is able to stay rich and still qualify as a disciple of Jesus. Apparently, he has chosen God as his master; consequently, he has begun to live the life of the beatitudes, and wealth has lost its power over him. The fact that he has the courage to identify himself as a disciple to the Roman prefect by asking for Jesus' body is a sign of this freedom. The point is not whether a follower of Jesus possesses wealth but how he or she relates to it. Jesus insists that the possession of wealth presents serious danger to a person's spiritual health. But submission to God through discipleship in the community of Jesus can liberate us from wealth's power. This is one of those things that is "possible with God."

Trust Your Heavenly Father!

Having illuminated the issue of ultimate human commitment with the images of the heart's treasure, the generous eye over the evil eye, and God over idolatrous mammon, the Sermon now provides encouragement for placing one's ultimate trust in the heavenly Father (verses 25-34; par. Luke 12:22-32).

6:25 "Therefore I tell you [plural], do not worry about your life, what you will eat [or drink], or about your body, what you will wear. Is not life more than food and the body more than clothing? 26Look at the birds in the sky; they do not sow or reap, they gather nothing into barns, yet your heavenly Father feeds them. Are not you [plural] more important than they? 27Can any of you by worrying add a single moment to your life-span? 28Why are you anxious about clothes? Learn from the way the wild flowers grow. They do not work or spin. 29But I tell you that not even Solomon in all his splendor was clothed like one of them. 30If God so clothes the grass of the field, which grows today and is thrown into the oven tomorrow, will he not much more provide for you [plural], O you of little faith [*oligopistoi*]? 31So do not worry and say, 'What are we to eat?' or 'What are we to drink?' or 'What are we to wear?' 32All these things the pagans [*ethnē*] seek. Your heavenly Father knows that you need them all. 33But seek first the kingdom [of God] and his righteousness, and all these things will be given you besides. 34Do not worry about tomorrow; tomorrow will take care of itself. Sufficient for a day is its own evil."

At first this teaching sounds like naïve advice. Is Jesus here advising his followers that if they trust the Creator sufficiently, they ought to be able to live like flower children? Is Jesus really presenting the birds of the air and the lilies of the field as practical examples of the humane life? How does that square with St. Paul's insistence that members of the community who do not work should not eat (2 Thessalonians 3:10)? The discourse obviously argues from the patterns visible in creation. That may seem to work out in the nonhuman part of nature, but how does this apply to humanity? We need to be clothed with more than our skin.

The answer lies in the kingdom saying of verse 33. The talk of birds and flowers turns out really to be about human *priorities*. *"Seek first the kingdom [of God] and his righteousness, and all these things will be given you besides."* The whole Sermon is a description of the shared life of a group that has become a community because it has become a family under a heavenly Father by doing the Parent's will. An inevitable "side effect" of living that life—especially as summarized by the Golden Rule of 7:12 and the mandate to love neighbor as self in the spirit of Jesus (19:19-21)—is that the needs of all (surely including food, drink, and clothing) will be met. Placing this saying (verse 33) in the context of the Father's feeding of birds and "clothing" of flowers is a way of saying that the kind of *community* to which Jesus calls his disciples is how the human creature was created to live and the ordinary means by which the Father cares for them.

The anxiety against which the teaching warns is not the prudent attention to meeting the normal needs for food, drink, and clothing. The target of the teaching is any distracting *preoccupation* with these things—the kind of preoccupation identified with the thorns in the explanation of the parable of the sower, the "worldly anxiety and the lure of riches" that choke the word of the kingdom before it can bear fruit (13:22). Doing our part in a community that is preoccupied with living the covenant of life with the Father—seeking the kingdom—liberates us from these other preoccupations.

The quality of "little faith" carried by the adjective that the Sermon applies to the listening disciples in verse 30 (*"O you* [plural] *of little faith"*) is expressed in the single word *oligopistoi*. Whereas Luke uses it only once in his gospel (at 12:28, the parallel to Matthew 6:30), for Matthew it becomes a key theme in his portrayal of the disciples. In all four gospels, when the evangelists portray Jesus' disciples, they are not so much interested in conveying the historical experience of those first followers; the gospel writers seem more interested in using their portrait of the early followers as a vehicle for helping their audience (or readers) gain insight into what following Jesus means in any age—not just then, but *now*. Mark, for example, does not shrink from picturing the disciples as spiritually blind and deaf. At every turn they are clueless regarding the true nature of what it means for Jesus to be the Messiah and the place of suffering in his life and work. This is likely Mark's way of addressing what his audience needs to learn. For Matthew, on the other hand, the disciples understand Jesus and his mission quite well. In his gospel, Jesus can say to the disciples, "Blessed are your eyes, because they see, and your ears, because they hear" (13:16). At the close of the speech on the parables of the kingdom (13:51), Jesus asks, "Do you understand all these things?" They answer, "Yes," and Matthew gives us no reason to doubt the truth of their answer.

For Matthew, the disciples' main problem is something else. They are "of little faith." In the context of his gospel, this means that they do not trust the Father enough to *act* upon their understanding of Jesus' person, message, and mission. Besides the saying about "little faith" that he shares with Luke, Matthew introduces the notion four more times into the tradition he has from Mark. When the disciples panic at the seismic storm on the Sea of Galilee, Jesus again chides them as *oligopistoi* (8:26). Later, when Jesus warns them to "beware of the leaven of the Pharisees and Sadducees," their concern about the lack of literal bread is such that Jesus again calls them *oligopistoi* (16:8). And when Jesus, Peter, James, and John come down from the mountain of transfiguration, and the other nine ask why they were unable to drive out the demon from the boy, Jesus says, "Because of your *oligopistía*" (17:20). In Matthew's version of the "walking on the water" episode, when Peter starts to walk toward his master, becomes frightened, and begins to sink, Jesus, as he rescues him, asks, "*Oligopiste*, why did you doubt?" (14:31). You might say that for

Matthew, the disciples have a nasty case of *oligopistía*. Yet, as mentioned above, that little faith coexists with understanding.

The response of the disciples in the boat on the occasion of the walking on the water is another example of such a juxtaposition. Mark's version of the episode concludes by saying, "They were [completely] astounded. They had not understood the incident of the loaves. On the contrary, their hearts were hardened" (Mark 6:51b-52). In Matthew's version, however, after Peter is accused of being "of little faith" and *doubting*, the whole boatful of disciples is able to *worship* Jesus, and in words that anticipate Peter's confession of faith two chapters later, they proclaim, with astonishing insight, "Truly, you are the Son of God" (Matthew 14:33). Matthew's theme of knowing disciples who fail in faith climaxes in the final scene of his gospel, and in a way that resonates richly with the water-walking episode. Again they knowingly "see" Jesus, but now it is in his risen state (28:17; see 14:26). Again, as in the becalmed boat, they *worship* Jesus (28:17; see 14:33). And again, remarkably, like the sinking "Rock," Peter, they *doubt* (expressed in a Greek word used only twice in the New Testament, *distazō*, 28:17; see 14:31). Yes, worship and doubt somehow coexist in the same persons. Evidently Matthew's audience was a people who understood Jesus and his teaching just fine but who were hesitant to act on that knowledge with a full, bold trust. When we take this theme back to its first occurrence in the Sermon (at 6:30), the implication is that the audience is urged to *act* on the understanding they are being given by throwing themselves into the community life as it is sketched right here in the Sermon. If they do that, they will experience the care of the Father through one another.[73]

LUKE ON WORRY AND THE KINGDOM

We have just wrestled with the Q sayings about anxiety over food, drink, and clothing and the priority of seeking the kingdom, and we came to recognize the importance of the context that Matthew supplies in his presentation of those teachings in his gospel. Luke, too, is wonderfully deliberate in his presentation of that same material. He treats the passage not in his Sermon on the Plain but as part of Jesus' teaching on the road to Jerusalem. He introduces the passage with an incident (the request to intervene in a fraternal dispute, 12:13-15) followed by a parable unique to the Third Gospel (the rich fool, verses 16-21), and ends it with a kingdom saying also unique to his gospel ("Your Father is pleased to give you the kingdom," verse 32) and heart and treasure sayings that parallel Matthew 6:19-21.

If the Q sayings about worrying over food, drink, and clothing seem to call for a lifestyle lacking in normal prudence and responsibility, Luke forestalls that misunderstanding by first addressing one of the most distracting preoccupations of all—*greed*, one of the ways that concern for personal needs can go wrong.

12:13Someone in the crowd said to him, "Teacher, tell my brother to share the inheritance with me." 14He replied to him, "Friend, who appointed me as your judge and arbitrator?" 15Then he said to the crowd, "Take care to guard against all greed, for though one may be rich, one's life does not consist of possessions."

In his usual way (see 15:1-3), Luke prepares for the teaching of a parable by providing a narrative setting in Jesus' ministry. The fraternal quarrel over inheritance raises the topic of greed and the question of the place of possessions in a person's life. With wonderful irony, Jesus' response—"Friend, who appointed me as your judge and arbitrator?"—echoes the question posed to Moses by his fellow Hebrews in Exodus 2:14 and included in Stephen's speech in Acts 7:35: "Who appointed you ruler and judge?"

¹²:¹⁶Then he told them a parable. "There was a rich man whose land produced a bountiful harvest."

The beginning of this parable is carefully phrased. Whatever contribution the landowner or his workers have made in the process of farming, it is indeed *the land*—a gift of God together with the God-given seeds, rain, and sunlight—that has produced the abundant harvest.

¹²:¹⁷"He asked himself, 'What shall I do, for I do not have space to store my harvest?' ¹⁸And he said, 'This is what I shall do: I shall tear down my barns and build larger ones. There I shall store all my grain and other goods ¹⁹and I shall say to myself, 'Now as for you [literally, "Self"], you have so many good things stored up for many years, rest, eat, drink, be merry!'"

Let us pause here a moment. Notice that the man sees the abundance of the harvest as a personal crisis of storage. His Jewish tradition would have taught him that as a landowner, he was a mere steward for the real owner, God; and his charge was to see that the land served the needs of all in the community. But he wants to grab it all for himself. The way his response is described is full of irony. In the very communal culture of the Mediterranean world, this man has no one to speak with but himself. The Greek text underscores his self-imposed isolation humorously. A more literal translation of verse 19 would be this: "And I shall say to myself, 'Self, . . .'" The only dialogue in this man's life is an interior dialogue, and he is so caught up with self-preoccupation that he addresses himself as "Self"! A final irony comes in the next verse, where he discovers that he is not as alone as he had thought. He has forgotten about the divine Presence!

¹²:²⁰"But God said to him, 'You fool, this night your life will be demanded of you; and the things you have prepared, to whom

will they belong?' ²¹Thus will it be for the one who stores up treasure for himself but is not rich in what matters to God."

What God says in verse 20 might more literally be translated, "Fool, this night *they will foreclose on this self of yours*; and the things you have stored up, to whom will they belong?"[74] Notice how this parable has put in narrative form the teaching we met in Matthew 6:19-21 (about treasuring up treasure and the location of one's heart), which Luke will place later in his gospel at 12:33. This little (and often neglected) parable is a masterpiece, sketching in four verses the image of a person whose greed has led him to break all of the covenant relationships:

- He has lost his sense of his relationship to the land, which he should steward for its ultimate owner, the Creator.
- He appears to have lost any connection with the community, his only dialogue partner being himself.
- He has no sense of his own life as a gift of God meant for the service of others.
- He has lost any awareness of his relationship to God as present to his life.

By introducing the Q sayings on anxiety regarding food, drink, and clothing in this manner, Luke has provided the framework for a special understanding of this teaching. Except for a few minor differences in wording, verses 22-30 record this teaching as it was expressed in Matthew 6:25-33. As in Matthew's version, a kingdom saying brings the teaching on anxiety into the ultimate perspective: *"Instead, seek his kingdom, and these other things will be given you besides"* (Luke 12:31). Matthew integrates the kingdom saying with his Sermon by linking it with his thematic word *dikaiosynē* ("righteousness"—the doing of God's will). Luke, on the other hand, integrates the kingdom saying with his own gospel in another way. He inserts the following verses:

> [12:32] "Do not be afraid any longer, little flock, *for your Father is pleased to give you the kingdom.* [33]Sell your belongings and give alms. Provide money bags for yourselves that do not wear out, an inexhaustible treasure in heaven that no thief can reach nor moth destroy. [34]For where your treasure is, there also will your heart be."

This assurance of the Father's gift of the kingdom resonates with several other passages unique to the Third Gospel and finds its fulfillment in Luke's second volume, the Acts of the Apostles:

1. At the Last Supper, Jesus confers on his disciples a kingdom such as his Father has conferred on him, so that "you may eat and drink at my table in my kingdom; and you will sit on thrones judging the twelve tribes of Israel" (Luke 22:30).

2. During his appearance to his disciples in Jerusalem after his resurrection, Jesus' final words are "And [behold] I am sending *the promise of my Father* upon you; but stay in the city until you are clothed with power from on high" (Luke 24:49). In the context of the Third Gospel, "the promise of my Father" entails both Luke 11:13 ("If you then, who are wicked, know how to give good gifts to your children, how much more will the Father in heaven give the holy Spirit to those who ask him?") and 22:28-30 (the conferral of the kingdom promised at the Last Supper). So "the promise" entails both Spirit and kingdom.

3. These threads come together at the beginning of Acts. Before the ascension, Jesus tells the apostles to "wait for '*the promise of the*

Father about which you have heard me speak; for John baptized with water, but in a few days you will be baptized with the holy Spirit'" (Acts 1:4-5). The Jerusalem community of Christians, drawn from Jews who have come from the Diaspora to celebrate Pentecost, is portrayed as the end-time restoration of Israel. The restored twelve apostles "judge" (in the Old Testament sense of exercising charismatic leadership like the twelve leaders in the book of Judges) the restored twelve tribes.

In the narrative framework of Luke–Acts, then, the Spirit-filled Christian community is a manifestation of the kingdom of God. It is in this context that the words of Luke 12 are to be understood. Thus, Luke teaches in his own way what Matthew teaches in the Sermon on the Mount. The freedom from concern about food, drink, and clothing entails no abdication of responsibility. It is a side effect of cooperating with the Spirit of God in the formation of community and the enterprise of continuing Jesus' mission.

CHAPTER 10

JUDGE NOT, BUT USE YOUR HEAD AND HEART

(MATTHEW 7:1-12 AND LUKE 6:31, 37-42; 11:9-32)

This chapter could be subtitled "hand-eye coordination." That phrase describes a basic skill that is part of human development, and here I want to apply it to the psycho-spiritual dimension that Jesus addresses in the Sermon when he uses imagery about the eye and heart. This imagery is biblical language for how we perceive or focus our attention (eye) and what is the root orientation of our desires and actions—habits of the heart. In one way or another, the whole Sermon has been about these fundamental relationships, and the next twelve verses continue the exploration.

MEASURE FOR MEASURE: VARIETIES OF JUDGMENT

7:1"Stop judging [*mē krinete*], that you [plural through verse 2] may not be judged. ²For as you judge, so will you be judged, and the measure with which you measure will be measured out to you. ³Why do you [singular through verse 5] notice the splinter in your brother's eye, but do not perceive the wooden beam in your own eye? ⁴How can you say to your brother 'Let me remove that splinter from your eye,' while the wooden beam is in your eye? ⁵You hypocrite, remove the wooden beam from your eye first; then you will see clearly to remove the splinter from your brother's eye."

The verb used here by Matthew, *krinō*, is as rich and various in meaning as the English word "judge." It can mean any of the following: make a selection, select, prefer; judge, pass judgment upon, express an opinion about, criticize, find fault with, condemn; think, consider, look upon; reach a decision, decide, propose, intend; engage in a judicial process (either in a human court or, in the passive voice, to be judged in the divine tribunal).[75] If we allow the immediate context to govern our understanding of the word in the first verse, the second clause (*"that you may not be judged"*) helps us understand what "judge" means in the first clause. The passive voice in "that you may not be judged" indicates an act of God. There is no way of avoiding the judgment of God in the sense of the divine evaluation of one's life in the final judgment, vividly portrayed in Matthew's gospel, for example, in the parables of "sorting out" the good and bad (13:30, weeds and wheat; 13:48, fish in the net; 25:1-13, wise and foolish virgins) and in the language of receiving reward—now or later—throughout the Sermon. No one escapes the divine judgment understood in this general sense. So the meaning intended in the words "that you may *not* be judged" must be the kind of judgment that one can hope to avoid: condemnation. It must be, then, that Godlike ultimate judgment that the first command (*"Stop judging!"*) forbids disciples. The sense would be "Do not presume to exercise that Godlike judgment (particularly condemnation) regarding your brother or sister." We can recognize here the same kind of divine-human reciprocity that was expressed in the statements about forgiveness in the Lord's Prayer ("Forgive us our trespasses as we forgive those who trespass against us") and its positive and negative reiteration in 6:14-15. It is also similar to the example at Matthew 5:23-24 (your worship of God is as good or as poor as your relationships with your fellow community members).

The second verse broadens that mandate to an even more general principle. *"As you judge, so you will be judged"* leaves an opening for a meaning of judging that is positive and merciful. Luke's parallel in his Sermon on the Plain expresses both the initial meaning and the positive possibilities in his version:

"Stop judging and you will not be judged. *Stop condemning and you will not be condemned. Forgive and you will be forgiven. Give and gifts will be given to you; a good measure, packed together, shaken down, and overflowing, will be poured into your lap.* For the measure with which you measure will in return be measured out to you." [Italics mine to indicate what is unique to Luke's version.] (Luke 6:37-38)

Luke has taken the image of a measuring scoop, presumably available in the text of Q, which he and Matthew are using independently, and has developed it into the picture of scooped grain being poured abundantly into a garment open on one's lap. While affirming the negative edge of the initial "measure for measure" saying, Luke has also made explicit, and expanded, the positive possibilities of being judged (by God) as one judges (other human beings).

It is interesting that Mark uses the "measure for measure" saying in a different context at 4:24, in connection with the "lamp on the lampstand, not under a bushel" saying in the midst of the three parables of growth. In this context what is being measured out seems to be the response to the word through mission. One receives light in the measure that one lets the light shine by passing it on.

Matthew's text continues in verses 3-5 with the wonderful and famous parabolic image of a person noticing and offering to remove a splinter from a brother's eye and not noticing the *wooden beam* in his own. The humorously exaggerated language matches the hyperbolic metaphors in other sayings of Jesus. Consider, for example, the one about straining out the gnat and swallowing the camel (23:24), or the warning to the rich at 19:24—"It is easier for a camel to pass through the eye of a needle than for one who is rich to enter the kingdom of God." The Sermon on the Mount itself contains other examples of hyperbole, including the following: "If your right eye causes you to sin, tear it out and throw it away" (5:29).

Verse 5 brings two surprises. First, the application of the term "hypocrite" to a member of the community ("your brother") is startling and reminds us that even fellow members of the community can act hypocritically with respect to one another. Second, note the conclusion: If you attend to the beam in your own eye first, *"then you will see clearly to remove the splinter from your brother's eye."* This conclusion allows for the kind of prudential judgment that *can* be exercised lovingly ("remove the splinter") provided one has humbly dealt with one's own faults.

This passage is a good reminder of something often observed regarding human nature: The flaws we most easily detect in others are often the very flaws that others see in us. The next saying vividly takes the matter of perceptions to another dimension.

DOGS AND SWINE

7:6"Do not give [plural] what is holy to dogs, or throw your pearls before swine, lest they trample them under foot, and turn and tear you to pieces."

In the biblical cultures, dogs (because strays are generally unclean) and pigs (because they were legally impure) easily became derogatory terms for outsiders and "others." Think of Jesus' (playful?) characterization of gentiles as "dogs" (Matthew 15:26-27; Jesus' word to the Canaanite woman, *kynarion*, the diminutive, suggesting house dog as opposed to street dog). Or consider Paul's dismissive epithet in Philippians 3:2 for his "Judaizing" rival Christian missionaries: "Beware of the dogs!" Or Revelation 22:15, referring to those excluded from the heavenly Jerusalem, which states, "Outside are the dogs, the sorcerers, the unchaste, the murderers, the idol-worshipers, and all who love and practice deceit." As for pigs, they are *the* primary unclean animal in Hebrew dietary law. Most of us can recognize that the names of these animals still serve as insulting terms across cultures. Indeed, this very text may have helped popularize "pig" and "dog" as terms of abuse.

Standing alone, the saying of 7:6 has a proverbial ring and is applicable to a variety of situations. For example, *Didache* 9:5 applies it to a circumstance obviously different from Matthew's context, the Eucharist. After quoting a prayer of thanksgiving used in the Christian ritual of the Lord's Supper, this early Christian text concludes: "But let no one eat or drink of your Eucharist except those who have been baptized into the name of the Lord, for the Lord has also spoken concerning this: 'Do not give what is holy to dogs.'" Simply reading that application and then returning to the source, Matthew 7:6, helps one realize that the context of Matthew 7:6 gives the saying a different meaning. Following upon the delicate advice about fraternal correction, the point seems to be something like "Make sure you don't offer your 'pearls' of fraternal correction to the unready or the unwilling. You could open yourself to disaster."[76] If it seems extreme to use the metaphors "holy things" or "pearls" to describe one's insights into the kind of correction a brother or sister needs, recall the hyperbole of the wooden beam in the eye. A little human experience reveals that attempting to improve those close to us is always a delicate and dangerous matter.

If we continue to take Matthew's context seriously and not treat the "pearls before swine" saying as a free-floating maxim that bears no connection to its present setting, we have to acknowledge that it takes *some* kind of judgment to call (at least mentally) another person a dog or a pig. If there is any coherence in verses 1-6, the judgment forbidden in verse 1 (*"Stop judging!"*) is not the prudential judgment of intelligent human interaction. What is forbidden is the judgment of condemnation (something only God can do accurately).

It is also possible that in Matthew 7:6, the strong language of "pig" and "dog" may refer to those outside of the community, whose spiritual blindness and hardness of heart may render them thoroughly resistant to the word of the gospel (like the people referred to in Jesus' mission speech: "Whoever will not receive you or listen to your words . . . "—10:14). If so, the point may be something like this: "Do not judge. Do not be arrogant and hypocritical in your prudential judgments about your brother and sisters in the community. But do indeed use your judgment in your interaction with those *outside* the community. Try to share the gospel with all, to be sure, but when you encounter hardened hearts and total resistance, *'Don't throw your pearls before swine.'*"[77]

Regarding this delicate matter of making judgments about other people, especially about what they say, St. Ignatius of Loyola provides an important bit of Christian wisdom early in his *Spiritual Exercises*. As he begins his instructions for what he calls the First Week of the exercises, he states something he calls "Presupposition":

That both the giver and the maker of the Spiritual Exercises may be of greater help and benefit to each other, it should be presupposed that every good Christian ought to be more eager to put a good interpretation on a neighbor's statement than to condemn it. Further, if one cannot interpret it favorably, one should ask how the other means it. If that meaning is wrong, one should correct the person with love; and if this is not enough, one should search out every appropriate means through which, by understanding the statement in a good way, it may be saved.[78]

Ignatius may have included this principle in his printed edition of *The Spiritual Exercises* to remind officials of the Inquisition to exercise Christian charity when they inspected his writings for possible heresy. But the presupposition is universally applicable to any human communication, especially among those committed to love of neighbor and, yes, even to love of enemies. Our own age does not lack those who would operate from a posture and presupposition of "more orthodox than thou."

LUKE'S TAKE ON JUDGING OTHERS
AND DIVINE RECIPROCITY

Luke's version of Jesus' teaching of judgment comes with a different emphasis. Whether he finds this difference in his source, Q, or whether he provides it in his redaction, the important thing is to hear this text on its own terms. As Luke's text, it is Luke's voice as he interprets the Jesus tradition for his audience. For the purpose of our study, I will italicize the parts that differ significantly from Matthew's parallel.

6:37 "Stop judging and you will not be judged. *Stop condemning and you will not be condemned. Forgive and you will be forgiven. ³⁸Give and gifts will be given to you; a good measure, packed together, shaken down, and overflowing, will be poured into your lap.* For the measure with which you measure will in return be measured out to you."

If there was any ambiguity regarding the meaning of "judge not" in Matthew's parallel to verse 37, Luke's understanding that it refers to the judgment of condemnation comes through clearly in verse 37b. He then asserts the opposite of condemnation: "Forgive and you will be forgiven." Matthew's gospel emphasizes this theme in its own way through the expansion of the Lord's Prayer and the parable of the unforgiving servant in chapter 18. For Luke, the emphasis comes here, in the Sermon on the Plain. The NAB translation of the first part of the next verse, "Give and gifts will be given to you," sounds like a reference to generosity in general, as in "Whatever way you are generous to others, God will reward you even more generously." A more literal translation of that clause, "Give, and it will be given to you," could be understood as a development of the call to forgiveness. In either case, the rest of the verse describes the reciprocal forgiveness (or generosity) of God in a lovely metaphor of abundance: a gift of grain poured out into an apron. In that context, the "measure for measure" saying has a different connotation than its parallel in Matthew (7:2b). In Matthew's Sermon the saying comes as a *warning* that you will experience from God the judgment that you render to others. In Luke's context, following upon the "grain in the lap" image, the "measure for measure" saying comes as a *promise*: Your generous forgiveness to others will be more than reciprocated in God's generosity to you. The text of Luke's Sermon on the Plain continues:

> 6:39And he told them a parable, "Can a blind person guide a blind person? Will not both fall into a pit? 40No disciple is superior to the teacher; but when fully trained, every disciple will be like his teacher."

These two verses are Q sayings, which Matthew parallels in quite different contexts, applying the "blind guides" image to the Pharisees at Matthew 15:14 and applying the disciple/teacher saying as a warning to the disciples about the rejection and persecution they will have to face. Luke apparently draws the sayings into the Sermon on the Plain here as an introduction to material on moving the beam from your own eye before dealing with the splinter in your brother's eye. The teacher/disciple saying serves to remind disciples that in matters of judging, forgiving, and fraternal correction, Jesus himself is the model. The saying about the beam in your eye and the splinter in your brother's eye (verses 41 and 42) parallels almost exactly

Matthew 7:3-5. Any difference in tone comes from context. Luke's passage on generous forgiveness and the model of Jesus as the Teacher ensures that the eye-clearing procedure is done in the right spirit. But Matthew's insertion of the Golden Rule immediately after his version should have a similar effect.

AGAIN, PRAY! YOUR HEAVENLY FATHER CARES

7:7 "Ask and it will be given to you; seek and you will find; knock and the door will be opened to you. 8For everyone who asks, receives; and the who seeks, finds; and to one who knocks, the door will be opened. 9Which one of you would hand his son a stone when he asks for a loaf or bread, 10or a snake when he asks for a fish? 11If you then, who are wicked, know how to give good gifts [*domata agatha*] to your children, how much more will your heavenly Father give good things [*agatha*] to those who ask him."

Someone looking for order and design in the Sermon on the Mount may wonder why this teaching on prayer in Matthew 7:7-11 was placed there. Why did Matthew not place this teaching with the passage on the Lord's Prayer as Luke did (possibly keeping it where he may have found it in Q)? The careful arrangement that we have found in the editing of the Sermon up to this point does indeed encourage us to ask this kind of question. In fact, there is a plausible way of seeing design in the ordering of 7:1-11. It has been observed that 7:1-11 is the structural twin of 6:19-34.

Matthew 6:19-34 has one subject (the appropriate Christian attitude toward material goods) treated in four parts:

1. A thesis (store up heavenly, not earthly treasure, verses 19-21), with two metaphorical illustrations;

2. Sound eye versus evil eye (verses 22-23);

3. The two masters, God and mammon (verse 24); and

4. An encouragement regarding God's care with two illustrations—God's feeding of the birds and his clothing of the fields with flowers (verses 25-34).

Similarly, Matthew 7:1-11 has a primary subject (the appropriate Christian attitude toward persons) treated in four parts:

1. A thesis (as you judge, so you will be judged, verses 1-2), with two metaphorical illustrations;

2. Deal with the plank in your own eye before you try to deal with the splinter in your brother's eye (verses 3-5);

3. Don't give holy things to dogs or throw pearls before swine (verse 6); and

4. An encouragement regarding God's care, illustrated with two examples of a human father's care for his children that God surely surpasses—bread, not stone; fish, not snake (verses 7-11).[79]

Had Matthew kept verses 7-11 close to the teaching of the Lord's Prayer, the speech would have lost the power it has within the present design. Whether or not we attend to the design, the arrangement teaches some important relationships: Just as a proper relationship to the *things* of creation requires that we relate trustingly to the Creator of all in our desires (the kingdom first!—6:19-34), so a proper relationship to other *persons* requires that we *pray* trustingly to our caring Father (7:1-11).

The clarity and power of this teaching is such that it hardly needs any commentary. Jesus asks his audience to examine their experience. This audience was mainly if not entirely male, because in that patriarchal culture, women were largely absent from public forums such as the one pictured in Matthew 5–7 ("the mountain"). What father does not recognize that no matter how flawed his character, he will surely look after the needs of his children? If this is true of you, how much more of the Father who is God? For contemporary Christians, "Father" can simply be the name of the first person of the Trinity. Jesus, however, wants his followers to take the implications of calling God "Father" quite seriously and as the term "Father" is understood in his social context. Matthew, Mark, and Luke each testify that Jesus used the kinship language of "brother," "sister," and "mother" to denote the new kind of "family" that came about when people accepted his teaching of the will of God as Father. Only to the extent that they become brother and sister of Jesus will they come to know the Creator as Father and themselves as adopted children of God.

Luke's Version

We have already noted that Luke places this teaching, quite naturally, close to his account of Jesus' teaching of the Lord's Prayer to his disciples on the road to Jerusalem, in chapter 11. Note also that the teaching follows immediately after the parable about the hospitality at midnight and the availability of bread (Luke 11:5-8).

When we compare Luke's version as it parallels Matthew 7:7-11, we notice that along with much similarity in wording, Luke differs from Matthew's version in two interesting ways. First, while both give the example about the fish ("What father among you would hand his son a snake when he asks for a fish?"—Luke 11:11; par. Matthew 7:10), they join this common example with different second examples. Matthew 7:9 says, "Which one of you would hand his son a *stone* when he asks for a *loaf of bread*?" while Luke writes, "Or hand him a *scorpion* when he asks for an *egg*?" The difference could simply lie in their use of variant versions of Q, but it is also possible that Luke has just introduced an entire parable focused on bread as the primary image (verses 5-8) and so provides an alternative to the bread-not-stone saying.

The second significant difference in Luke's version is the language he uses for the heavenly Father's gift. Where Matthew writes, "If you then, who are wicked, know how to give good gifts to your children, how much more will your heavenly Father give *good things* to those who ask him" (7:11), Luke's version says, "How much more will the Father in heaven give *the holy Spirit* to those who ask him?" (11:13). Luke's naming of the Holy Spirit as possibly the most desirable gift supports Luke's special emphasis on the Holy Spirit as the way the Father animates both the life and ministry of Jesus and the mission of the church as narrated in the Acts of the Apostles. When the risen Jesus speaks to his disciples about the coming fulfillment of "the promise of my Father" (Luke 24:49 and Acts 1:4), that promise entails both the Holy Spirit (Luke 11:13 and Acts 1:5) and the kingdom (Luke 12:32 and 22:28-30). This fulfillment is inaugurated during the feast of Pentecost (Acts 2).

THE GOLDEN RULE

[7:12]"Do to others whatever you would have them do to you. This is the law and the prophets."

Because of its presence in the Sermon on the Mount and because of its summary nature and simplicity of expression, this is one of the best known of Jesus' teachings. Commentators often note a parallel in extrabiblical Jewish tradition, a passage from the Babylonian Talmud attributed to Hillel: "What is hateful to you, do not do to your neighbor; that is the whole Torah, while the rest is commentary thereon; go and learn it" (*b. Shabbat* 31a).[80] Some, straining to find novelty in Jesus' teaching, point out that Jesus takes a traditional proverb expressed negatively (as here by Hillel) and puts it positively. But one can find in Scripture itself positive expressions of what is essentially the same teaching. Most obviously, there is Leviticus 19:18b, which Jesus teaches as the second greatest commandment, after the *Shema*: "You shall love your neighbor as yourself" (Matthew 22:39). And Sirach 31:15 says, "Recognize that your neighbor feels as you do, / and keep in mind your own dislikes."[81]

The truth of Jesus' teaching does not rest on its novelty. At the same time, the context of this teaching in the Sermon on the Mount shows that it is not simply to be taken in a flat "horizontal" sense, meaning simply that human-to-human relationships are what Christian faith is all about. By stating that "this is the law and the prophets" (7:12), Jesus ensures that the saying is understood in the context of a covenant with God. This covenant relationship is what enables people to understand and live out human relationships as part of their relationship with the Creator and his creatures. What is more, the rest of the Sermon teaches that this doing unto others entails love of enemies.

Missing in the NAB translation on the opposite page is a rendering of the Greek particle *oun* at the beginning of the verse, which means "therefore" or "so." This signals that the saying somehow follows upon what precedes it. Does the Golden Rule follow in a consequential way on the teaching that prayer will be answered? This reading does not seem obvious. It makes more sense to note that it really harks all the way back to 5:17: "Do not think that I have come to abolish the law or the prophets. I have come not to abolish but to fulfill," which introduces the passage on the greater righteousness, which in turn introduces 5:21–7:11, the great center of the Sermon that spells out exactly the behavior that greater righteousness entails. So the Golden Rule is a summary of that whole central section—the six antitheses, the teaching on the proper way to carry out the three major practices of piety, and the teachings on worry and judgment informed by trust in a caring God.

Luke's placement of the Golden Rule is striking—right in the center of his Sermon on the Plain at 6:31: "Do to others as you would have them do to you." Whether Luke placed it there or found it there in Q, the placement is telling. In the Sermon on the Plain, the location of the Golden Rule in the middle of the teaching on love of enemies (given *twice* in Luke's Sermon, at verses 27 and 35!) has powerful implications. It means that the way to love enemies is to place ourselves in their shoes—something for which most of us need the "outside help" that comes from prayer!

Chapter 11

Do What You Hear!

(Matthew 7:13-27 and Luke 6:43-49)

Having laid out the essentials of the Way of Jesus, Matthew uses three images from Jesus' sayings that dramatize the importance and wisdom of actually choosing to carry out this vision of Christian community, the life of the new covenant. The challenge of living this commitment is illustrated by three contrasts: the way to life versus the way of death; the fruitfulness of the true prophet as opposed to the ultimate failure of the false prophet; and the wise person who builds on rock as contrasted with the fool who builds on sand. Each set of contrasting images teaches the community something about the challenges to be faced and the urgency of acting on the vision that Jesus outlines.

The Two Ways

7:13 "Enter through the narrow gate; for the gate is wide and the road [hē hodos] broad that leads to destruction, and those who enter through it are many. 14How narrow the gate and constricted the road [hē hodos] that leads to life. And those who find it are few."

For contemporary North Americans, the translation "road" suggests a paved street, which may be a bit too concrete (no pun intended) to do justice to an image that means to suggest a "way of life," a notion better captured by "way" or "path." Whether we are to imagine a path that leads to a gate or a gate that opens to a path may be a false dilemma, since "path" and "gate" may be synonymous. In the

Fourth Gospel, Jesus speaks of himself both as the gate (of the sheep-fold, John 10:7) and the way (14:6).

The idea that a religious master teaches a *way* or *path* to life and light is common through the ages and across cultures, and this is true of the Hebrew Bible and Christianity. For example, Psalm 1—the gate, as it were, to the book of Psalms—contrasts delighting in the law of the Lord (associated with fruitfulness and fullness of life) with walking the way of sinners (associated with infertility and the impermanence of windblown chaff). The idea that life entails a profound choice between two ways—one leading to life, the other leading to disaster—is frequent in the Old Testament. See, for example, Deuteronomy 11:26 ("blessing" or "curse"); 30:15 ("life and prosperity" or "death and doom"); Jeremiah 21:8 ("a choice between life and death"); and Wisdom 5:6-7 ("the way of truth" versus "the light of justice," and "the way of the LORD" versus "the ways of mischief"). The manual of discipline used by the Essenes employs the image of the two ways. The *Didache* sets out Christian practice as a way of life as opposed to the way of death in its first six chapters.

All three synoptic gospels introduce John the Baptist by citing Isaiah 40:3: "Prepare the way [*tēn hodon*] of the LORD." Mark structures a whole section of his gospel—sometimes called "the way of discipleship" because Jesus instructs his disciples on the nature of his messiahship and what it means to follow him (Mark 8:27–10:52)—by punctuating this section with references to the "way" seven times (8:27; 9:33-34; 10:17, 32, 46, 52).[82] Mark's framing of this discipleship section with two cures of blindness is a way of illustrating the fact that any would-be follower of Jesus is spiritually blind until he understands that Jesus is not a warrior messiah but a Suffering Servant, as in Isaiah. To follow him is to walk the same road to Jerusalem in one's own life. This is a theme all four evangelists explore, each in his own manner.

Although Matthew does not carry over from Mark exactly these references, he does develop the "way" theme in his own style. Besides the "two ways" saying under consideration, the Sermon evokes the "way" image in the little parable of settling with one's opponent "on the way" (5:25). That detail is surely a reference to the pilgrimage of one's life on the way to final judgment: Your lifetime is a once-only opportunity for reconciliation with your fellow human beings; settle up on the way, and your way will be the way of Jesus!

Matthew touches both the "way" theme and his special emphasis on righteousness when he (uniquely) has Jesus describe John the Baptist as having come "in the way of righteousness" at 21:32. Even his adversaries, the Pharisees' disciples and the Herodians in this case, can (hypocritically, but with ironic accuracy) refer to Jesus teaching truthfully "the way of God" (22:16; par. Mark 12:14).

When Matthew narrates Jesus' third passion/resurrection prediction, Jesus speaks to the twelve "on the way" (20:17). After the two sons of Zebedee approach Jesus (through their mother!) to request the top spots next to Jesus in his kingdom, Jesus sets them straight (along with the other ten disciples) regarding the nature of true discipleship—it's about service, not about making one's authority felt (20:20-28). Then Matthew revises the account of the healing of blind Bartimaeus by telling instead of "*two* blind men" who are "sitting by the roadside" (20:30). In this passage Matthew underscores Mark's "way of discipleship" theme by doubling the blind man, perhaps to match the two Zebedee brothers and suggest that the worldly notion of discipleship implied in their ambition was a case of temporary blindness. And may the readers seek healing if they recognize that they suffer a similar spiritual blindness! Indeed, all who would enter by the narrow gate need such a healing from blindness if they are to follow the way of Jesus.

Luke, too, is fully aware of this theme of the way. Most important, he expands Mark's one-chapter journey (10) of Jesus and his followers into an extended central section of his gospel, from 9:51 to 18:14, placing there much of Jesus' teaching on discipleship (including, for example, the Lord's Prayer, in Luke 11). When Luke presents the story of the early church in the Acts of the Apostles, he shows that a common name for the Christian movement was "the Way [hē hodos]"; see Acts 9:2; 16:17 ("a way of salvation"); 18:25-26 ("the Way of the Lord"); 19:9, 23; 22:4; and 24:14, 22. All of this provides a context that lends depth to the "two ways" image embodied in Matthew 7:13-14. It is a way of expressing what contemporary theologians call the "fundamental option" that underlies the living out of a mature life.

TRUE AND FALSE PROPHETS

[7:15] "Beware of false prophets [pseudoprophētōn], who come to you in sheep's clothing, but underneath are ravenous wolves. [16]By their fruits you will know them. Do people pick grapes from thornbushes, or figs from thistles? [17]Just so, every good tree bears good fruit, and a rotten tree bears bad fruit. [18]A good tree cannot bear bad fruit, nor can a rotten tree bear good fruit. [19]Every tree that does not bear good fruit will be cut down and thrown into the fire. [20]So by their fruits you will know them.

[21]"Not everyone who says to me, 'Lord, Lord,' will enter the kingdom of heaven, but only the one who does the will of my Father in heaven. [22]Many will say to me on the that day, 'Lord, Lord, did we not prophesy [eprophēteusomen] in your name? Did we not drive out demons in your name? Did we not do mighty deeds in your name?' [23]Then I will declare to them solemnly, 'I never knew you. Depart from me, you evildoers.'"

Having addressed the audience of disciples and crowds directly with "you" plural in the Golden Rule ("Do unto others . . ."), that is, calling *them* to do something, the discourse moves to a mandate that seems to focus on *others* (*"Beware of false prophets"*). This is a powerful rhetorical strategy. The listener (or reader) is led at first to think of the consequences of *other people's* behavior: Like good trees or bad trees, people produce deeds, good or bad, that reflect their interior dispositions. So pay attention only to prophets who practice what they preach. Simple enough so far, and not particularly challenging to the audience, but then comes the kicker. The statements made by the "hypothetical" speakers in verses 21 and 22 turn out to be awfully familiar. In fact, they are saying things only plausible among the followers of Jesus. Who else would call Jesus "Lord"? Who else would prophesy, drive out demons, and do mighty works in the name of Jesus? Only insiders—Christians.

Once the audience recognizes that these are Christians speaking, they (we) have to ask why they deserve to be told *"I never knew you. Depart from me, you evildoers."* The answer can only be that they are the pseudoprophets described in the previous verses, who are fruitless and rotten trees, fit to be cut down and thrown into the fire. And if the audience (and we readers) wonder what makes for rottenness and fruitlessness, verses 24-27 make it perfectly clear: the fruitless false prophets who fail to do *"the will of my Father in heaven"* (verse 21) and everyone "who listens to *these words of mine* but does not act on them" (verse 26). At this point anyone with a ten-minute attention span recalls that the final beatitude at the head of this Sermon calls the followers of Jesus "prophets." Stunningly, the voices of the people who speak of prophesying, casting out demons, and doing mighty deeds in Jesus' name are disciples who carry out a charismatic ministry but fail to live the way of life taught in the Sermon.

Taken together, the sayings in this passage present a radical challenge, especially to persons who have a special role of ministry in the church. These teachings present a scenario in which one can have an effective ministry (the speakers can correctly claim to have prophesied, driven out demons, and done mighty deeds) and yet fail utterly in the eyes of Jesus. Fruitfulness entails the way of life sketched in the rest of the Sermon. This means embodying the beatitudes; practicing the greater righteousness by curbing anger and lust and through sexual fidelity, straightforward speech, nonviolent response to hostility, and love of enemies; practicing almsgiving, prayer, and fasting not for show but for the Father who sees in secret; and refraining from "playing God" in one's appraisal of others. In doing these things, one does the will of the heavenly Father as taught by Jesus. When that community life is lived faithfully, ministries of prophecy, deliverance from evil spirits, and the doing of mighty deeds have their place in the fuller context of the covenant life.

If we wonder how Matthew can think of false prophets as members of the intimate family of the church, we have only to recall that this same gospel presents pictures of a community of "good" and "bad" that will require a final divine sorting out. These include the parable of the weeds and the wheat ("Let them grow together until harvest," 13:30); the parable of the net ("The angels will go out and separate the wicked from the righteous," 13:49); and the parable of the wedding feast ("The servants went out into the streets and gathered all they found, bad and good alike, and the hall was filled with guests," 22:10). Many of the passages in the Gospel of Matthew are a kind of "wake-up call" addressed to an apparently complaisant community that needed to be reminded that mere membership in the group was not enough. God would judge all according to how they lived out what they had learned and professed. The final parable, about the two kinds of builders, will drive this message home.

LUKE'S TAKE ON GOOD AND BAD DEEDS AND WORDS AS FRUIT OF THE HEART

Both Matthew and Luke seem to work from material in the Q sermon about judging a tree by its fruit (Matthew 7:20 and Luke 6:44).

Matthew elaborates that idea with other Q sayings about true and false prophets; Luke focuses more simply on the reality that what people do and say flows from the kind of persons they have become— what we today call virtue ethics, which focuses more on character and its formation than on discrete acts. Without indulging in the fascinating guesswork of imagining Luke's rewriting process, let us simply read Luke's expression on its own terms:

> [6:43] "A good tree does not bear rotten fruit, nor does a rotten tree bear good fruit. [44]For every tree is known by its own fruit. For people do not pick figs from thornbushes, nor do they gather grapes from brambles. [45]A good person out of the store of goodness *in his heart* produces good, but an evil person out of a store of evil produces evil; for from the fullness of the heart the mouth speaks.
>
> [46]"Why do you call me, 'Lord, Lord,' but not do what I command?"

Like Matthew, Luke is careful to show Jesus' emphasis on the quality of an individual's *heart*, the core orientation of the person's relationships to God, to other persons, and to other creatures. The expression of verse 45 has the advantage of being applicable to both deeds and words. The repetition of "heart" [*kardia*] in this verse picks up a theme that is important to Luke throughout his gospel. The angel of the Lord describes the future mission of John the Baptist in words borrowed from Malachi 3:24: "to turn the hearts of fathers toward children" (Luke 1:17). The Magnificat speaks of the Mighty One scattering "the arrogant of mind and heart" (1:51). Mary is said to ponder things "in her heart" after key moments—after the visit of the shepherds in Bethlehem (2:19) and after finding the child Jesus in the temple (2:50). For Luke, encounter with Jesus reveals "thoughts of the heart"—see 2:35 ("so that the thoughts of many hearts may be revealed"); 5:22 (to the scribes and Pharisees, "What are you thinking in your hearts?" when Jesus forgives the paralytic); and 9:47 (Jesus perceives the rivalry in the hearts of his disciples). In his version of the explanation of the parable of the sower, Luke names the *heart* as the locus of the rejection or reception of the word of God; regarding the nonreceptive, the devil "takes away the word from their hearts" (8:12), and the receptive are said to "embrace [the word] with a generous and good *heart*" (8:15). Jesus warns, "Beware that your hearts do not become drowsy from carousing and drunkenness and the anxieties of daily life, and that day catch you by surprise like a trap" (21:34-35). (See also 24:25, 32, 38 regarding the responses of the disciples to the risen Lord.) The heart theme continues in Acts; for example, Luke says of Lydia that she "listened, and the Lord opened her heart to pay attention to what Paul was saying" (16:14). Like Matthew, Luke insists that the Christian life has a great deal to do with the habits of the heart, and those habits, traditionally called virtues, are delicate interactions of the grace of God (who "opened her heart") and the freedom of human response (she "listened").

Luke 6:46—"*Why do you call me, 'Lord, Lord,' but not do what I command?*"—introduces a parable that illustrates the folly of such behavior (the one who builds a house without a foundation). But notice that it also makes a fitting conclusion to the section on deeds and words flowing from the heart; words that are not supported by deeds betray a faulty heart, no matter how good the words sound.

THE WISE AND FOOLISH BUILDERS IN MATTHEW

Just as Matthew and Luke both reflect what they found in the Q version of the Sermon, beginning with a set of beatitudes emphasizing nonviolence and love of enemies and touching on judgment and integrity of heart, both also end with the parable of the two kinds of builders. Let us first consider Matthew's rendition:

7:24"**Everyone who listens to these words of mine and acts on them will be like a wise man who built his house on rock.**"

Already the essential meaning of the parable is available in the first verse. Everyone who carries out the teaching of Jesus taught in the Sermon on the Mount is like a person building his or her house on a solid foundation. In using this image of a house, Jesus draws upon what has been identified as one of the archetypal symbols of the human imagination. Dream analysts claim that when we dream about a house, the house symbolizes ourselves and mirrors our sense of the condition of our lives. Thus, an orderly house reflects a sense that our life is well ordered, and a disorderly house reflects a disorderly life. A flimsy or ill-constructed house symbolizes the awareness of one's vulnerability and a sense of being threatened by circumstances. Conversely, a solid house reflects a sense of security and strength. So as in the process of *construction*, a house becomes a powerful image of the whole project of one's life. Into that scenario Jesus introduces the idea that living according to the teaching of the Sermon is to build one's house on the most solid foundation possible—which is to say that living the vision of the Sermon is the way to meet the deep human need for security.

When one reflects on the contents of the Sermon—with its praising of meekness, mercy, and being persecuted for the sake of righteousness, and its advocacy of nonviolence, love of enemies, forgiveness, and utter dependence on God—they do not, on the face of it, look like strategies for achieving security. Indeed, they are the opposite of the world's way of seeking security. But is this not precisely the paradox that Jesus explicitly teaches twice in this gospel? Teaching about discipleship, Jesus says to the twelve, "Whoever finds his life will lose it, and whoever loses his life for my sake will find it" (10:39). Again, after the first prediction of his passion and resurrection, Jesus says to his disciples, "Whoever wishes to come after me must deny himself, take up his cross, and follow me. For whoever wishes to save his life will lose it, but whoever loses his life for my sake will find it. What profit would there be for one to gain the whole world and forfeit his life? Or what can one give in exchange for his life?" (16:24-26). We continue the parable:

> [7:25]"The rain fell, the floods came, and the winds blew and buffeted the house. But it did not collapse; it had been set solidly on rock."

And what do the rain, the floods, and the winds represent in this context? What threatens the construction of the house of one's life? It is reasonable for a reader of this gospel to think of what it is that threatens the growth of the plants springing from the seeds of the word of God in the parable of the sower (13:1-23). The threats in that parable are the things symbolized by the rapacious birds, the scorching sun, and the constricting thornbushes—temptations of the evil one, tribulation and persecution, and worldly anxiety and the lure of riches (verses 20-22).

> [7:26]"And everyone who listens to these words of mine but does not act on them will be like a fool who built his house on sand. [27]The rain fell, the floods came, and the winds blew and buffeted the house. And it collapsed and was completely ruined."

Had the parable ended at verse 25, the audience would have heard a complete message, one of profound encouragement: Put these teachings into practice and, paradoxical as it may seem, you will find the security that you desire; seek first the kingdom of God, and everything else you need will be given as well. If verses 24-25 offer a complete message of encouragement, verses 26-27 present the opposite: The fate of a person who hears but does not do is a sharp warning that such a life is not simply sad; it is utter disaster. This is very much in line with the judgment theme of this gospel that presents a stark contrast between the two possibilities of a human life, salvation and its opposite, what we have come to call damnation. While Jesus did not use that word or its Semitic equivalent, his imagery is clear enough. Think of the fates of the wise and foolish virgins, welcomed into the party or locked out (25:1-13). Or think of those who ministered to the hungry and the thirsty and those who did not (25:31-46). The first heard "Inherit the kingdom" (25:34); the second, "Depart from me" (25:25-41). The message throughout the Sermon is that the Father's gift of life entails a profound choice (sometimes called a "fundamental option"), according to which one's life will result either in fulfillment or in catastrophe.

Luke's Version of the Wise and Foolish Builders

6:47"I will show you what someone is like who comes to me, listens to my words, and acts on them. 48That one is like a person building a house, who dug deeply and laid the foundation on rock; when the flood came, the river burst against that house but could not shake it because it had been well built. 49But the one who listens and does not act is like a person who built a house on the ground without a foundation. When the river burst against it, it collapsed at once and was completely destroyed."

As we might expect, Luke's account of Jesus' life and teaching carries the same basic message, but in its own way. We saw how his treatment of the beatitudes balanced four congratulatory blessings with four corresponding and opposite "woes." If Matthew is content to provide nine positive beatitudes at the head of his version of the inaugural Sermon, he is careful to give his audience a series of seven "woes" prior to the fifth and final speech of his gospel (see 23:13-36).

Is there anything to be learned from a comparative scrutiny of Luke's version of the parable of the two builders? While the message and its expression are virtually the same, some differences are worth noticing.

1. Luke's version of the "Lord, Lord" saying provides a powerful introduction: "Why do you call me, 'Lord, Lord,' but not do what I command?" (6:46). In Matthew, the failure was not to do "the will of my Father who is in heaven" (Matthew 7:21). And then Matthew makes it clear, three verses later, that Jesus' teachings are expressions of the will of the Father. Luke's way of phrasing it ("what I command") focuses immediately Jesus' authoritative mediation of the Father's will.

2. Luke's description of the work of the prudent builder is more complicated, involving digging deeply and laying a foundation (*themelion*) on the rock, and the survival of the house is attributed to being "well built" (*dia to kalōs oikodomēsthai*) rather than to being founded on the rock. Similarly, the work of the imprudent builder involves building "on the ground without a foundation," thus putting the emphasis more on the foundation, or lack thereof. These details of Luke may well reflect the local geology and building practices familiar to him (or his source).

3. If these differences are due to the Q source, it is clear that Matthew has simplified the details and thus sharpened and simplified the contrast between the wise and foolish builders by making the difference a matter of building on rock and building on sand, leaving aside any distractions about the quality of the structure or the presence or lack of a foundation (separate from rock or earth).

In any case, there is no missing the import of this parabolic ending of the Sermon as both Matthew and Luke present it. The teaching of Jesus presented in this Sermon—especially the call to nonviolence and love of enemies (climactic in Matthew's antitheses and central in Luke's version of the Sermon)—is not a mandate addressed only to the heroic few; it is the very heart of Jesus' moral vision and of what it means to follow him. Moreover, this teaching is not a special set of religious practices; it is a blueprint for participating in the reign of God and living human life fully.

CHAPTER 12

POSTBIBLICAL RESPONSES TO JESUS' TEACHING ON NONVIOLENCE

A BRIEF HISTORY OF A DEVELOPING TRADITION

When we take the long retrospective view of Christian practice, it becomes clear that few have seriously doubted that Jesus advocated nonviolence for his followers in their personal daily lives. Where the teaching becomes a matter of doubt and debate is with respect to the larger context of public life, especially participation in war-making. This is a story worth trying to tell, even briefly. Here is how I summarize this fascinating development.

In his teaching about nonviolence and love of enemies in the Sermon, Jesus makes no explicit reference to participation in military service. In the first century, of course, military service was not an issue for Jews living under Roman occupation. As for the question of armed *resistance* against the empire, there is no indication in the gospels that Jesus advocated armed revolt. His lament over Jerusalem's failure to recognize "what makes for peace" and his prediction of Rome's destruction of the city suggest quite the opposite (Luke 19:40-44). Moreover, the examples Jesus uses to illustrate his teaching on nonviolence and love of enemies present interpersonal scenarios, not international conflicts.

It was inevitable, however, that postbiblical Christians would eventually have to deal with the issues of military service and the use of military force to address international conflicts. These issues are of such importance in our day that we would be remiss if we did not reflect on the various ways that people—Christians and non-Christians—have applied Jesus' teaching to questions of war and peace.

The Paradoxical Portrait of Jesus: A Nonviolent Messiah

To a people expecting a warrior messiah like David, Jesus came preaching the advent of the long-awaited "kingdom of God"—this to a people living under the occupation of the "kingdom" or empire of Caesar, recently Augustus, currently Tiberius, and for Matthew and Luke, most likely Caesar Domitian. After Jesus' death by Roman crucifixion and his resurrection by the Creator God of Israel, whom Jesus called Father, his followers recognized that the power of the heavenly empire of God that had been present and working through Jesus was now working through them as they spread his Way in the formation of faith communities called churches. In their interpretation of Jesus, the gospel writers affirm his messianic credentials as son of David. At the end of the day, however, the evangelists prefer the model of Isaiah's Suffering Servant over the figure of warrior King David. (See, for example, the fulfillment citation of Isaiah 42:1-4 at Matthew 12:17-21; the allusion to Isaiah 42:1 at Matthew 3:17 ("my beloved son, with whom I am well pleased"); and the allusions to Isaiah 42:6 and 49:6 ("a light for revelation to the Gentiles") at Luke 2:32 and Acts 13:47.

The Early Church

In the first two centuries after Christ, noncitizens of the empire (and that included most Christians) were not recruited for the Roman legions, and the idolatry and rough personal morality of army life made military service unattractive to Christians. So the morality of war and military service was generally a nonissue for the early church. Jesus' teachings on nonviolence and enemy love were understood, taught, and practiced on the level of daily personal encounters.

Justin Martyr, writing around A.D. 150, is able to pray for the emperor and the empire and still claim that the Christian community already lives in a way that fulfills the messianic age prophesied by Isaiah 2:4 ("swords into plowshares, spears into pruning hooks"), even though the world around that community practices war. Tertullian, writing at the end of the second century, is the first Christian writer to address the question of Christians serving in the military; he does not see how Christian soldiering is warranted: "Even if soldiers came to John and got advice on how they ought to act, even if the centurion became a believer, the Lord, by taking away Peter's sword, disarmed every soldier thereafter. We are not allowed to wear any uniform that symbolizes a sinful act" (*On Idolatry*, 19:3).[83] Early in the third century, Hippolytus of Rome writes in the *Apostolic Tradition* that Christian soldiers were not allowed to kill, that judges with the power of capital punishment who become Christian must give up their office, and that no catechumen might join the army. Writing *Against Celsus* around A.D. 248, Origen insists that Christians are good servants of the empire and can "fight as priests and worshippers of God while others fight as soldiers. Though they keep their right hands clean, the Christians fight through their prayers to God on behalf of those doing battle in a just cause and on behalf of an emperor who is ruling justly in order that all opposition and hostility toward those who are acting rightly may be eliminated" (8:73).[84]

THE "CONSTANTINIAN TURN" AND THE EMERGENCE OF THE JUST WAR CRITERIA

When Emperor Constantine (reigned 312–336) legalized Christianity and, later in the century, Theodosius established it as the religion of the empire, Christians found themselves challenged by a different relationship to the world around them. Many became public officials with a responsibility for the common good. These Christians had to face the responsibility of using military force to defend the innocent, and this situation prompted the church's more gifted leaders, such as Ambrose and Augustine, to do some serious thinking and writing about using police and military force in a way that was consistent with following the teaching of Jesus. They recognized the right of a nation to defend itself against aggression and the need to ensure that such defense was in the spirit of love of neighbor and enemy.[85]

A set of criteria eventually emerged for adjudicating when the use of military force was warranted and how such a war must be conducted—what has come to be known as the "just war" theory. Building on principles already articulated by Cicero, the just war tradition that began to receive Christian application in the fourth century later was refined by the work of Aquinas (1225–1274), Vitoria (1486–1546), and Suarez (1548–1617). Most Christians today are familiar with the just war tradition in its now classic list of criteria for judging whether a possible war is just: It must be (1) a defensive war warranted by a *just cause;* (2) declared by *legitimate authority* (not a private individual); (3) for a *right intention;* (4) as a *last resort;* (5) with a reasonable *probability of success;* and (6) with a *proportionality* between the likely destruction and the good sought. Two more criteria are required in the actual conduct of the war: first, again *proportionality,* and second, *noncombatant immunity.*[86] Underlying these criteria is a presumption against the use of force that goes right back to Jesus' teaching on nonviolence and love of enemies in the Sermon mediated by Matthew and Luke.[87]

Recent Developments in the Nuclear Age: From Just War to Nonviolence

In the past century, certain charismatic individuals have brought Jesus' teaching on nonviolence and love of enemies back into international public discourse. Gandhi's reading of Tolstoy brought Jesus' teaching on the Sermon on the Mount to his attention. In his search for a practical truth about addressing violence and fighting injustice, he was inspired by the provocative examples that Jesus uses to illustrate the fifth antithesis. His own application took dramatic forms that engaged millions of his fellow nationals. Among these were his program of recovering the Indian art of homespun cloth in order to free the people of India from the British monopoly in that industry, and his great salt march, in which he led thousands in a two-hundred-fifty-mile march to the sea to symbolically "make salt" to expose the English domination of that human necessity.

Later it was Martin Luther King's reading of Gandhi in his seminary days that led King to interpret Jesus' teaching in Matthew 5 in the spirit of Gandhi and to creatively apply Jesus' examples to his own struggle to overcome entrenched racism in the United States. He used the tools of disciplined nonviolent boycotts and sit-ins.

The response of most Christians to the rise of Nazism in Germany illustrated how a misapplication of one part of Scripture, Romans 13 (empire as instrument of God when implemented rightly), could dull the power of other parts—Matthew 5, Luke 6, and also Revelation 13 (empire as tool of the demonic). Yet others, like the Lutheran Dietrich Bonhoeffer and the Catholic Franz Jägerstätter, heard Jesus' teaching as a call to resist Nazism and Hitler even at the risk of their lives. Since the Second World War, the desire to follow Jesus' teaching on nonviolence on the international level has found group expression among Catholics in the peace movement called Pax Christi International, founded in France in 1945. A United States chapter, Pax Christi USA, was founded in 1972 and has now grown to more than twenty thousand members.

In the Second Vatican Council document *Gaudium et spes* (Pastoral Constitution on the Church in the Modern World), the Council fathers developed the church's teaching on war and peace in a variety of ways:[88]

1. They affirmed the connection between justice and peace: "Peace is not merely the absence of war, nor can it be reduced solely to the maintenance of a balance of power between enemies; nor is it brought about by dictatorship. Instead, it is rightly and appropriately called an enterprise of justice." (78).

2. They expressed support for those who "renounce the use of violence in the vindication of their rights and who resort to methods of defense which are otherwise available to weaker parties too, provided this can be done without injury to the rights and duties of others or of the community itself" (78).

3. They evoked Isaiah 2:4 as realizable in the Christian era: "Insofar as men are sinful, the threat of war hangs over them, and hang over them it will until the return of Christ. But insofar as men vanquish sin by a union of love, they will vanquish violence as well and make these words come true: 'They shall turn their swords into plough-shares, and their spears into sickles. Nation shall not lift up sword against nation, neither shall they learn war any more'" (78).

4. They reasserted the primacy of conscience in the case of individual soldiers given immoral commands (79).

5. They affirmed the need to honor international agreements regarding wounded and imprisoned soldiers and to "make humane provisions for the case of those who for reasons of conscience refuse to bear arms, provided, however, that they agree to serve the human community in some other way" (79).

6. They acknowledged the traditional right of national self-defense: "As long as the danger of war remains and there is no competent

and sufficiently powerful authority at the international level, governments cannot be denied the right to legitimate defense once every means of peaceful settlement has been exhausted" (79).

7. They affirmed a legitimate role for Christian participation in military service: "Those too who devote themselves to the military service of their country should regard themselves as the agents of security and freedom of peoples. As long as they fulfill this role properly, they are making a genuine contribution to the establishment of peace" (79).

8. The sole condemnation by the assembled bishops of Vatican Council II was addressed to wars against total populations: *"Any act of war aimed indiscriminately at the destruction of entire cities or extensive areas along with their population is a crime against God and man himself. It merits unequivocal and unhesitating condemnation"* (80).

9. They acknowledged that the mere possession of "scientific weapons" *may* act as a deterrent to possible enemy attack (81).

10. But they hastened to add that reliance on such deterrence promotes an arms race that endangers the world and exhausts resources needed to address social ills (81). As we will see below, during the past twenty years, church leaders have declared that the present context has rendered the possession of nuclear arms as a deterrent no longer legitimate—indeed, as "morally abhorrent."

The document then proceeds to develop the insight that lies at the heart of the Sermon on the Mount, namely, that real progress toward disarmament and the abolition of war requires nothing less than the conversion of hearts. For followers of Jesus, this means yielding to the graces petitioned in the Lord's Prayer and modeling in the faith community the peace we hope will be realized in the whole human family. It is instructive to note that these statements on war and peacemaking occur in the larger context of a chapter entitled "The Fostering of Peace and the Promotion of a Community of Nations." The governing value that the Council fathers call "the universal common good" derives from the vision implied in Jesus' portrayal of the Father's inclusive love, which makes his sun rise on the bad and the good and causes rain to fall on the just and the unjust (Matthew 5:45). This vision is evident in statements such as the following: "Therefore, to encourage and stimulate cooperation among men, the Church must be clearly present in the midst of the community of nations both through her official channels and through the full and sincere collaboration of all Christians—a collaboration motivated solely by the desire to be of service to all" (89).

In the 1983 pastoral letter *The Challenge of Peace: God's Promise and Our Response,* the U.S. Catholic bishops reiterate the teaching of *Gaudium et spes* eighteen years later, complementing the document with a review of the fuller Catholic tradition on war and peace, including biblical background, philosophical principles, and recent papal teaching, especially that of John Paul II. They speak of two traditions, *pacifism* and *the just war theory,* and apply these streams to the formation of consciences in our day. They reiterate the Second Vatican Council's support of conscientious objection. They also renew their earlier (1968) call for a legislative provision to recognize *selective* conscientious objectors (those who refuse to participate in a particular war). They conduct a moral analysis of the arms race, the use of nuclear arms, and the possession of nuclear weapons as deterrence. They are skeptical that there is any valid use of nuclear arms and, with Pope John Paul II, accept the possession of nuclear weapons as a deterrent only as a *temporary* strategy, as a part of efforts toward eventual nuclear disarmament.

Ten years later, in the 1993 document *The Harvest of Justice Is Sown in Peace*, the U.S. Catholic bishops reviewed these questions and *rejected the possession of nuclear weapons as a valid deterrent, and specified that progressive disarmament must mean a commitment to the total elimination of nuclear weapons, not just as an ideal, but as a concrete policy goal.* The bishops espouse nonviolence as a guiding principle of international policy. Five years later seventy-five bishops in Pax Christi USA published a more radical assessment:

Nuclear deterrence as a national policy must be condemned as morally abhorrent because it is the excuse and justification for the continued possession and further development of these horrendous weapons. We urge all to join in taking up the challenge to begin the effort to eliminate nuclear weapons now, rather than relying on them indefinitely.[89]

In 2005 Archbishop Celestino Migliore, Vatican ambassador to the United Nations, leveled this definitive critique:

The Holy See has never countenanced nuclear deterrence as a permanent measure, nor does it today when it is evident that nuclear deterrence drives the development of ever new nuclear arms, thus preventing genuine nuclear disarmament. Nuclear weapons assault life on the planet, they assault the planet itself, and in so doing they assault the process of the continuing development of the planet. The preservation of the Non-Proliferation Treaty demands an unequivocal commitment to genuine nuclear disarmament.[90]

Summarizing the current state of church teaching on war and peace, one commentator notes "a shift in Catholic social teaching away from just war and toward nonviolence. The church's official teaching now embraces . . . a composite position: nonviolence but when that fails, just war—the justified, limited, and accountable use of force."[91]

When the *Catechism of the Catholic Church* summarizes Catholic teaching on war and peace under the fifth commandment in paragraphs 2302–2330, it draws on the first antithesis, focusing on anger and hatred as the source of violence, and describes peace as the product of justice (Isaiah 32:17; *Gaudium et spes,* 78) and the fruit of the "peace of Christ" (Ephesians 2:16). It also affirms that followers of Jesus are committed to being the peacemakers named in the seventh beatitude. The *Catechism*'s three-page summary of the just war doctrine affirms that "all governments are obliged to work for the avoidance of war," and also grants that "as long as the danger of war persists and there is no international authority with the necessary competence and power, governments cannot be denied the right of lawful self-defense, once all peace efforts have failed."[92]

One insight that emerges from even a cursory review of the post-biblical Christian response to Jesus' teaching on nonviolence and love of enemies is that new historical contexts require fresh responses. The minority status of the Christian movement within the world of the Roman Empire during the first two centuries after Christ was such that it was a clear choice for followers of Jesus not to participate in the militia of the empire to avoid the pressures of idolatry as well as the possibility of shedding blood. With the "Constantinian turn," the empire became at least nominally Christian, and many Christians had leadership roles in the government and therefore had to make decisions regarding the defense of the common good against external threats and attacks. The rationales for using military force for the defense of the empire (Augustine) provided warrant for the Crusades for the majority of Christians in the Middle Ages.

In the first half of the twentieth century, U.S. Roman Catholics often saw themselves as a distinct minority group within the nation because of their immigrant status or descent. The pressure to prove themselves as patriotic citizens, combined with the clear evil of Hitler's project, made it difficult to closely scrutinize the morality of some of the means of war, such as the quarantining of Japanese Americans or the carpet bombing of cities that destroyed infrastructure and targeted whole populations indiscriminately, climaxing in the nuclear destruction of Hiroshima and Nagasaki. These events provided a new context for reflection and teaching within Christian communities. It was precisely this context that has led the Roman Catholic Church to the understanding that found magisterial expression in the writings of John XXIII, Paul VI, the Council fathers in *Gaudium et spes*, and John Paul II.

Now those of us who are Roman Catholics and citizens of the United States find ourselves in a context whose "distant mirror" is the Constantinian turn of the early fourth century in the Roman Empire. Now that we are mainstreamed, we are no longer pressured to prove our patriotism. Baptized followers of Jesus have been in charge of the U.S. government for some time; the largest group of Christians, Roman Catholics, populate the houses of Congress in numbers exceeding the proportion of the people they represent. Yet we find that the stated public policy of our government conflicts in major ways with our church's best efforts to implement the teaching of Jesus; this was evident in the run-up to the U.S. invasion of Iraq. Regarding military presence in the world, the stated objective of "full-spectrum dominance"—that is, the domination of land, sea, air, and even space—remains in place. "Space" here, of course, does not mean the entire cosmos, which is beyond human reach, but *orbital* space— the space around planet Earth that hosts the hundreds of satellites that serve our communications, scientific, and intelligence-gathering needs (think global-positioning systems and cellphone transmission). No nation has yet put weapons in orbital space, but we have refused to rule it out.[93] Meanwhile, we have moved into warfare by drones without substantial congressional debate.

This talk of global space technology seems so far removed from the intimate personal context of Jesus' teaching in first-century Palestine (those examples of one-on-one encounters) that we may be tempted to think there is no connection between the two. But notice that Jesus speaks with an authority of a new Moses, indeed one far greater than Moses—the Son of God. And he speaks not simply to individuals but to individuals healed and gathered in community and bent on doing the will of the Creator addressed as Father. His invitation to respond to oppression and hostility with creative nonviolence animated by love of enemies is framed by a vision of human solidarity that understands God as desiring the good of all—bad and good, just and unjust. The mandate to love neighbor calls us to attend to the needs of all, not only the mugging victim by the side of the road, but anyone touched by the reach of our city, state, nation, and the international corporate entities that we host. Paying attention to and doing what we can to influence what our nation does in our name must surely be part of our efforts to follow Jesus today.[94] This is the very thing our bishops have addressed in their quadrennial pastoral letters on faithful citizenship over the past thirty years. Matthew and Luke have passed on this teaching for all of us to take to heart as we respond to the story of Jesus that they have mediated for all of us.

Conclusion
"O Help Us Listen Now, As Then"

You never know where you are going to find insight. Wondering how I might structure a concluding chapter for this book, I came across a hymn in the Office of Readings for Liturgy of the Hours that captures our relationship with the Sermon on the Mount/Plain with brilliant simplicity. The words are cast in the conventional four-beat, rhyming format of a mid-twentieth-century hymn. I found this unpretentious text to be a remarkably simple and full response to the teaching of Jesus that we have received in Matthew's Sermon on the Mount and Luke's Sermon on the Plain.

Lord Jesus, once you spoke to men
Upon the mountain, in the plain;
O help us listen now, as then,
And wonder at your words again.

We all have secret fears to face,
Our minds and motives to amend;
We seek your truth, we need your grace,
Our living Lord and present Friend.

The Gospel speaks, and we receive
Your light, your love, your own command.
O help us live what we believe
In daily work of heart and hand.[95]

Jesus is addressed precisely as "Lord Jesus," the exalted title used first by the post-Easter community who had come to know Jesus of Nazareth as *Kyrie*—LORD, the risen Lord now acknowledged as divine. This is surely how Matthew and Luke intend us to hear the Jesus presented in their respective gospels.

Even the "men" of the first line, which inevitably carries a patriarchal ring to most twenty-first-century North American ears, fit what we know about first-century Palestine. It was indeed mainly adult males who gathered in public places to listen to itinerant preachers; women and children stayed at home. Matthew and Luke know that *their* audiences include women as well as men. We have tried to hear these words in their original cultural setting as well as we can, the better to hear them in our own context.

"Upon the mountain, in the plain" crisply acknowledges that we have two versions of the "inaugural address" in which Jesus expressed the essence of his moral teaching—the Sermon on the Mount in Matthew 5–7 and the Sermon on the Plain of Luke 6:20-49. We have tried to listen to the integrity of each rendition in its respective gospel context, our purpose being to better hear what those words say to us now. And taught by Matthew's version about the centrality of prayer, we do indeed pray with the hymn, *"O help us listen now, as then, / And wonder at your words again."*

"We all have secret fears to face" recalls Jesus' teaching of God as a compassionate Father whose universal gifts of rain and sunshine are signs of his inclusive love for all. The line also suggests that God can be trusted for "daily bread" and forgiveness, and also for the food, drink, and clothing we need, if we commit ourselves to the communal enterprise of first seeking together the reign of God and the gift of his Spirit.

The acknowledgment that we have "minds and motives to amend" captures Jesus' emphasis in the Sermon on the proper nurturing of our inner life, managing our anger and our sexual imaginings, seeking first the kingdom, using the gift of speech to say what we mean, loving the enemy, inventing ways to respond nonviolently to hostility and injustice, and doing religious practices not for show but for our heavenly "Father who sees in secret" (Matthew 6:7).

"We seek your truth, we need your grace, / Our living Lord and present Friend" captures the Sermon's emphasis on the importance of prayer if one is to live Jesus' vision. That centrality comes through in the teaching of the model, the Lord's Prayer in Matthew 6:6-15, and in the assurances of the Creator's paternal care in Matthew 6:25-34 and 7:7-11.

"The Gospel speaks, and we receive / Your light, your love, your own command." What a wonderfully simple way to express the complex reality of the revelatory text! Indeed, the Gospel—in the form of the written gospels—does indeed speak. These texts, Matthew's Sermon on the Mount and Luke's Sermon on the Plain in this case, are the privileged and normal way we hear the Word of God. And our faith is that these human texts do indeed mediate the Jesus we address directly in prayer, such that we can speak to him of "your light, your love, your own command." Our study of the human words, the authors' redaction and arrangement, the implied background from the earlier Scriptures, and the context of the ancient world generally—this study is finally at the service of hearing the One to whom we pray, "our living Lord and present Friend."

"O help us live what we believe / In daily work of heart and hand." This petition takes us right to the point of the Sermon's end, especially as expressed in the parable of the wise and foolish builders. "Daily work of heart and hand" is a perfect summary of the challenge. Living the vision of the Sermon is truly a work of the *heart*. It is the "pure of heart" who are congratulated in the sixth beatitude of Matthew (5:8); the heart is also where adultery can begin (5:28). Where the heart is, there is our treasure (6:21), for better or for worse, which is also echoed emphatically in Luke's Sermon on the Plain (6:45).

As the heart goes, so goes the *hand*. *"Daily work of heart and hand"* summarizes aptly the spending of a life. Drawing on experience and reflection, the community of Jesus' followers, the church, is still laboring to apply the Sermon's vision to the shifting contexts of contemporary life. That is why our leaders, in concert with the "sense of the faithful," continue to apply the teaching of Jesus to issues such as abortion, immigration, entrenched poverty, preventive war-making, land use, climate change, capital punishment, violence against women and children, and the management of economies.

The prayer rightly ends on the final note of the Sermon, with the parable of the builders on rock or sand. Doing what Jesus asks results in building a life that endures; hearing and not doing what one hears from Jesus results in absolute disaster. The choice is ours, and it is a scary one. But sufficient help is available. The "you" addressed in the Sermon is not a lonely individual; it is "you" in the plural, a community, and a healed and praying community to boot. And the One we pray to is not a long-ago and faraway Jesus of Nazareth; the One we address is "our living Lord and present Friend."

ENDNOTES

1. For a recent and thorough effort to read Luke's Sermon on the Plain on its own terms, see L. John Topel, SJ, *Children of a Compassionate God: A Theological Exegesis of Luke 6:20-49* (Collegeville, MN: Liturgical Press, 2001).

2. An excellent example of this kind of analysis is the work-in-progress of John P. Meier, *A Marginal Jew: Rethinking the Historical Jesus* (four volumes, with a fifth to come; New York: Doubleday, 1991–).

3. The story of this consensus has been nicely summarized in many places. See, for example, Raymond E. Brown, *An Introduction to the New Testament* (Anchor Bible Reference Library; New York: Doubleday, 1997), 99–125.

4. Throughout this book I am using the name Matthew for the author of the Gospel of Matthew quite apart from the question of the relationship of this document to the tax collector Matthew mentioned at Matthew 9:9—the man called Levi, son of Alphaeus in Mark 2:14. The earliest manuscripts of the gospels name no authors. The attributions to Matthew, Mark, Luke, and John come later. The idea that the author of the Gospel according to Matthew is someone other than the tax collector is based on (a) the author's dependency on the work of Mark and the Q collection of sayings (why would an eyewitness depend on the work of a non-eyewitness?) and (b) the absence within the text of any claim that the author was a participant in the events recorded. In the present book, as in contemporary scholarship generally, referring to Matthew as the "First Gospel" and to Mark as the "Second Gospel" pertains to their traditional place in the arrangement of the canon and not the chronological order of their compositions.

On the authorship question, see Brown, *Introduction*, 208–212, where he states the following: "By way of overall judgment on the 'Matthew' issue, it is best to accept the common position that *canonical Matthew was originally written in Greek by a non-eyewitness whose name is unknown to us and who depended on sources like Mark and Q*" (italics in the original).

5. Some years ago, I wrote a shorter book approaching the beatitudes from this perspective, *The Beatitudes in Context: What Luke and Matthew Meant* (Zacchaeus Studies: New Testament; Wilmington, DE: Michael Glazier, 1990). The present book recapitulates that project and carries it forward through the whole Sermon.

6. For an excellent introduction to and commentary on the whole of the First Gospel, see Daniel J. Harrington, SJ, *The Gospel of Matthew* (Sacra Pagina Series, vol. 1; Collegeville, MN: Liturgical Press, 1991). And for the same regarding Luke–Acts, see Luke Timothy Johnson, *The Gospel of Luke* (Sacra Pagina Series, vol. 3; Collegeville, MN: Liturgical Press, 1991); *The Acts of the Apostles* (Sacra Pagina Series, vol. 5; Collegeville, MN: Liturgical Press, 1992).

7. Where an idea or interpretation is not my own or something generally known, I will provide a footnote indicating the source. The main dictionary I use is W. F. Bauer, F. W. Danker, W. F. Arndt, and F. W. Gingrich, *Greek–English Lexicon of the New Testament and Other Early Christian Literature* (3rd ed.; Chicago: University of Chicago, 2000). **Hereafter, this lexicon will be referred to as BDAG**, the conventional way of referring to this tool by the first letters of the editors' names.

8. This interpretation of Matthew's preference for "kingdom of heaven" is argued in detail by Jonathan T. Pennington, *Heaven and Earth in the Gospel of Matthew* (Grand Rapids, MI: Baker Academic, 2009).

9. For a treatment of this dimension of the Gospel of Matthew, see Warren Carter, *Matthew and Empire* (Harrisburg, PA: Trinity Press International, 2001).

10. See Terrence L Donaldson, *Jesus on the Mountain: A Study in Matthean Theology* (Sheffield: JSOT Press, 1985).

11. This is a thesis defended in the Donaldson book mentioned in the previous note.

12. The Greek adjective *makarios* shows up in English in "macarism," a scholarly synonym for beatitude.

13. In both sets of beatitudes, including Luke's "woes," "you" and "yours" are the *plural* form of the second-person pronoun. Thus, from the beginning, it is clear that Jesus addresses his teaching to a group. This grammatical cue is simply lost in English translation.

14. This is the definition given in the standard lexicon in BDAG, 896.

15. There are *ptōchoi* in Acts, but see Acts 4:34: "There was no needy person [*endeēs*] among them"—a clear allusion to LXX Deuteronomy 15:4, describing the Jubilee practice.

16. Scholars of Isaiah agree that chapters 1–39 were mainly written before the Babylonian exile, chapters 40–55 written during the exile, and chapters 56–66 after the return. Accordingly, it has become conventional to refer to Isaiah 1–39 as First Isaiah, Isaiah 40–55 as Second Isaiah, and 56–66 as Third Isaiah.

17. D. P. Seccombe (*Possessions and the Poor in Luke–Acts* [SNTU Series B. vol. 6; Linz, Austria: Harrachstrasse 7, 1982], 24–69) develops this in some detail.

18. W. D. Davies and Dale C. Allison (*The Gospel according to Saint Matthew* [International Critical Commentary; New York: T & T Clark, 1988; in three volumes], 1:436–439) develop this interpretation at some length.

19. I borrow this idea from Robert A. Guelich, *The Sermon on the Mount: A Foundation for Understanding* (Waco, Texas: Word Books, 1982), passim.

20. J. Dupont (3:336) makes this observation.

21. Guelich, *Sermon*, 74–75.

22. BDAG, 861.

23. While Matthew's description of Jesus as *praüs* at 11:29 and 21:5 are the passages most pertinent to our discussion of *praüs* in the third beatitude, his citation of Isaiah 42:1-2 at 12:18 is surely part of the picture. Note especially Matthew 12:20: "A bruised reed he will not break, / a smoldering wick he will not quench, / until he brings justice to victory."

24. Helpfully, the 1986 revision of the NAB renders Matthew's sevenfold use of *dikaiosynē* "righteousness" in each instance.

25. See M. L. Barré, "Blessed Are the Pure of Heart," *Bible Today*, 22 (1984), 236–242.

26. *The Spiritual Exercises of St. Ignatius*, no. 38.

27. See W. Foerster, "*Eirene, ktl.*," TDNT 2 (1964), 419.

28. The phrase ("children *of God*" [*tekna tou theou*]), however, turns up only in Pauline and Johannine writings (see John 1:12; 11:52; Romans 8:16, 21; Philippians 2:15; 1 John 3:1, 2, 10; 5:2).

29. The point here is not to challenge the pastoral appropriateness of the NAB 1986 rendering of this phrase as "children of God" but to attend to the way Matthew's phrase in the Greek associates the Christian peacemaker with Jesus as the Son of God.

30. The summary nature of this eighth Matthean beatitude was so obvious to some patristic writers, e.g., Augustine and Hugh of St. Victor, that they simply treated the beatitudes as seven. See Jeffrey P. Greenman, Timothy Larsen, and Stephen R. Spencer (eds.), *The Sermon on the Mount through the Centuries* (Grand Rapids, MI: Brazos Press, 2007).

31. It is interesting that the sole instance of the verb *eirēnopoieō* ("I make peace") in the Greek Old Testament is in a commendation of the person who confronts where confrontation is called for: "He

that winks with his eyes deceitfully procures griefs for men; / but he that reproves boldly is a peacemaker," LXX Proverbs 10:10.

32. These uses are itemized by Davies and Allison, I:472–473.

33. I was alerted to this background by my colleague Bruce Malina, who notes it briefly in B. J. Malina and R. L. Rohrbaugh, *Social Science Commentary on the Synoptic Gospels* (Minneapolis, MN: Fortress, 1992), 50. My discussion is partly a summary of their source, R. De Langhe, "*Judaisme ou Hellenism en rapport avec le Nouveau Testament*," in L. Cerfaux et al., *L'Attente de messie* (Desclee de Brouwer, 1985), 65–67.

34. A couple of passages in the Old Testament seem to use the cognate Hebrew word *eretz* ("earth") to refer to this kind of kiln, at Job 28:5 and Psalm 12:6 ("The words of the Lord are pure words, / as silver purified in the earth seven times" to use the LXX, which seems to come closest to the Hebrew), and Job 28:5 ("As for the earth, out of it comes bread, / but underneath it is turned up as by fire," NRSV).

35. The NAB 1986 rendering, "But if salt loses its *taste*, with what can it be *seasoned*"—reflecting the verb in Mark 9:49 and Luke 14:34 (*artyō*, "I season")—moves from catalyst to condiment. But Matthew's word is *halisthēsontai*, literally "to be re-salted." Thus Matthew keeps the language open to the kiln metaphor. Similarly, rendering *mōranthē* (literally, "becomes foolish"; possibly here "becomes dull") "loses its taste" also takes us unnecessarily from catalyst to condiment, whereas the Greek is open metaphorically to the idea of a catalyst growing dull in the sense of losing its former power as a catalytic agent.

36. "Law" here means the Torah, the first five books of the Bible with its 613 laws embedded in the story of ultimate origins and of Israel's liberation from slavery and life with God in the wilderness.

37. Davies and Allison, *Matthew*, 1:492–493.

38. *Nostra aetate*, 4; *Catechism of the Catholic Church*, 597. See also *The Jewish People and Their Sacred Scriptures in the Christian Bible* (2001), accessible online at the Vatican Web site.

39. "A distinction is to be observed between general contrast (*dè*) and that which is directly contrary (*allá*)" (F. Blass and A. Debrunner, *A Greek Grammar of the New Testament and Other Early Christian Literature* [University of Chicago Press, 1961], § 447).

40. The contemporary Jewish scholar Pinchas Lapide (in *The Sermon on the Mount: Utopia or Program of Action?* [Maryknoll, N.Y.: Orbis, 1986], 46) insists on the continuity of Jesus' teaching with Jewish tradition and emphasizes the point by referring to the so-called antitheses as "supertheses."

41. Since the variation in numbering the Ten Commandments is often a source of confusion, especially in interdenominational and interreligious conversations, a clarifying note is appropriate here. All traditions treat the commandments of Exodus 20 and Deuteronomy 5 as ten in number (a decalogue) because the Torah itself refers to the "ten words" (Exodus 34:28; Deuteronomy 10:4). But how the traditions divide the text of the commandments into ten parts varies. The Jewish, Orthodox, and Reformed Christian traditions count the prohibition against graven images as a separate commandment, the second; then they combine the coveting of the neighbor's wife and the coveting of the neighbor's goods as a single commandment, the tenth. The Roman Catholic, Lutheran, and Anglican traditions follow Augustine's numbering; they include the prohibition of graven images as part of the first commandment, and they divide the tenth commandment (in the Jewish numbering) into two—the coveting the neighbor's wife (called the ninth) and the coveting of the neighbor's goods (called the tenth).

42. *Gehenna* is the Hebrew name for the ravine south and west of ancient Jerusalem, the Valley of the Sons of Hinnom. Because this place was associated with the evil of child sacrifice (Jeremiah

7:31-32) and also because it became the Jerusalem garbage dump where fire often smoldered continually, Gehenna became the name for the place of punishment in the next life. Jesus uses the language and imagery familiar to his audience. "Gehenna" occurs three times in Mark (in one passage, 9:31, 33, 37); once in Luke (12:5 = Matthew 10:28); once in James (3:6). It occurs seven times in the First Gospel (5:20, 22, 29; 10:28; 18:9; 23:15, 35). The word is often rendered "hell" in English. The crude and concrete source of the name "Gehenna" has no bearing on the spiritual reality that is named.

43. I first encountered this interpretation in the popular treatment of biblical interpretation by Gerhard Lohfink, *The Bible: Now I Get It! A Form–Criticism Handbook* (trans. by Daniel Coogan; New York: Doubleday, 1979), 149.

44. For a full exploration of this idea, see Dale C. Allison, *Studies in Matthew* (Grand Rapids, MI: Baker Academic, 2005), 65–78.

45. As it happens, this passage is absent from the Gospel of Luke, where it is part of his so-called Little Omission (of Mark 9:41–10:12).

46. Hebert Danby (editor and translator), *The Mishnah: Translated from the Hebrew with Introduction and Brief Explanatory Notes* (Oxford: Oxford University Press, 1967).

47. For a full discussion of the bearing of these Essene documents on the meaning of *porneia* in the New Testament, see Joseph A. Fitzmyer, "The Matthean Divorce Texts and Some New Palestinian Evidence," *Theological Studies* 37.2 (1976), 197–226.

48. On the connection between Matthew 1:18-19 and the divorce practice of first-century Palestine, see Allison, *Studies in Matthew,* 163–172.

49. Luke describes a number of women traveling with Jesus and the twelve and providing for the group "out of their resources" (Luke 8:1-3), so we have evidence that some women had recourses to act

independently. But none of these were described as divorced, and Suzanna was the wife of Chuza. And recall that Jesus understood his network of followers to be a family (Mark 3:31-35; Matthew 12:46-50; Luke 8:19-21). Martha, Mary, and Lazarus, for whom no spouses are named, seemed to live as a family unit, possibly as celibate urban Essenes.

50. The translation is that of George E. Ganss, SJ, *The Spiritual Exercises of Saint Ignatius* (St. Louis: The Institute of Jesuit Sources, 1992), 36–37.

51. *Washington Post* report of a vengeance trial appearing in *The Omaha World Herald*, January 21, 2008.

52. This is the translation offered by Walter Wink. My treatment of this passage draws heavily from his article, "Beyond Just War and Pacifism: Jesus' Nonviolent Way," *Review and Expositor* 89 (1992), 197–214. Wink employs this interpretation in a number of subsequent works, but this article contains his fullest exegesis of Matthew 5:38-42.

53. BDAG, 80. The following are all the NT instances of the verb *anthistemi*: (1a) to be in opposition to a person, *to set oneself against, oppose* (as in Matthew 5:39 [sole use in Matthew]; Acts 13:8; Galatians 2:11 [Paul to Peter]; 2 Timothy 3:8 (2x); James 4:7 [the devil]; 1 Peter 5:9 [the devil]); (1b) *to oppose a thing* (as in Luke 21:15 [wisdom]; Acts 6:10 [wisdom]; Romans 9:19; 13:2; 2 Timothy 3:8; 4:15 [our preaching]; and (2) to be resistant to power; *resist* (as in Ephesians 6:13 [the devil, implied in context]; and Romans 13:2b [what God has appointed]).

54. Wink, "Beyond Just War and Pacifism," 199.

55. Ibid., 208. The careful analysis of Hans Dieter Betz (*The Sermon on the Mount* [Minneapolis, MN: Augsburg Fortress, 1995], 280) supports a similar translation: "Do not retaliate."

56. Davies and Allison note the resonance between these seven words and Isaiah 50 (*Matthew*, I:554).

57. Translation from Florentino García Martínez (ed.), *The Dead Sea Scrolls Translated: The Qumran Texts in English* (New York: E. J. Brill, 1996; second edition).

58. I spell out Luke's theme of "hearing" in "'Watch How You Hear': The Healing of *kōphoi* ("Deaf-mute") Persons in Luke," in Mary F. Foskett and O. Wesley Allen, Jr. (eds.), *Between Experience and Interpretation: Engaging the Writings of the New Testament* (Nashville, TN: Abingdon Press, 2008), 147–173.

59. It is Luke's "lend, expecting nothing back" that was the basis of the church prohibition of usury, the taking of interest on loans, during the Middle Ages. On this, see John T. Noonan, Jr., *A Church that Can and Cannot Change: The Development of Catholic Moral Teaching* (Notre Dame: University of Notre Dame Press, 2005).

60. I analyze this passage more fully in "Acts 4:23-31—A Neglected Biblical Paradigm of Christian Worship (Especially in Troubled Times)," *Worship* 77 (May, 2003), 225–237.

61. *The Apostolic Fathers; Greek Texts and English Translations* (third edition; edited and translated by Michael W. Holmes after the earlier work of J. B. Lightfoot and J. R. Hunter; Grand Rapids, MI.: Baker Academic, 2008).

62. It is interesting to note that these three practices are also three of the five pillars of Islam, the other two being (a) the affirmation of the one God and Muhammad as his Prophet and (b) the Hajj (the pilgrimage to Mecca).

63. The word occurs once in Mark at 7:6 ("Well did Isaiah prophesy about you hypocrites, as it is written: 'This people honors me with their lips, / but their hearts are far from me'"). In Luke it occurs three times: 6:42b (par. to Matthew 7:5 "You hypocrite! Remove the wooden beam from your eye first"); 12:56 ("You hypocrites! You know how to interpret the appearance of the earth and sky"); and 13:15 (to the people in the synagogue, "Hypocrites! Does not each one of you on the sabbath

untie his ox or his ass from the manger and lead it out for watering?"). Matthew loves the word, employing it fourteen times, incorporating seven of them into the woes against the Pharisees that he inherits from Q and places in Matthew 23. These hypocrites shut the kingdom of God against people (23:13); devour widows' houses and make a pretence of long prayers (verse 14); will transform a proselyte into a "child of Gehenna" (verse 15); tithe mint and dill and cumin but neglect justice, mercy, and faith (verse 23); cleanse the outside of the cup and the plate but inside are full of extortion and rapacity (verse 25). As for the abstract noun *hypokrisis* ("hypocrisy"), that word occurs once in each of the synoptics: Matthew 23:28 (where the hypocrites are said to be "full of hypocrisy and evildoing"); Mark 12:15 (where Mark says that Jesus perceives *hypocrisy* in the questioners about tribute to Caesar, and Matthew calls it "their malice" and Luke "their craftiness"); and Luke 12:1 (where Luke alone identifies "the leaven of the Pharisees" as hypocrisy, while Matthew 16:12 later explains the leaven as "the *teaching* of the Pharisees and Sadducees.")

64. Carolyn Osiek ("'When You Pray, Go into Your *tameion*' (Matthew 6:6): But Why?" *Catholic Biblical Quarterly,* 71 [October 2009]: 723–740) surveys the cultural data regarding references to this domestic space. She concludes, in part: "Matthew's admonition to 'pray to your Father in secret' in your *tameion* continues the theme of secrecy in Matthew 6:18,

that is, deliberate concealment, so as not to be seen by those human beings who might bestow honor. It is an exhortation not to be alone but to receive one's most important guest. It is quite understandable, therefore, that it becomes in some exegesis a metaphor for the human heart (e.g., Augustine, *conf* 8.8; 12.16), a secret chamber that is accessible anywhere by the one in whom it dwells" (p. 740).

65. BDAG, 376–377.
66. BDAG, 793.

67. Bruce M. Metzger, *A Textual Commentary on the Greek New Testament* (second edition; New York: American Bible Society, 1994), 130–131.

68. The cultural observations and interpretation come from Kenneth E. Bailey, *Poet and Peasant: A Literary–Cultural Approach to the Parables in Luke* (Grand Rapids, MI.: Eerdmans, 1976), 86–118.

69. BDAG, 508–509.

70. Matthew's redaction of Mark 7 emphasizes the *mouth*. Where the Markan Jesus refers to what goes in and what comes out of a *person*, the Matthean Jesus refers to what "enters *the mouth*" and what "comes out of *the mouth*" (15:17, 18). This is in line with his stress on the true and simple use of speech in the antithesis about oath-taking. Moreover, Matthew's introduction of "false witness" (*pseudomartyria*) into the list of what comes out of the heart (15:19) resonates with his highlighting false witness in the Jewish inquest, where the chief priests and Sanhedrin are said to seek "false testimony" (*pseudomartyria*) against Jesus and "false witnesses" (*pseudomartyres*) do indeed come forward (Matthew 26:59, 60).

71. Malina and Rohrbaugh, *Social-Science Commentary on the Synoptic Gospels*, 125–126.

72. The KJV and the Rheims translations give this literal translation, and the NRSV includes it in a note.

73. For a more detailed treatment of this theme in Matthew, see Dennis Hamm, "Matthew's Portrait of the Disciples," *The Bible Today* (September 2004), 287–291.

74. For this translation note, as well as for the exegesis of this passage, I am especially indebted to Bailey, *Through Peasant Eyes*, 57–73.

75. These meanings are gathered from the entry under *krinō* in BDAG.

76. Regarding this verse, the entry in BDAG under *kyōn, kynos*

("dog") includes this observation: "Mt 7:6 must be a proverbial saying, and in its present context appears to be a warning against untimely or imprudent approaches to those in need of counsel or correction."

77. This interpretation follows Davies and Allison, *Matthew*, I:676.

78. *The Spiritual Exercises of St. Ignatius: A Translation and Commentary by George Ganss, SJ* (St. Louis: Institute of Jesuit Sources, 1992), no. 22.

79. Davies and Allison (*Matthew*, I:625–626) spell out this design in even greater detail.

80. Ibid., 687.

81. Davies and Allison (*Matthew*, I.687) note that Greek and Roman parallels include Herodotus, Isocrates, and Laertius and that the idea of doing to others as one wishes to be done to is "an almost universal sentiment," to be found in Buddhist, Confucian, and Islamic texts.

82. These references point to instances of the Greek word *hodos*, which is sometimes obscured in English versions, as for example in the NAB at Mark 10:17, where *eis hodon* is rendered "on a journey"—an accurate translation, but one misses the road/path/way theme; see the NIV's "on his way."

83. Quoted in Louis J. Swift, *The Early Fathers on War and Military Service* (Message of the Fathers of the Church, vol. 19; Wilmington, DE: Michael Glazier, 1983), 42. Much of my résumé of early church reception of Jesus' teaching derives from Swift's excellent survey of patristic writing on war and peace, which includes abundant samples of their writing in English translation together with his running commentary.

84. Swift, 55.

85. For a helpful review of recent research in early Christian attitudes on military service, see David G. Hunter, "A Decade of Research

on Early Christians and Military Service," *Religious Studies Review,* vol. 18, no. 2 (April 1992), 87–93.

86. For a further discussion of the criteria, see the *Catechism of the Catholic Church,* §2309; and for a fuller discussion, see the National Conference of Catholic Bishops, *The Challenge of Peace: God's Promise and Our Response, A Pastoral Letter on War and Peace* (Washington, DC: U.S. Catholic Conference, 1983), §§ 80–110. See also the authoritative *Compendium of the Social Doctrine of the Church* (Pontifical Council for Justice and Peace, Libreria Editrice Vaticana; Washington, DC: United States Conference of Catholic Bishops, 2005), §§ 500–520. Also instructive is Todd D. Whitmore, "The Reception of Catholic Approaches to Peace and War in the United States," in Kenneth R. Himes, OFM, et al. (eds.), *Modern Catholic Social Teaching: Commentaries and Interpretations* (Washington, DC: Georgetown University Press, 2004), 493–521.

87. The strength of the just war tradition within Roman Catholic teaching accounts for the readiness with which Pope John Paul II and national conferences of bishops spoke against the use of military force in the run-up to the invasion of Iraq. For a helpful résumé of the responses of the Vatican to the war in Iraq and the issue of "preventive" war, see John L. Allen, *All the Pope's Men* (Garden City, NY: Doubleday, 2007), 370–378.

88. The English language text of *Gaudium et spes* can be accessed on the Vatican Web site.

89. "The Morality of Nuclear Deterrence: An Evaluation by Pax Christi Bishops in the United States," October 1998. Accessible at http://www.ccnr.org/pax_christi.html.

90. Statement by Archbishop Celestine Migliore, delivered to the 7th Review Conference of the States Parties to the Treaty on the Non-Proliferation of Nuclear Weapons (NPT), 2005.

91. Drew Christiansen, SJ, "Of Many Things," *America* (October 20, 2008), 2.
92. *Catechism*, 2308, quoting *Gaudium et spes*, § 78, paragraph 5.
93. See "United States Space Command's *Long Range Plan,*" available at http://www.fas.org/spp/military/docops/usspac/lrp/toc.htm. The document is dated April 1998, but nothing suggests that it does not represent current policy. For a careful assessment of this policy by the former editor of *The Bulletin of Atomic Scientists,* see Mike Moore, *Twilight War: The Folly of U.S. Space Dominance* (Oakland, CA: The Independent Institute, 2008). This Mike Moore is not to be confused with the documentary filmmaker or the former prime minister of New Zealand.
94. For an instructive analysis of the options and challenges facing U.S. Catholics in the current context, see the prize-winning book of Kristin E. Heyer, *Prophet & Public: The Social Witness of U.S. Catholicism* (Washington, DC: Georgetown University Press, 2007).
95. Text by H. C. A. Gaunt, in *The Liturgy of the Hours,* vol. 2, English translation by the International Commission on English in the Liturgy (New York: Catholic Book Publishing Co., 1976), 1472.